The **Guardian**

Guide to the
internet

D1080957

For Kim, Lee and Cameron

The **Guardian**

Guide to the internet

A beginner's guide to the digital age

by Jim McClellan

FOURTH ESTATE • LONDON

First published in Great Britain in 1998 by
Fourth Estate Limited
6 Salem Road
London W2 4BU

Copyright © Jim McClellan 1998

1 3 5 7 9 10 8 6 4 2

The right of Jim McClellan to be identified as the author of
this work has been asserted by him in accordance with the
Copyright, Designs and Patents Act 1988.

A catalogue record for this book is available from the British Library.

ISBN 1-85702-665-9

Designed and typeset by Blackjacks, London

Printed in Great Britain by WBC Book Manufacturers, Bridgend

CONTENTS

• •

Foreword 12
Introduction 19

SECTION 1
BEFORE YOU CONNECTED 29

Get your bearings online 29
Net addresses. 32
Mapping the net 35
Try before you buy 38
Net myths deconstructed 40

SECTION 2
GETTING CONNECTED 59

Hardware 59
    The computer 61
    The modem. 70
Your connection 74
    Online services or ISP's 74
    Which ISP 79
    Signing up with an ISP. 87
Connecting for the first time. 88

Installing your modem. 90
Connection software 90
Get online with Online Services 93
Get online with Internet Service Providers 95
Doing it yourself 96
Troubleshooting 97

SECTION 3
GETTING TO GRIPS WITH THE NET 103

THE WORLD WIDE WEB 104

Software 110
Surfing the web for the first time 118
Mouse menus 121
Frames, Image Maps and Forms 123
More complex navigation. 124
Getting to your favourite sites faster 127
Troubleshooting 132
Customising your browser 135
The Cache, saving documents and images from the web 140
Next step 144
Searching the web 144
Search sites on the web 147
Using a Search Engine 149
Using an Online Directory 156
Listings, Awards and Web Rings 159
Research online. 163
Future directions 165
Next step 166

E MAIL AND MAILING LISTS 167

What software do you need 171
   Configuring your mail software 172
Your first message 174
   Email style 175
   TLA'S and Smileys 177
   HTML or Plain Text Mail 179
Sending your first message 181
   Troubleshooting 182
Getting your mail 183
Replying to your Mail 185
   Carbon Copying and Forwarding 187
   Address Book and Email Directories 188
   Email and Attachments 189
   Managing your email 193
   Free mail, Redirections and other mail services 195
Mailing Lists 199
   How not to be a slave to your email 203
   Next step 205

USENET NEWSGROUPS 206

Choosing a Newsreader 212
   Configuring your Newsreader 213
Getting started 215
Subscribing to and reading a newsgroup 220
   Newsgroup style and netiquette 225
Posting Messages 228
   Getting answers from newsgroups 231

Attachments and HTML 232
Coping with newsgroups 234
Where to next? 235

FTP AND DOWNLOADING FILES FROM THE NET 236

How free is free software? 237
Freeware 242
Shareware 243
Beta Versions 243
Getting Started 244
Downloading files from the web with your browser 245
Downloading files from an FTP site with your browser 248
Downloading files with an FTP programme 249
Troubleshooting 253
Working with downloaded files 254
File Types 260
Where to next? 263

ONLINE CHAT 264

Places to chat online and the software you need 270
Online Services 270
Internet Relay Chat aka IRC 270
Web chat 272
Chat style and netiquette 273
Chat on the Online Services 275
Internet Relay Chat 279
Chat on the web 286
Instant Messages 291

Graphic Chat 293
MUDs. 294
Where to next? 298

SECTION 4
TAKING THE WEB TO THE NEXT LEVEL 299

Multimedia and the Web 299
Getting started 300
Getting plug-ins and ActiveX controls 302
Helper Applications. 307
Java 308
Offline Browsing 310
Shopping on the Net 314
Making an Online Purchase. 317
Net Shopping in the UK and US. 319
Electronic Cash, Online Auctions and Shopping Bots 322
Next step 325

ESSENTIAL CLICKS. 326

Search 327
Research. 328
Software 329
Culture 329
Entertainment 331
Games. 333
News and Weather 334
Computers and Technology 335

Webzines. 336
Sport. 338
Travel 338
Shopping. 339
Weird 341
Net Culture. 342
Women 345
Kids 346
Politics/Net Politics 346
Relationships. 348
Science 348
Health 349

SECTION 5
LOOKING AFTER YOURSELF ON THE NET 351

Pornography, free speech and protecting your kids online 351
Setting guidelines and boundaries for children online 360
Privacy on the net 366
Privacy online at work. 367
ISP's and privacy 368
Email and privacy 368
Newsgroups, Mailing Lists and privacy 372
The web and privacy 373
Harassment on the net. 377
Email and harassment 378
Spam 379
Trust and security 383

Viruses and hackers. 385
Copyright and libel on the net 387
Next step 391

SECTION 6
POWER USERS 393

Power connections. 394
Power Mail 397
Power Browsing 399
VRML 400
Internet Telephony and Video conferencing 401
Push 404
The Active Desktop. 407
Accelerators, Search Agents and Offline Browsers 408
History 413
Do it Yourself 415
Starting you own Mailing List 416
Starting A Usenet Group 418
Creating your own Webpage 419
HTML basics 419
HTML editors 420
Some general advice. 422
Publishing and publicising your page 423
Next step 425
Further reading 427
Internet Service Providers and Online Services 437
Glossary 439

Acknowledgements

Thanks to Ian Katz for persuading me to do this book in the first place. I would never have got started without his encouragement. I would never have managed to finish without the advice and help of my editor, the infinitely patient Mathew Clayton. Thanks to my agent Cat Ledger, for all the obvious reasons. Various people read the manuscript at different stages in production and helped to weed out mistakes (and if any remain don't blame them, blame me) – thanks in particular to Simon Waldman and Mike Bracken. On occasion, I have reworked bits of the journalism I've cranked out over the years. So thanks to the various editors who have (a) made my copy much better with their various suggestions and (b) put up with my hopeless deadline surfing: Matthew Collin, John Godfrey, Sheryl Garratt, Charles Gant, Bill O'Neill, Kevin Wilson and Jack Schofield of the *Guardian* Online, Ekow Eshun and the rest of the guys at *Arena*, Peter Howarth, Jo Glasbey, Amy Raphael and Viv Groskop at *Esquire*, Tom Hodgkinson of the *Idler*, Lindsay Baker, Joe McGee, Andrew Anthony and Mike Pilgrim from the old *Observer* Life magazine, Simon Rogers at the *Big Issue*, Hari Kunzru, Jim Flint, Avril Mair, Richard Barbrook and Dylan Jones – apologies if I've forgotten anyone. Big shouts to friends and family who were roped into long conversations about this book – George and Janet, Graham and Moira, Sheryl and Mark, Nicky and Russell, Andy and Sonia, Phill and Graham, Helen McClellan, Jon and Rob, Kodwo Eshun, Steve Beard and Steve Bode. Finally thanks to my kids, Lee and Cameron, for putting up with me while I did this and, most of all, thanks to Kim – I couldn't have done this without you.

FOREWORD

● ●

I got my first taste of the online world in March 1995 when a profoundly dull American politician called Lamar Alexander had the attention-grabbing idea of launching his campaign for the presidency in cyberspace. As the *Guardian*'s New York correspondent, I was assigned to cover the event and dutifully logged into the Coliseum, an online chat 'auditorium' operated by America Online.

It was billed as a momentous occasion, the first significant American political event played out in bits and bytes. The candidate declared in ringing keystrokes that the hundred or so digital citizens gathered in the Coliseum were 'making a little history'. But it didn't feel much like history. As Mr Alexander droned on about the importance of education, most of his audience debated the relative merits of Hole and Nirvana. That was the good bit. When an intrepidly serious user inquired what others thought of the candidate, he received just one reply that can be reproduced here: 'He types too slow.'

It was a profoundly unedifying experience and I reported scathingly that the internet was not all it was cracked up to be. If Mr Alexander's cyber campaign launch constituted a high point in the development of the

< 13 >

new medium, I figured, I would be able to live without it. Barely two years later, though, I was heading back to London, to take over the reigns of the *Guardian*'s nascent internet publishing effort, to the bafflement of most of my friends and colleagues.

Somewhere between Lamar and London, I had become convinced that the net was quite simply the most exciting thing since Neil Armstrong's small step across the lunar landscape. There was no 'eureka' moment, but two experiences in particular opened my eyes to the unique power and potential of the medium.

The first came after members of the Heaven's Gate cult committed mass suicide in San Diego in March 1997. Within hours of the news breaking, I was listening to the group's leader, 'Ti', explaining why he and his followers had chosen to ascend to 'the level above human' – apparently from inside my computer. It was an utterly transporting experience, and I felt something similar a few weeks later when I tapped in the address of the newly launched web site of the North Korean Press Agency. Scanning the succession of headlines about the failure of the western economies and the boundless achievements of North Korean's valiant armed forces, it was as though I had been beamed from my Manhattan office into the topsy-turvy world of Kim Il Sung.

Not much has changed in Pyongyang since then but a lot has changed on – and around – the net. In the last year it has edged stealthily but firmly into the mainstream of British life. The telltale trio of 'w's has crept on to advertising hoardings, TV screens and even the self-promoting cards which practitioners of the oldest profession leave in London telephone booths.

Even supposedly traditional institutions like the royal family, MI5 and

< 14 >

Wisden have set out their cyber-stalls - the latter, I am delighted to report, in association with the *Guardian*. And barely a week seems to go by without some internet-related story in the news.

Amid the exaggerated claims and hysterical headlines, the net has quietly established itself as one of the most useful tools of modern life. It is, quite simply, the easiest way to check a train timetable or to buy a recondite book. It is the quickest way to find out the lyrics of a half-remembered song, to check the side effects of a prescription medication, or to look up a Belgian telephone number. There are web sites that will automatically translate prose into French, Japanese and even Jive. And of course email has all but taken over from the paper variety as the dominant form of written communication.

For all its efficiency, though, much of the net's appeal derives from its wilder, more chaotic reaches. It is the ultimate theatre of the absurd, a hothouse of eccentricity and obsession where you can find sites devoted to dramatic bus accidents or find a romantic partner in an American jail. On the net you can watch a woman giving birth live – or Californian police blowing up a beached whale with dynamite (something of a classic, this one). To paraphrase Henry James and suggest that 'all human life is there' would be a certain understatement.

You don't need to be a cyber-theorist to see that, beyond the endless stories of quick riches and cyber hoaxes, the net is beginning to effect our lives in quite profound ways. It may have done more to empower the individual – at least the individual who can afford a net connection – than anything since universal suffrage. I don't mean the set-piece displays of digital democracy like Lamar Alexander's virtual campaign launch or

< 15 >

Tony Blair's hotly hyped online interview. The truly democratising power of the net is the way in which it subverts the control of information.

At its simplest, the net gives individuals easy and often free access to information that was once available only to an information elite – librarians, reporters, academics, those wealthy enough to afford access to powerful online databases like FT Profile or Lexis Nexis. The United States' Federal Aviation Authority may not release any document electronically that it would not in print, but the fact that air travellers can now check the safety record of any commercial aircraft at the click of a mouse represents a significant shift of what you might call info-power.

Still more exciting, and potentially far-reaching, are the many ways in which the net is making available information that was once safely corralled by governments, companies and other groups. Take Harry Knowles, the portly Texan movie buff who infuriates Hollywood by publishing guerrilla reviews of new films long before they have been formally released. The subject matter might seem trivial but the studio bosses understand very well the dizzying power shift that Knowles and his computer have managed to effect – through gritted teeth they concede that a 26-year-old geek sitting in a darkened room now has the power to make or break a multimillion-dollar new release. It's not hard to see why many autocratic regimes count the net among their most dangerous enemies.

If there is one thing the net respects less than authority it is geography. We can only guess at the long-term consequences of a medium that collapses nationality to a two- or three-character code at the end of a web or email address. In a recent discussion thread on the *Guardian*'s football website, we counted contributions from no less than nine countries

< 16 >

including the United States, Norway, China and South Africa. It is hard to see how this kind of accidental internationalism can fail to effect our ideas of nationality, race and our place in the world.

For all the net's efficiency and power, though, it can be profoundly frustrating. It is often difficult to establish the reliability or provenance of material, much of which would never pass the tests applied to information published by more traditional means.

Since the net is not presided over or organised by any controlling intelligence (the so-called search engines come closest to fulfilling this role), it can be fiendishly difficult to sort the wheat from the chaff. And though there are almost certainly no more prats in cyberspace than in real space, it often seems that way.

Undoubtedly the largest single source of net-related frustration, though, is the comparative frailty of its technology. For a medium that is moving rapidly into adolescence if not adulthood, the technology on which it is based remains almost laughably primitive. Much vaunted net 'landmarks' like the release of the Louise Woodward ruling have reliably descended into farce as computer users have jammed lines or toppled servers.

But trials like these await only those who have already managed to find their way on to the information superhighway. Things have improved a lot since the early days when you had to be a veritable computer whiz simply to set up your email address, but connecting to the net isn't quite like switching on a new video recorder either. Hence this book, a comprehensive and easy to use manual that will take you from net virgin to cyber sea dog in 467 pages. Happy surfing.

IAN KATZ
Associate Editor of *New Media*

< 17 >

INTRODUCTION

● ●

The aim of this book is to help you make use of the net. The idea is to get you online and reaping the benefit as quickly and easily as possible. At the same time, I suspect that you'll want to know a little bit more about the net than just the straight 'how to' advice. Most net guides effect what you might call a 'dummy-ing' down of their readers. You agree to identify yourself as an 'Idiot' and then are led very slowly, step by step, through the confusing world of the net and the software you need to use it.

I agree with the need for clear and simple instructions on how to do things but I don't think people are dumb just because they don't know how to work a web browser. And I don't think that you need to switch off the bulk of your brain when you sit down to read a net manual. Some cultural/historical information can make it easier to grasp certain aspects of the net. My hope is that, by the end of this book, as well as knowing how to use certain programs, you'll have accumulated a measure of what we could call net literacy, or perhaps 'net savvy', a more general knowledge of the online world which ought to help your dealings there run more smoothly.

Unlike most net manuals, this guide is not written from an American perspective. Obviously, part of the hype about the net is that it's a global

< 19 >

thing, but geography still matters. Many American manuals are written for people who don't have to pay for local telephone calls and hence can spend the whole day online without too much worry. In the UK, where we pay through the nose for local calls, people use the internet very differently. They go online quickly, grab the stuff they need, log off and read it offline. They're less likely to be enthusiastic about net ideas like push technology, which sends information to you at regular intervals but requires you to be online an awful lot for it to work properly. So, this guide will take account of the cultural and technical differences between UK and US net culture, and will look at sites of UK interest as well as some of the impressive American efforts.

Unlike many other net manuals, this one won't be mindlessly gung-ho about the net. I am pretty enthusiatic about the online world. But there are plenty of things online I don't find that convincing (e.g. Push) and plenty of net activities I don't personally devote that much time to (online chat, for example). It may be that the stuff that I don't like will be the stuff that particularly draws you in. That is one of the good points about the net. Whatever some techno-gurus might suggest, getting online is not like signing up for some monolithic crusade. You don't have to buy into the whole program. You can pick and choose.

This book is aimed primarily at absolute beginners. My aim is to help you progress – or should that be regress – from upstanding healthy examples of Homo Erectus to stoop-shouldered, screen-eyed, mouse-clutching versions of that lesser known but quickly growing species – Homo Connectus. That said, I hope there will be useful information in here even for those who are comfortably navigating the web.

< 20 >

Section 1 – **Before You Get Connected** gives you some general advice about getting your bearings online. It also takes apart some of the things people have said about the net over the years. If you're in a hurry to get online, you could skip the latter and save it for later. **Section 2 – Getting Connected** gives advice on the hardware and software you need, getting an internet connection and connecting for the first time. If you already have a computer, modem and net connection, go straight to **Section 3 – Getting to Grips with the Net,** which offers detailed advice on how to get the most of out the main net activities:

The World Wide Web

The web is usually the thing people immediately 'get' when they go online. The multimedia part of the net, the web is made up of sites (or pages) put up by everyone from multinational media corporations to charities, pressure groups and, yes, ordinary people like you. On the web, you can read online magazines which feature text and graphics, or you can watch videos, download music, buy books and CDs, book flights and holidays, even play games. You can move between sites by clicking on hypertext links, wandering far from the pages you originally accessed. This section will tell you how to find your way round the web and how to work with your browser (the software program you use to move around the web) so that your time online is more productive.

Searching the Web

One of the hardest things online is finding your way to the information you're interested in. Here's where you need search sites – online resources

< 21 >

which keep track of what's out there and point you in the right direction, usually. This section will tell you how to use search engines, online directories and other search sites. There are also a few tips about using the web as a general research tool.

Electronic Mail

Email is one of the things people immediately latch on to when they first get online. The attractions of being able to communicate with friends around the world for the cost of a local telephone call are pretty obvious. This section tells you how to send and receive email, looks at web-based mail and mailing lists and concludes with some advice on how to get the best out of email without it ruining your life.

Usenet newsgroups

Like the web, Usenet is just one part of the net proper, a collection of thousands of 'newsgroups', online forums where people discuss a variety of subjects. You post your thoughts on something, someone else reads them and posts a response and gradually over time you build up a kind of conversation (or 'thread', as the online jargon has it). This section will tell you what software you need to access Usenet, how to select and use the newsgroups you're interested in, how to cope with the huge amount of information that appears there everyday and how to survive in one of the wilder, more raucous parts of the net.

< 22 >

Downloading files and software via FTP

The internet is packed with interesting files and useful bits of software. Using your web browser or FTP software (FTP is a bit of compuspeak which stands for File Transfer Protocol), you can find files and software you're interested in and download them on to your own computer. You can also upload files and software of your own. This section will give you the basics on using FTP and offer some general advice on keeping track of material downloaded from the net.

Online chat

For many people, chat is one of the most compelling parts of the net. You can talk, or rather type, to people in real time online, in special chat rooms. Yes, people often talk dirty, creating private rooms where they can indulge in collaborative one-handed typing. But they also talk about much else, swapping news and ideas. This section will point you to the best places to chat online, tell you the software you need and offer advice on how not to let online chat take over your life (or your telephone bill).

I've put the web and email at the beginning of this section because they seem to be the most popular online activities. However, it may be that chat will be the thing for you. In other words, feel free to read this section in any order. Strictly speaking, it might even be sensible to start off with the section on downloading software online. It's up to you. In this section I've concentrated on giving detailed advice about version 4.x of the two most popular browsers – Netscape Navigator (which is part of the Communicator package of net tools) and Microsoft's Internet Explorer. New versions of browsers

< 23 >

appear all the time and by the time you read this, version 5.x of each may be available. However, I think it's likely that if you sign up with one of the major internet service providers, you'll get version 4.x of either Navigator/Communicator or Internet Explorer for the forseeable future. If you don't, and you're using something newer or older, don't worry. Browsers don't change that much and you should still be able to follow the advice.

You can use your browser to handle email and newsgroups and to download files, so I've also concentrated on these in the relevant chapters. However, I've also included pointers to alternative standalone programs you could use instead. So don't feel you have to use the browser for everything. This section goes into things in a fair amount of detail. The idea is to help you to minimise hassles when you're just getting started. The later sections are less detailed – the assumption being that you will be more comfortable with the net.

Section 4 – Taking the Web to the Next Level deals with web multimedia, offline browsing (a way of downloading web pages so that you can read them whilst offline and thus save money) and shopping on the web. It also features the *Guardian*'s **Essential Clicks**, a listing of 100 indispensable web sites.

Section 5 – Looking After Yourself Online offers advice on protecting yourself and your kids online. It covers privacy, censorship, junk email, legal issues and features some general survival tips.

< 24 >

Section 6 – Power Users is for those of you who decide to get really serious about the net. There's advice on starting mailing lists and newsgroups and putting up your own web page, along with details of yet more web multimedia and pointers to some of the countless 'cool tools' you can buy to beef up your web browsing.

Finally, at the back of the book you'll find information about UK internet service providers, a glossary and a list of links to web sites with information about the history of the net.

Throughout the book you will see various captions boxed-off from the main text, featuring useful bits of information – look out for:

Read About It Online

The net is often the best place to find out about the net, especially the latest developments. So every now and then, I'll include details of sites on the net where you can find more information on a particular topic. If you're just starting out, these might look a bit confusing at first, but once you're familiar with the web you can always come back and check them out.

Jargon File

Brave new worlds require brave new words. The net and its related technologies come with all manner of slanguage, jargon and puzzling technical terminology. Some of it is amusing, some of it is irritating. Check these boxes to find out what it all means.

< 25 >

Tips

These feature bits of advice I've found useful, tricks of the trade, rules of thumb and all that. Perhaps we should kick off with a sort of all-purpose tip, which is: if you feel a little nervous about getting online, don't worry. Self-induced technophobia is often the biggest problem people face when dealing with computers. It's true that connecting to the net is still a lot harder than it should be but it's nowhere near as hard as it used to be. If you know how to use a PC running Windows or an Apple Mac, you will crack the net.

As proof, I cite myself. I've never studied computers or computer science. I've got a vague idea how they work, but no deep technical knowledge. In fact, I got interested in computer culture and the net via literature. In 1986, I read *Neuromancer*, the novel in which SF writer William Gibson first developed his vision of cyberspace, and became interested in computer networks. I read more about the net, made some geeky friends and shoulder-surfed a bit in the early nineties, eventually getting online properly at the start of 1994.

This may not be what you want to hear from the author of a net guide on which you've spent good money. But the point is, if I managed to figure out the net, so can you. I did it in part by flicking through the odd manual, although there weren't that many when I started and most read as if they were compiled by malfunctioning artificial intelligence programs. But mostly I just tried things out, messed about with software, clicked buttons and pulled down menus to see what would happen.

With some net pursuits, you do need to learn some technical text commands (some chat programs for example), but most online software

< 26 >

is pretty intuitive. Tinkering is the way to learn. People who aren't familiar with computers are often worried that they will 'break' them if they press the wrong button. Once again, it's true that computers are not as robust and reliable as they should be, but they're not that feeble. And there are always support lines and guarantees to fall back on. So get stuck in and you'll soon be hooked.

Once you find your telephone bills going through the roof and your social life in ruins, if you're looking for someone to blame, feel free to drop me a line - **jim.mcclellan@guardian.co.uk**. In fact, if you find any mistakes in the book or new web sites that you think might be useful, it would be great to hear from you. Though I've done my best, there are bound to be a few errors in the book you're about to read - if only because things are constantly changing on the net. Just as this book was about to go to the printers, the news broke that the online service AOL had bought Netscape, the company that makes one of the big two web browsers. At a more basic level, web sites go offline or even change addresses. Consequently, we've decided to put up a special Guardian Net Guide web page at url to follow. This is the place to go for updates, news on new software and details of web addresses that have changed or were printed inaccurately in this book.

At the back of this book you will find a CD ROM. It works with both PC and Mac computers and will connect you to the internet via BT Click, a service provider that has no monthly fee but simply charges you at 1p per minute more than your local telephone rate. To get online load the CD then simply click on the words, "Get online now" and follow the instructions. You can find details of all the other service providers on Page 74.

< 27 >

The CD also gives you a brief intorduction to the internet and details of the Guardian's Unlimited websites. Things change pretty rapidly in the online world, with large companies swallowing up smaller ones, etc, so to make sure the information in this book stays current we will be posting updates on the Guardian's internet site **http://guardianunlimited.co.uk**.

< 28 >

1
BEFORE YOU GET CONNECTED

• •

Get your online bearings

Some net guides and manuals start with lengthy histories of the development of the internet and even detailed technical descriptions of how it all works. This can be pretty interesting. Really. And it can help you use the net in a more productive way. However, I'm not sure it's the best idea in the world to force beginners to bone up on the history of US Cold War research institutions and the intricacies of packet-switching before they've even had a chance to look around online.

To get started online, to orientate yourself on the net, you only need to know a few basics. You don't need a detailed knowledge of the net, but it helps to have some sort of mental picture of it. One way of thinking of the internet is as a network of networks. This gets across the fact that the net isn't one coherent, unified entity, it's a multiplicity. It's always good to remember this when people try to boil the net's variety down into one

< 29 >

Jargon file – Packet-Switching

When messages are sent via a network, they are broken up into individual packets of bits which are then sent separately. Packets contain details of the place they came from, and the address they're going to, amongst other things. ▲

thing, and tell you that, for example, the net is naturally libertarian in its political outlook.

At a very basic level, a computer network is a collection of computers – say in an office – connected in such a way that they can communicate with each other and share information. The net takes this to a global scale. It's a kind of global network that has emerged as more and more local and national networks hook up with each other. To connect to and communicate with each other, computers rely on shared standard languages, or, to use the technical term, protocols. When you're online, you'll encounter different sorts of protocol. For example, there's FTP, aka File Transfer Protocol, which allows you to upload or download files to and from the net. The World Wide Web, the multimedia part of the net,

Jargon file – Protocol

A shared language used by computers so that they can communicate with other computers. ▲

< 30 >

Jargon file – Top Down, Bottom Up

Two related terms you hear a lot online. The former refers to
authoritarian/hierarchical structures in which order (and other things)
are imposed by the people at the top. The latter refers to more open
grass-roots structures in which order (and other things) emerge from
the actions of ordinary users and trickle up. ▲

relies on something called HTTP – Hyper Text Transfer Protocol. The
basic protocol which enables the net to work by letting computers round
the world communicate with each other is TCP/IP – aka Transmission
Control Protocol/Internet Protocol. All these letters may look like the left-
overs from a game of Scrabble, but after a while you will get used to them
and will use them without thinking.

Another way to think about the net is as a many-to-many network.
This is shorthand for the fact that, when online, everyone can send as well
as receive messages. In contrast, broadcast TV is often characterised as a
one-to-many network – meaning one node or station sends messages and
all the rest of us can do is consume those messages. Some businesses are
attempting to bring the top-down, one-to-many model of TV to the net
(the theory being that this will bring ordinary users online). But never
forget – the net lets you send messages, publish your own ideas, upload
your own videos. ▲

< 31 >

Net addresses

So how do you and your information know where you are and where you're going on this wonderfully various many-to-many network of networks? Thankfully, the net, like the real world, has a system of addresses. All computers that are connected to the internet have a unique IP (as in Internet Protocol) address. This is a collection of four numbers, separated by full stops/periods (e.g. 123.4.56.891). Incidentally, there are plans afoot to extend and expand this system, since there are worries that shortly the net will run out of available addresses.

Obviously large groups of numbers are not the easiest thing to remember (or type). So, as well as the IP addresses there is also something called the Domain Name System which translates all those numbers into words. Along with an IP address, each computer connected to the net has its own unique domain name. These may look just as forbidding as IP numbers at first but you will soon get used to them.

Take the address for the *Guardian*'s web site –
http://www.guardianunlimited.co.uk.

The first part – **http://** – refers to the protocol used to access this address, in this case Hyper Text Transfer Protocol

The second part – **www** – indicates which part of the net we're talking about – in this case, the World Wide Web.

< 32 >

The third part – **.guardianunlimited** – is the name of the institution or people running the site/the computer it's stored on.

The fourth part of the address – **.co** – is known as a 'top level domain'. It tells you what sort of institution is behind the site. So .co indicates that it's a commercial/business site.

A variety of other identifiers could appear here:

.ac indicates a college, university or other sort of academic establishment

.edu also indicates academic establishments, used mainly in the States

.gov a government-run site

.mil a site run by the military

.org used by non-profit organisations

.com the American version of '.co', though increasingly used by companies all round the world

.net used by internet service providers.

There are plans to add a variety of new top-level domains in the near future – things like **.firm** and **.store** – but at the time of writing, these haven't been finalised.

Finally the fifth part of the address – **.uk** – tells you in which country the site is located. These are generally pretty easy to figure out – **.jp** is Japan, **.de** is Germany, as in Deutschland, and so on. For the most part, American sites (or sites that use the **.com** domain) can get away without indicating which country they're in.

< 33 >

Read about it online - Domain Names

If you want to find out more about domain names on the net –
how to register them, how to sell them, who runs them and much
else – or if you want to catch up on a little net name history, try
Internet Goldrush – **http://www.igoldrush.com**. For something more
businesslike, you could try Net Names – which will help you
register the domain name you need for your company –
http://www.netnames.co.uk. ▲

The addresses for electronic mail work in the same way, with the
name/nickname of the person (or department) you want to contact
appearing before the basic domain name, as in **netguide@guardian.co.uk**.

Once you get used to it, the domain name system is pretty easy to use.
And that's what most people do – just get on with things without giving it a
second thought. However, domain names and the things people do with
them are a source of endless fascination, or irritation, for some net users. The
result is a kind of net name subculture, which encompasses blaggers, politicians and artists. For example, some people took advantage of the slowness
of the mainstream business world to understand the net and bought up
famous domain names e.g. **www.bootsthechemist.co.uk** in the hope of forcing
the company in question to cough up serious money to get its name back –
a practice now known as domain squatting.

Some net users have advanced conspiracy theories about the CIA
connections of one of the organisations that makes a fat profit from
running the domain name system (Network Solutions Inc.). Everyone

< 34 >

from artists to gamey entrepeneurs have attempted to set up alternative domain name systems. Currently the US and the European Community are engaged in an ongoing political wrangle about how best to administer and extend the domain name system in the future. Once you get online, you'll be able to read a lot more about all this. In fact, a keen interest in net addresses is probably one of the key signs that you're well on the way to becoming a screen-obsessed Homo Connectus. ▲

Mapping the net

Addresses only go so far when it comes to finding your way around online. It's also helpful to construct a kind of mental map of the net. By this, I don't just mean something as practical and accurate as an A–Z – although there's some fascinating work being done at the moment on producing workable maps for the net. It's more a question of conceptual images or the metaphors you use when you think and talk about the net.

If you use a standard computer with a graphic interface (i.e. a screen full of little cartoon icons) and a mouse, you'll be used to what computer

Read about it online – Mapping

If you want to have a look at some recent efforts to provide visual maps of cyberspace, go to **http://www.cybergeography.org/**. ▲

< 35 >

Jargon file - Interactive TV

Much hyped in the early nineties before the net came along. This was supposed to be a TV set you could use to order pizza and videos and generally control when you saw certain TV shows. Some people think interactive TV was killed off by the net, but it remains the holy grail for certain big tech companies. ▲

types call the desktop metaphor. This means all the images of folders, files and trash cans you see on your screen. By making your PC seem familiar, these symbols help you to interact with your computer. Much net software continues the desktop metaphor, even when it doesn't seem that good a fit – for example, though awash in travel imagery, the Netscape web browser lets you 'bookmark' your favourite web sites.

However, some net theorists have argued that at a higher level we use a few general metaphors when using the internet and that these metaphors make this strange new technology seem more accessible. Hence, we think of the net as being like a huge global library, or a community meeting place, or a souped-up shopping mall, or as a new frontier, or even a kind of prototype interactive TV delivering something approaching video (or rather thirty-second video clips) on demand.

You could argue that the first example of a net metaphor is to think of it as a space in the first place, to think that, to rework Gertrude Stein, there is a 'there' there. In a way, that awful cliché of the early nineties – the information superhighway – was also a kind of net metaphor (the net

< 36 >

as digital motorway), used by American Vice President Al Gore when he needed to sell the American public the more intangible (not to say dry) idea of a National Information Infrastructure. The contagious spread of I-way imagery back then showed that we do need concrete, familiar images to help us get a handle on the immaterial realm that crackles into life over the wires. Metaphors like the net as library or community help us first grasp the online world, then get things done.

Some critics (e.g. Mark Stefik in his book, *Internet Dreams*, published in 1996 by MIT Press) argue that we need to choose our net metaphors carefully, because they will determine what sort of net we end up building. You can see what he means. As mentioned above, many big media companies have invested heavily in the mainstream-friendly idea that the net might be 'like television' and have pushed development in that area (e.g. in sending real-time video over the net). Whilst it's true that some areas of the net are a bit like television, overall the net as television metaphor offers a drastically diminished, rather passive idea of what the online world is and might be in the future.

Perhaps the best thing here is to be flexible. No single metaphor tells the whole story about the net. And all of them can apply at the same time. You can shift between them, depending on what seems useful at the time – whatever gets you through the net, as it were. ▲

< 37 >

Try before you buy

After getting a little conceptual, perhaps we should end by coming back down to earth. If you haven't actually been online before, the only sensible thing to do is to try the net before you spend any real money. You need to get an idea of what it's really like. It may be that you'll discover that the net isn't really for you. It's more than likely that this won't be the case. But it isn't guaranteed. So be sensible and try before you buy.

The easiest option is to go round to a friend who's already online and blag a few hours on his or her computer. People often suggest you persuade a wired-up buddy to give you a guided tour. I've done a few of these site-seeing sessions and people always start looking slightly glazed midway through – usually somewhere between the online bookstore amazon.com and Need to Know, the UK zine/mail-out that serves up a weekly shot of hip geek tech news, wind-ups and gossip. It may be my choice of sites. Then again, the net is not something you watch other people doing. The point is that you find your way around. You connect to the information and people you choose. So if you do head round to your net-literate friend, take a copy of their favourite video and a six-pack with you. Ask them to show you round for a while. Then sit them down

---

Jargon file – Spyware

Software used by companies to log exactly what their employees do on the net. ▲

< 38 >

Jargon file – Cybercafé

A café complete with a few terminals where you can buy coffee and access the net for a hour or so. Very popular a few years ago, cybercafés will need to develop and offer something more than net access if they are to survive over the next ten years. ▲

with the video and beers. They will be there if you get stuck but will leave you alone for a couple of hours and let you get on with things.

If the computers at work are hooked up to the net, you could try it out there. Remember, though, that your boss is paying and is more than likely using a piece of spyware to check on what the office drones do online. So you might want to check if it's OK to fool around for a bit.

The other place to go for a test run in cyberspace is a cybercafé. Most towns and cities now have one. You generally pay around £6 for an hour online. A tad expensive and perhaps a little confusing if you've never been online, but there should be help on hand to get you started (alternatively, you could take this book along and cut to the later sections). The better cybercafés also tend to have reasonably quick connections and the latest software. There are plenty of online lists of UK cybercafés (admittedly, if you're not connected, they're not going to be that much use). For more info, try Internet Magazine's list **http://www.internet-magazine.com/resources/welcome.htm** or the list at **http://www.cyberiacafe.net/cyberia/guide/ccafe_uk.htm**. Alternatively look for the Internet Cafés section on the UK Yahoo.

< 39 >

Net myths decontructed

People have said a lot of apparently sensible, vaguely contentious, mildly dubious or just plain daft things about the net over the last few years. Before we go any further, it might be helpful to clear your head of some of what's been said. Think of this chapter as a quick debriefing session, a Pass Notes for cyber babble. Once you have read it, I hope you will (a) be able to tell when the latest high-tech guru is talking out of his or her serial port, and, more importantly, (b) know a bit more about the way things really are online.

When you're on the net, national boundaries don't matter any more, distance is dead and where you are physically is completely irrelevant

True enough. The net helps people on different sides of the world communicate relatively cheaply. You can stay in the loop even if you're off the map, as a BT ad might put it. You can access information from Chinese dissident sites, download reports by Australian activists about Nike factories in South-East Asia, read American showbiz gossip rags days before their paper versions make it across the Atlantic. But location is still important. In the UK, where we pay for local phone calls and suffer under ludicrous libel laws, your net life is likely to be different from that enjoyed by American users.

< 40 >

Read about it online – Net Surveys

If you want to read the latest surveys of the net population and what they get up to, go to the site maintained by the Irish net consultancy Nua **http://www.nua.ie/surveys/index.cgi**, which features details of, and links to, most recent net surveys. ▲

Everyone talks about the net being a worldwide phenomenon but really it's just an American thing

Americans remain the most sizeable national presence on the net and they often act as if they own the thing, setting 'global standards' without bothering to consult the rest of the world (though perhaps we should be understanding about this since they did invent it). It's also clear that claims for the net's global reach are overstated. Most of the Southern hemisphere isn't connected. Even in the West, most people are not online. That said, more and more non-English-language web sites are coming online. If you take the time to look, you'll see that the net no longer begins and ends with American corporations and Texan conspiracy nuts.

The net is a sort of digital locker room, a toy for the boys

There are still more men online than women, though some areas are more balanced – AOL recently claimed that over 50 per cent of its users were women. Unfortunately, many men on the net do behave exceedingly badly,

< 41 >

Jargon file – Flame

An abusive/insulting online message fired off in anger at some mistake or perceived slight. People often get hold of the wrong end of the stick online, and send a response without engaging their brains. This leads to flame wars – raging arguments which can disrupt newsgroups and mailing lists. ▲

---

especially the troglodytes in some online chat rooms. But things are changing as more women get online. And there's nothing inherently male about the net. The theory that it is 'a guy thing' often seems like something dreamt up by boys who don't want to share. Women shouldn't stay offline because of worries about online sexism. In some ways it can be easier to deal with than the real world variety. You can always flame persistent male pests or set your software to make them disappear.

The net is a youth thing. If you're over forty you won't get it

It's no surprise that older people are vaguely net-phobic. Many don't have any experience of computers or the net. Some techno-gurus get paid a lot to tell them they wouldn't understand it all anyway. But think of the benefits of getting online: staying in touch with family and friends, accessing useful information (e.g. on health, holidays and finance), shopping without leaving home. Older people could get as much out of these as the young. Many have the time and the money for

< 42 >

the net. If you are an older reader, forget the prevailing wisdom and have a go.

The net is packed with geeks and nerds. So it can be of little use to ordinary, well-adjusted people like me

The media don't seem to like geeks. Perhaps journalists are subconsciously afraid of them. After all, geeks understand the computers that journalists rely on (but are largely clueless about). Really we should be grateful to the computer geeks who were obsessive enough to get something like the net up and running, though that doesn't mean you have to spend hours talking to them about rebel operating systems. Obviously there are lots of geek-oriented resources online. But the net is now a mainstream thing as well. There's plenty to interest people who don't spend their lives pondering continuity errors in *Star Trek*.

Jargon file – Chat Room

An online space where you can chat (i.e. exchange text messages in real time) with a group of users. ▲

< 43 >

**Most of the information on the net is rubbish – just not worth
bothering with**

There's an awful lot of witless stupidity on the net. But before you use
that as a reason to stay offline, wander into your nearest bookshop. What
do you see? Jeffrey Archer novels, ghosted autobiographies by B-list
sportsmen, shelves of *Men are from Mars, Women are from Venus*
claptrap. Milton, Blake, Joyce and Jane Austen don't usually take up the
bulk of the display space. The net is just like TV, radio and print. There
is a lot of rubbish but there's good stuff too, if you look.

**Thanks to the net, people from around the world will soon realise that
they are all just the same really and a new era of world peace will dawn**

A few techno-gurus still spout this routine. In theory, the net can help
broaden horizons. In practice, it often leads to a narrowing of perspective,
as people log into newsgroups devoted only to their interests or customise
their software so that they are only exposed to the news they choose. A few
years ago, some net users eulogised about how the artificial barriers of race,
colour, gender, creed and class faded away online. In fact, in the absence of
obvious visual signs, people assumed you were a white, middle-class bloke.
If you indicated you weren't, prejudice and hate often returned. Go online
now and you can find Christian fundamentalists disrupting online forums
run by gays and web sites run by racist groups – in other words, all the old-
world prejudices and conflicts, but in a slightly different form.

< 44 >

Log on to the net and you will immediately be assaulted by pornographic images, perverts and paedophiles

There is a lot of porn online – some of it foul stuff. Generally it doesn't leap out at you when you log on. You're more in danger of being 'assaulted' by the images peering down from the top shelf in your local newsagent. You usually have to go looking for porn online (though not always – for more on this, go to page 353). A hormonal teenager would have no problem finding it. Of course, in pre-net days, hormonal teens generally found ways to get hold of pornographic images. It is one of the standard male adolescent pursuits. Still the net does make it easy – the barriers that exist in the real world – the top shelf, shop assistants willing to enforce the over-eighteen rule – aren't there yet. However, there are plenty of things parents can do to protect their children and further frustrate their teenage sons. As for paedophiles, they use the net, just as they use telephones and the mail. They go online to swap pornographic

Read about it online – Illegal material

Under pressure from the police and the government, the UK net industry has made attempts to deal with the problems posed by child pornography. If users find child porn (or other illegal material online), they are encouraged to report it to The Internet Watch Foundation, who will then attempt to take some sort of action. Read more about what they're up to at **http://www.iwf.org.uk/**. ▲

< 45 >

Jargon file – Filterware

A software package designed to block access to certain sites: either those the maker of the program deems unacceptable or sites specified by the user. ▲

imagery and there is also evidence that some hang out in chat rooms popular with teenagers and children. However, paedophiles are not online in anything like the numbers some alarmists claim. Parents should ignore the panicmongers but take sensible precautions – as they would with the real world. This whole area is covered in more depth on page 351.

The government should do something to protect our children from the horrors of the net

Where material online is clearly illegal, as with child porn, action is already being taken by many UK internet service providers who choose to block access to newsgroups that circulate it. Most people can agree on the need to do something about child porn, but other areas (hardcore porn for the over-eighteens, political 'hate speech') remain more contentious. Protecting children without ruining all the good things about the net remains a difficult problem. It won't be solved by rushing in some new kind of law. A better way forward might be to let individual users control what their computers can access via online ratings systems and filterware,

< 46 >

but this certainly isn't the problem-free solution some claim. Again, there's more on this on page 351.

If you give out your credit card details online, hackers will get hold of them and use your account to subsidise their crack habits

Online security still isn't quite what it could be, but many of the worries about using credit cards online have more to do with the novelty of the technology than a sensible appreciation of the risks involved. You don't usually worry about giving out your credit card number over the telephone, but do you know where the card number you handed over will be stored? Hackers tell stories of swapping stolen card numbers, but they often get them by breaking into poorly protected computers at companies who collected them in normal ways (via mail and the telephone).

If you connect your PC to the net, it will soon be awash with strange computer viruses

I once worked at a magazine where the editor thought that if he got connected, viruses would instantly flow down the telephone lines and into his office network. Viruses don't jump down the telephone line and deliberately seek out your PC like some malevolent killer bug. (And I don't think the editor really believed this. He was more worried about his staff wasting too much time online and was using the virus story as cover.) If you get a piece of email entitled "!!! This is a Virus – Your Machine is already infected !!!", it's a wind-up. The only thing in danger of being

< 47 >

infected is your mind – with groundless worries. However, be careful about software you download from the net. Always run a virus check on it.

On the net no one knows you're a dog

The punchline from a famous cartoon showing two dogs in front of a computer. The net does let you communicate in relative anonymity. In an online chat room, people know as much about you as you choose to tell them. Hence, one of the great male online pursuits – going to a chat room and pretending to be a woman. All harmless fun – usually – but the anonymity afforded by the net can be abused and some of the most enduring spaces on the net are those where people give their real names and take responsibility for their words. That said, the net is not as anonymous as it might seem. Everywhere you go in cyberspace, you leave trails that can be followed fairly easily. There's more on this on page 373.

Using the net makes you sad and depressed

It is true that, once you're online, the arrival of the quarterly telephone bill can lead to a certain sinking feeling. However, there were suggestions earlier this year that using the net led to a marked increase in real depression, according to a survey done at Carnegie Mellon University. Various newspaper pundits seized on this and ran glib 'told you so' sneers disguised as opinion columns. It was left to various online magazines to look more closely at the study's conclusions. They pointed out that it did measure feelings in a rather vague way and that the people in the survey group – who

< 48 >

Read about it online – Net Surveys

The Carnagie Mellon Home Net Survey is online at **http://homenet. andrew.cmu.edu/progress/research.html**. The best attempt to debunk it was by Scott Rosenberg of the American webzine Salon **http:///www.salonmagazine.com/21st/rose/1998/09/03straight.html**. Long term net booster Howard Rheingold offered a more rueful meditation on the possible truths behind that survey in the webzine Feed **http://www.feedmag.com/essay/es102_master.html**. ▲

had never used the net before and took it up for the study – were perhaps not that representative. Many critics suggested that it was misleading to lump all online activities together. Getting involved in supportive long-term online relationships is not the same as drifting through anonymous chat rooms where people mostly trade insults. However, whilst treating the survey with scepticism, a fair few net writers and pundits did admit that they recognised a grain of truth in the survey, that some net activities (pointless flame wars, surfing for porn) can be pretty grim. Perhaps the thing to take from this is the realisation that the net is not one thing, good or bad; it's a whole variety of things. Some may get you down. Some may make your life more worthwhile. However, doing any of them to excess, to the point where your real-world relationships start to dwindle, is not a good idea. ▲

< 49 >

The net is a functioning anarchy – no one's in charge and that's why it works so well

One of the great net clichés, and true, up to a point. A Cold War invention, the net was conceived as a decentralised communications network. The idea was that without an obvious centre through which all messages on the system passed, it would be less vulnerable to enemy attack. OK, so there is no central command. And the committee of boffins – the Internet Engineering Task Force **http://www.ietf.org/** – that sets the technical standards that keep the net running is a very open and democratic structure. However, there is a central organisation in charge of administering the system of net addresses. The rather scarily named WorldCom may soon control over half the net's infrastructure. And whilst the government doesn't control the net, if you keep posting reports on your web pages about what MI5 are really up to, you may receive an unwelcome dawn wake-up call.

The net is a creation of the free market. If governments get involved, they will only mess it up

The 'decentralised' technology of the net is often cited as an argument for similarly decentralised political systems. You'll encounter plenty of techno-libertarians online who see the net as both symbol and proof of the superiority of the free market and argue that government has no role in cyberspace. It can be amusing to point out to them that the net was only developed thanks to government funding and taxes. It's true that govern-

< 50 >

ment hasn't always been that constructive in its dealings with the net. But as multinational corporations use the net to gather more and more information about us, we may need the government to stand in their way.

The net will lead to the collapse of the nation state

The net causes problems for national governments. They can't stop their citizens accessing sites they don't like. They're unsure how to collect tax on shopping done online. Some computer types – known as cypherpunks – see this as just the beginning. They believe that Nation states will inevitably disappear as people use the net to keep their finances secret (frustrating tax collection). Worse, thanks to the net, people will begin to cut themselves off from their physical neighbours and will feel closer to people online whose interests (economic, political, sexual, whatever) they

---

Jargon file – Cyberpunks

Skilled programmers with a libertarian bent who believe in free speech (and the free market, usually) and defend the right of individuals to use encryption technology to protect their privacy online. When they're not writing/distributing encryption programs, they compose rants about the evils of big government, its future collapse and the coming of crypto-anarchy. For an introduction, try the cypherpunks' homepage at **http://www.csua.berkeley.edu/cypherpunks/Home.html**.

< 51 >

share. This may happen in some form. But, to shift the terms of the debate slightly, watch out for people claiming that this new technology means the end of that old technology, like the fools who go on about computers and the end of the book. New technologies do not simplistically replace old technologies. What usually happens is that the older technologies get reinvented in response. When TV appeared, radio and cinema changed, they didn't disappear. The same goes for political or cultural technologies. The net will lead to a change in the nation state and how we think and feel about it. It's already happening. But it won't finish it off.

The net will lead to the collapse of big multinational corporations

While the late-night pipe-dreams of cyber-libertarians involve the collapse of 'Big Government', those of left-wing libertarians usually concern the fall of the hated multinational corporations. Apparently, armed with the net, smaller nimbler outfits will naturally see off these hulking slow dinosaurs. Actually Disney, Time Warner and the rest have in fact been reasonably effective online. And faced with the confusion of the online

---

Jargon file – Cyberspace

A term first coined by SF writer William Gibson, for the consensual hallucination people encountered when they logged on to computer networks. Now taken to mean the place you're in when you're on the net. ▲

< 52 >

world, many newcomers seek out the names and brands they recognise from the real world – in other words, the big multinational corporations.

Thanks to the net, no one will ever leave their homes again but will be sucked into the unreal world of cyberspace

The net-hating neo-Luddites who say this also go on about how much rubbish there is on the net. Some contradiction here, maybe? Remember, we're talking about the net, about web pages which often take ages to load and then seize up for no reason. Will this keep us hypnotised before our screens, like moths to the flame? However, parts of the net can be very compelling, especially to adolescents of all ages. Parents should keep tabs on their teenagers' use of the net, in particular chat rooms. As for the rest of us, we seem to be using the net to get away from it all in a fairly conventional way. Hence the popularity of web sites enabling you to book holidays.

The net is a living thing, an emergent global mind in which we are all mere neurons.

This kind of pseudo-sixties, techno-mystic chatter is popular online amongst those who get over-excited by the speed with which the net allows us to communicate. They look at the swiftness with which ideas spread across the net and conclude that those ideas must be alive. Underneath, this is often a crude kind of anti-humanism which holds that technology is calling the shots, not us, that people didn't build the net,

< 53 >

Jargon file - Neo-Luddites

Latterday descendants of the Luddites. This crew sometimes take a hammer to computers – if they need a publicity gimmick to sell their new product. Mostly they confine themselves to knocking out book deals about the superhighway to hell. ▲

that it somehow built itself. Personally I think that, without people, the net is just a load of wires in the ground.

The net is a new frontier, a brave new world, a separate country cut off from the old world

Ever since it exhausted the real frontier (and its implied escape from the problems of the past), America has been looking for a replacement. In the sixties, space was the new frontier. Now cyberspace is the place where Americans can play out their manifest destiny and reconnect with the American Dream. New-frontier rhetoric is pretty harmless, providing journalists with a chance to rabbit on about cybercowboys. It becomes irritating when people take it literally and start claiming that the net really is another country. It is true that there is a net culture, a self-selected group who think about the net in a particular way, who are pro-free speech, anti-government and libertarian in their outlook. And often when you go online you feel you're wandering through some sort of parallel universe. But to start campaigning for secession is to get caught up in your

< 54 >

Read about it online - John Perry Barlow

The prime example of this was net guru John Perry Barlow's rather silly 1996 'Declaration of the Independence of Cyberspace' in which, angered by the US government's admittedly stupid attempt to censor the net via something called the Communications Decency Act (now happily defunct), he donned Jeffersonian drag to tell Ye Governments of Ye Olde Industrial World that they had no jurisdiction over the net. You can read it at **http://www.eff.org/pub/Publications/ John_Perry_Barlow/barlow_0296.declaration**. ▲

own metaphors. Behind all this chatter is a kind of technological escapism, a desire to leave the messy real world behind for the ideal realm of cyberspace. The interesting and important thing about the net is that it can help you reconnect with the real world in new ways.

The net will empower ordinary citizens and remake democracy

Claims about online democracy look slightly hollow given that, even in the West, the net is still the plaything of the few. That said, the net is changing

Jargon file - Intranet

A private corporate or institutional network which uses the technology and protocols of the internet. ▲

< 55 >

politics at a practical level. Westminster now has its intranets, virtual think tanks and mailing lists. However, being able to email MPs does not make party politics automatically more involving. People get interested if political ideas have substance, not because they can hang out in an online chat room with Tony Blair. Enthusiasts suggest that soon we'll use the net to vote on all sorts of issues. As it is, people can barely be bothered to vote every four years, so they're unlikely to spend their evenings voting away, however easy point-and-click technology makes it. That said, the net is changing politics – by involving people beyond simple party lines, by helping them to form different sorts of associations and groups. You can see it in the way the net is already used by environmental activists or to campaign against multinational corporations like McDonald's and Nike.

If we wire our schools, our education worries will be over

Obviously children need to be taught about computer networks. And the net can be a wonderful educational resource. But on its own, it won't solve the problems our schools have. Money that might be better spent elsewhere (on decent textbooks, repairing facilities, paying teachers enough to enable them to regain some sense of self-worth and purpose) will be lavished instead on the rather nebulous 'national grid for learning'. This may do some good but it will also bring Microsoft and other big companies into our classrooms. It may also create a new set of problems. Once the 'national grid for learning' is up and running, teachers will need to be trained to use it. It will also need to be upgraded on a fairly regular basis, which will cost yet more money.

< 56 >

If you don't get online now, right now, you'll be left behind, you'll be toast, roadkill on the superhighway

A variation on standard computer industry ad hype – that if you don't buy a PC now, you'll never catch up, you'll be history. And if you do buy a computer now, you'll need to buy another one in two years' time or you'll be history again. Recently, net critics have cannily taken cyber-hypesters at their word and asked about those who will be left behind because they can't afford the net, suggesting that a two-tier society of information-haves and information-have-nots will be created. The cyber-hypesters response was that no one will really be left behind, there won't be information-have-nots, just information-have-laters. Their new idea is that we should all be grateful to the info-have-nows because they're testing out bug-ridden products, paying through the nose for things that will eventually be sold much more cheaply to the mainstream when they actually work. This is pretty glib. Access to the net for those who are less well off remains a problem. As for the claims that you have to get online or risk being info-highway roadkill, there are now lots of good reasons for getting online. Worrying that you'll be 'left behind' if you don't is not one of them.

< 57 >

2 GETTING CONNECTED

So you're ready to get online. You want that twenty-first-century, information-at-your-fingertips cyber-blast and you want it now. Unfortunately, before you surf anywhere, you will have to spend some money, especially if you don't already have a computer. Even if you do have a PC of some sort, you'll need to buy a modem and get a connection to the net. The online world doesn't come cheap at the moment. Handing over wads of money to salespeople, especially computer salespeople, is never a happy or painless process. However, in the next section we'll help you to find a reasonable deal when it comes to kitting yourself out for the internet. ▲

Hardware

You can now use all sorts of things to access the net – natty digital personal organisers, cutting-edge mobile phones, TVs fitted with special

< 59 >

set-top boxes. There's even a souped-up home telephone (it looks like it has ambitions to grow up to be a laptop one day), which will let you read web pages and email as well as make standard voice calls. Undoubtedly, many of these gizmos will be very useful in the future, but at the moment you should leave them to the geeks. The net-friendly mobile phones and personal organisers are getting better but these are still really only for gadget boys or business people – in other words, for people who already have a computer at home or in the office but need to check email on the move. You wouldn't want to have one of these as your first choice for accessing the net.

The new breed of web-capable TVs have become better in the last year and are being hyped (again) as perfect for non-computer types, but they still probably need a while to develop. I'm still not sold on the basic idea

Read about it online – Web TV

The big player, when it comes to accessing the web via TVs and set-top boxes, is the American company Web TV (owned by Microsoft). On their web page **http://www.webtv.net** they sell themselves as not so much an internet thing, more a way to make TV more interesting. The British competitor is the NetStation which was launched in 1997. They emphasise how easy it makes getting online – no modems to configure or software to get. However it also relies on its own rather creaky web browser. For more information, go to **http://www.netstation.co.uk/netstation/**.

< 60 >

of checking out web pages and sending email via the TV. The problem isn't just that TV monitors still aren't best suited to delivering legible text (and there's still an awful lot of text online). It's more that accessing the web via the TV set raises the wrong sort of expectations. The web isn't like TV yet, though these new web TVs might encourage that assumption. Yes, you can see video via the web, but it will be low resolution and pretty jerky – nothing to compare with the images on even the most knackered goggle box. In addition, the net is still nowhere near as reliable as TV at the moment and will suffer from the comparisons that will inevitably be made if you start accessing it via the same machine you use to check out *The Simpsons*.

Beyond that, watching TV and wandering round the net are two very different experiences. The former is more passive; the latter is more active. You need to be up close to the screen, figuring out what to do and where to go next. And it's not easy writing email perched on the couch pecking away at a cross between a TV remote control and a miniature keyboard. Undoubtedly, in the future, the TV will become more intelligent, will merge with the computer in some way and you will use this new piece of kit to access some part of the net. Too many people with a lot of money want it to happen. But it isn't going to happen for a while. So your best bet if you want to get online is still a home computer.

The Computer

Perhaps we should address the Mac versus PC thing first. When it comes to buying a home computer to access the net, you have a choice between a Apple Macintosh or an IBM-compatible PC running Microsoft

< 61 >

Windows. (Of course you could go for one of the other machines – Acorns, Amigas and the rest – which are fine, but less well supplied when it comes to net software.) Though some people pursue it with religious intensity (mainly Mac owners – most PC owners don't love their machines enough), the Mac/PC debate is one of the more boring things about computer culture. Actually the choice is pretty simple. If you want to be able to swap files and other bits and pieces with friends and work colleagues, you should buy the same sort of computer as them, which will usually mean a computer running Windows (Microsoft has 90 per cent of the PC market). If you want something easy to use, the Apple Mac is still the best bet, despite the advances made by Microsoft. The

Read about it online – Operating Systems

For a dated but still amusing piece about the battle between rival operating systems, try the satirical analysis offered by Italian semiologist/novelist Umberto Eco. He argued that the Macintosh was a Catholic machine – in that it was 'cheerful, friendly and conciliatory', dealt in 'simple formulas and sumptuous icons' and assumed that 'everyone has a right to salvation'. MS DOS PCs, on the other hand, are Protestant – they 'allow free interpretation of scripture', demand 'difficult personal decisions' and do not assume that 'all can achieve salvation' or even get their files printed. Apparently, Windows represents an Anglican-style heresy. You can find it at **http://www.isi.edu/~nomdenet/eco.html**. ▲

< 62 >

Mac is also still the choice of many creative professionals – artists, journalists, designers, publishers. If that's what you do (or hope to do in the future), the Mac is probably what you want.

However, this is a book about the net and at the moment the bulk of new net software comes out first for the PC. Some of it never comes out in a Mac version. That may not bother you, though recently several Mac-using pundits have written newspaper columns about how they've bought a PC because they were fed up at not being able to use the latest nifty net software (maybe it was a slow news week). Perhaps the real difference between what we might call Macolytes and PC clones is that the latter accept that they're buying a fallible piece of machinery. They expect it to break down and malfunction. People who buy Macs know that they are buying more than a machine. They are buying into a kind of cult based around a piece of technology that once promised to change the world, a cult obsessed with the superiority of its icons and interface, that religiously reads all those articles in the technology press headlined 'Rotten to the Core – Will Apple Fall?'

You shouldn't spend too much time pondering all this. A more pressing concern is how much computing power you need to get online. So long as you don't expect the multimedia animations and video feeds, so long as you're happy with reading and writing text and don't want pretty pictures, you can actually get by online with something very low tech – an old 486 DX PC that runs Windows 3.x and has 8 Mb of RAM and a couple of hundred Mb of hard disk space or an old Mac from two or three years ago. But I wouldn't advise it. After a while, struggling along with this may become more than a bit tiresome.

< 63 >

If you want to see a bit more of what's on offer online, the minimum requirements are:

RAM You can just about get by with 16 Mb but you're better off with 32 Mb. It will make the latest versions of the web browsers run a lot quicker.

Hard Disk Web browsers and other bits of software are getting ever more bloated and once online you might find yourself amassing a sizeable collection of software. So although you can get by on something smaller, realistically you'll need at least a 1 Gigabyte hard disk. Most new machines come with much more.

Multimedia If you want to check out online multimedia – listen to music or watch video clips – you need a decent soundcard and speakers, a video-card with a megabyte or two of video RAM and graphics accelerators. Most new computers now carry this kind of thing as standard. If you want to telephone people via the net, you might find a microphone useful.

Processor Speed This isn't as much of an issue as some make out, but a reasonable Pentium won't hurt. Even if you buy second-hand these days, you're likely to get something like that.

Monitors Size is up to you, though there's something slightly domineering about some of the huge computer monitors now appearing on the market. More important, if you're going to use a creaky old PC or buy second-

< 64 >

hand, check that your monitor has at least 256 colours. If you're buying new, don't worry about this.

Operating Systems Though you can get by with a computer that runs an old operating system (i.e. Windows 3.x), everything becomes that bit more fiddly. You have to get separate bits of software for different tasks. Windows 95/98 and NT have the programs you need to get online already built into them. The same goes for Macs from System 7.5 on. Windows 98 takes everything one step further, introducing something called 'web integration'. There's more on this in the section on the web on page 407.

CD ROM Drive This has been a standard on new PCs for years now, but if you are running an older computer which doesn't have one, getting software on old 3.5 floppy discs may become a problem.

If all you're planning to do online is send email and check out the web, if you don't intend to wander through any 3D online environments and you don't mind if the video you see online is a little jerky, you'll be fine with an entry-level home/multimedia PC. Prices and specs change month by month in the computer business, but as this book was going to press, spending around £1,000 would get you a PC with a 333 MHz Pentium II processor, at least 32 Mb of RAM, a 3 Gigabyte hard disk, 32-speed CD ROM drive, 4 Mb 3D video card, 15-inch monitor, soundcard, speakers and 56.6k fax modem, plus software. For the average net user this is more than adequate.

If you move around a lot and need to take your PC with you, you could go for a laptop. It's pretty easy to find something that fits most of

< 65 >

Tips – Buying a Computer

Before you buy, think about what else you plan to do with your computer. If all you're going to do, aside from going online, is word processing, you don't need a screamingly fast processor and Gigabytes of disk space. On the other hand, if you want to play computer games (especially the latest generation of 3D efforts), then a faster machine with a lot of memory and special graphics cards is a big help. ▲

the above requirements (though you might have to take a drop on processor speed if you're on a budget, and you won't get an internal modem). However, laptops are significantly more expensive than home PCs. You pay a lot for mobility.

When it comes to buying new computers, computer magazines sometimes tell you to look at something mid-range, which tends to mean shelling out around £1,500 or so, plus VAT. Apparently you should do this to ensure a bit of future proofing. Put simply, this means taking action to ensure that, in the eyes of the industry at least, your shiny new PC doesn't become a worthless piece of junk the day after you buy it.

In the computer business, obsolescence doesn't have to be deliberately planned. It's the way of the world. Chip speeds increase and the cost of memory falls almost month by month. Matching this, software developers continually increase the size of their products to take advantage of these gains, resulting in what cynics refer to as 'bloatware'. So whilst

< 66 >

Read about it online - Moore's Law

Why does your PC feel like a worthless piece of junk a year after you bought it? Blame Moore's Law, the principle first laid down in 1965 by Gordon Moore, co-founder of the chip company Intel, who suggested that the number of transistors you can pack on to a single chip will double every eighteen months. Actually he didn't quite say that, but that's what people decided he said, and he went along with them. Moore's Law is the reason that computers that cost the same get faster and faster each year. Tech journalists often claim that Moore's Law no longer applies or is about to, in the jargon, 'hit a wall'. For the record, Gordon Moore thinks it's good 'til 2012. Read his thoughts on Intel's site **http://www.intel.com/solutions/issue/feature**. ▲

everything seems to be changing, everything also seems to be standing still. What all this apparently means for the ordinary punter is that you need to buy mid-range if you want your machine to have enough power to handle the new software programs that come out the year after you buy it – hence future proofing.

Actually many people make do with the software bundled with the computer when they bought it. They don't always go out the next year and buy the new version of Microsoft Office or whatever. That said, it is nice to feel that the machine you bought a few months ago hasn't already been dismissed as an antique by the industry. If you do have the money to 'future proof', the thing is go for first is extra RAM – you can never have

< 67 >

enough of that stuff. Then go for a big hard disk. Processor speed isn't that important unless you're going to play lots of computer games – in which case, the faster the better. One of the irritating things about the computer industry is that if you buy a home computer and it becomes a useful part of your life, you will probably have to reconcile yourself to upgrading it or trading up to a newer machine in a few years' time. That said, you don't need to chuck out old machines anywhere near as often as the computer business and its sponsored hacks would have you believe.

If you don't want to buy a completely new computer, you can upgrade your existing model. If you're reasonably handy, you can do this yourself. Inserting extra chunks of RAM into a PC is actually pretty easy. As ever, it's easier still for Mac owners. However, if you are a computer innocent, the idea of fiddling with computer innards will undoubtedly seem a little daunting. You can get people to upgrade for you, though by the time you've paid for them and the extra components, you might find you could have bought a new machine for the same money.

Buying a computer

Be sensible – do a bit of research before you buy. Read the consumer computer magazines. Scope out the prices and specifications on different brands and models. Think a bit about what you want. Once you've done this, you can either go to a shop or buy direct from one of the big manufacturers. This is a matter of taste. Some people like to play around with something before they pay. I've always bought direct and had no problems. More and more, you can specify exactly what you want. If you are tempted by brilliant deals advertised in a computer magazine, think a bit

< 68 >

about the companies behind them. You want reliability from your PC. You want to be able to take it back to the manufacturers if problems occur (or at least give them a call). Some of the companies offering those great prices look like they might not be around that long.

Many new PCs are now sold as 'net ready' and come bundled with a year's access to the net and the software you need. That's fine, but check to see that you're not paying extra for this kind of thing. When you sign up with an internet service provider they should provide you with all the software you need as part of their introductory package.

Should you buy a second-hand computer? Obviously this will save you a lot of money, though it can be a minefield for beginners, worse than second-hand car dealing. If you are going to buy an old machine, take along a computer-literate friend so you don't get conned. That said, this could be worth investigating. The computer world is full of speed junkies who sell off perfectly good machines so they can get the latest, fastest thing. So you may find a real bargain.

Tips – Guarantees

Wherever you buy your computer, it's worth spending money on extending guarantees or service warranties. Computers remain unreliable machines. It shouldn't be that way. They should be as reliable and robust as the average TV set. But at the moment, they still aren't – another irritating thing about the computer business – so it's a good idea to cover yourself. ▲

< 69 >

The Modem

Once you have your computer, the next thing you need is a modem. For those with a home PC, there are two different types – internal and external. As you might expect, the former is installed inside your computer. The latter sits on your desk next to your computer and you have to connect it via one of the serial ports at the back of your machine. Internal modems don't require an extra power source, which may be an issue if you're short of power sockets at home. They also save on desk space and mean a little less cable spaghetti at the back of your computer. External modems need to be plugged into the mains (at the moment) but they are generally easier to install and easier to replace if they go wrong or you buy something newer and faster. You can also watch their status lights flashing on and off and kid yourself you know exactly what's going on.

Jargon file – Modems

A modem converts the digital information your computer works with into audio signals that can then be sent down a standard telephone line. Apparently the name is a compression of the technical term, Modulater Demodulater. The modem was something of a lifesaver for struggling newspaper subs looking for a punning headline for yet another piece about net culture. However, it is believed that to avoid government regulation, the newspaper industry is now enforcing a self-imposed ban on headlines like 'It's the Modem World!' ▲

< 70 >

Personally, if I were starting from scratch and had to choose, I'd always go for an external modem – they're just much easier to deal with. These days, you don't always have to choose. Most new PCs come bundled with a pre-installed internal modem, which for non-DIYers and computer virgins will be an attraction. If you're planning to access the net via a laptop, you'll need a PCMCIA modem, which is about the size of a credit card and slots into the back of your machine. As with laptops in general, it costs more than ordinary PC modems.

You can spend up to £200 on a top-of-the-range modem, which these days is a multi-purpose beast which doubles as a speaker phone and does your voice mail and faxes. However, the first thing you should think about when buying a modem isn't that snazzy voice mail feature but the speed at which it can send information, measured in bps (or bits per

Tips – Serial Ports

If you are going to use an older machine to get online, you need to check that it can cope with modern modems. Look in the manual and check that the serial port you are going to hook your modem up to (usually COM2) has something called a 16550 UART. Alternatively, if you've got a PC, go to the DOS prompt and run msd.exe, which should tell you what you need to know. If you don't have a 16550 UART, you'll need to upgrade your serial port – possibly not something you want to get into if you're not that comfortable with computers. ▲

< 71 >

second). The higher the speed, the faster data gets sent back and forth between you and whatever you're accessing online. So in this case, speed is good. The minimum modem speed you should put up with is 28.8 Kbps (which means data gets sent at 28,800 bits per second).

Your speedfreak nethead buddy will probably have (and will already be complaining about) a 56.6 Kbps modem. More and more new computers come bundled with them. There are two things you should know about what the computer mags like to call '56K sizzlers' (everyone has to get excited about something). First, for various technical reasons, they receive data at 56.6 Kbps but send it back at 36.6 Kbps. In addition, only in ideal conditions will they receive data at 56.6 Kbps. Most of the time they'll chug along at something between 40 and 50 Kbps.

Second, for the first year they were on the market there were two competing sorts of 56.6 Kbps modem – x2 produced by US Robotics/3Com and K56flex which was developed by Rockwell and Lucent. A committee of transnational suits resolved this dispute and agreed on a common standard known as V.90. Manufacturers promised

---

Read about it online – 56k Modems

There's nothing geeks like doing better than reading and arguing about competing standards. Hence there were plenty of web sites pondering the 56K question. Best of the bunch and still worth a look is 56k.com at **http://www.56k.com/**. For more general modem info and help, try Modem Help at **http://www.modemhelp.com/**. ▲

< 72 >

Tips – Modem Speed

Is it that important? Yes, but . . . Sometimes things are just slow online and it's nothing to do with your connection. A 28.8 Kbps modem is still fine for most non-graphics-intensive online pursuits, but most people wish they had a 56.6 Kbps machine. Whatever you get, you'll wish you had something faster. ▲

that punters who had already bought their 56.6 Kbps modem would be able to upgrade them to the new standard free of charge. However, this process has taken a while. It has also taken a while for modems built to the new standard to appear in the shops. Check with manufacturers if you're confused at all.

Thanks to the competing standards problem the first people who bought 56.6 Kbps modems had to check that their internet service provider could support their choice. It's still probably a good idea to call your ISP (when you choose one) to make sure that your modem will be OK with them. There are other modems on the way that promise even faster connections but at the moment, 56.6 Kbps is probably the easiest option if you want something vaguely speedy. ▲

< 73 >

Your connection

You have your computer and modem. The next thing you need is a connection to the net. The best bet for the beginner is the telephone line. It's simple and just about everyone's got one. If you become seriously keen on the net, you may want to try something different. There's more about other options on page 394. If you are using your home telephone line, disable call waiting if you have it. Otherwise it may break into your net calls and cut you off. You could also try the 'Call Minder' service, which takes voice messages while your line is engaged, then calls you afterwards to tell you that you have voice mail. If you become a heavy net user, it's probably worth getting an extra line. That way, you can keep track of how much you are spending.

Online Service or Internet Service Provider?

Your computer is hooked up to your modem which is plugged into your phone line. Next you need to dial up someone who can provide you with a connection to the internet. Here you have a basic choice between internet service providers and online services. The former provides you with a connection to the net and the software you'll need to get about. The latter give you access to the net and to their own private networks of services – databases of information, online editions of well-known magazines and newspapers, cinema listings, travel information, shopping, user forums, live chat rooms, online celebrity chats in which you can quiz 'the stars' about their new product and much else.

< 74 >

Tips – Family and Friends

Look at the latest pricing offers from BT, if you get your telephone service from them. It's probably a good idea to put the number of your internet service provider on your Family and Friends list and save a bit of money. Not much, admittedly, but every bit helps. If you do become a serious user, check out their Premier Line deal. ▲

There are over 200 ISPs in the UK. Among the better known are Demon Internet, who pioneered the market here and are responsible for the basic charges being so cheap, UUnet Pipex Dial, Global Internet, BT Internet, Netcom and Easynet. The big online services are AOL, Compuserve, the Microsoft Network (MSN) and, in the UK, Line One (a joint venture between Rupert Murdoch's News International and British Telecom).

The difference between an online service and some internet service providers can sometimes be less than clear. Take Cix, which started out as a sort of huge bulletin board system/virtual community. When you dialled up, you could access the conferences run by members on various subjects, read what they had to say and post your own thoughts. A few years ago, Cix moved into providing access to the net. When you sign up with them now, you can just get net access or pay a little more for access to the conferencing system. Also Virgin Net sells itself as an internet service provider but when you sign up with them, you get access to various members-only services.

Online services are generally very easy to use (and their software is easy to install). They're family-oriented and their conferences and chat

< 75 >

Jargon file – Bulletin Board Service, aka BBS

The precursors to the online services and virtual communities today and still used by elements of the tech community. A BBS is a computer hooked up to a telephone. You dial it up directly and can upload and download files and post messages for other people to read, amongst other things. ▲

rooms are moderated. In other words, in theory, there's someone around to deal with the pests that pop up occasionally in the online world. They are both local and global in scope. Though AOL is an American company, it has worked hard to provide a lot of dedicated British content and services. In addition, it claims that it's one of the more balanced spaces online – women apparently comprise over 50 per cent of its users. If you sign up with an online service, you will also be able to travel round the world (OK, the Western world) and still access the net and pick up your mail. In the past, Compuserve has been particularly strong on this.

The bad things about the online services are the things that might attract some people. They are very modern-mainstream, very commercial – the corporate towns of cyberspace. This might start to rankle, especially when you become more familiar with the net and realise that much of the information you're paying for is available elsewhere for free. Online services, in particular Compuserve and AOL, have suffered badly from spam – net slang for unsolicited junk email – though they have been aggressive in attempting to tackle the problem.

< 76 >

The main attraction of the internet service providers is that they're cheap. They generally charge a flat monthly rate for unlimited access. They also offer a freer, less controlled, less censored experience. That can be a problem for some, especially beginners, who might feel a little at a loss. That said, many of the big ISPs now have homepages which will point you in the direction of interesting services and sites. Some ISPs can also be rather unreliable. The industry hasn't built up a great reputation when it comes to customer service, though things are improving. Some operations continue to offer a terrible basic service. It can be impossible to connect at peak times and when you do get online, things move incredibly slowly.

That said, things are getting a lot better. A few years ago people were prepared to put up with a bit more from their ISPs. The whole thing felt like a bit of an adventure. But now, it's clearly a business. ISPs present themselves as the kind of serious companies who advertise on TV and

Read about it online – AOL

This certainly isn't a reason not to choose AOL, but you should be aware that AOL users are still the subject of significant prejudice and occasional abuse online. The hardcore geek élite assume all AOL users are incompetent and accuse the company of delivering a bad service and of being anti-net and pro-censorship. If you want to know why a significant proportion of the online population thinks that 'AOL sucks', try **http://www.aolsucks.org/**. ▲

< 77 >

sponsor football teams. As a result, you have a right to expect a certain level of service, especially from the bigger names in the market.

If you think an online service might be what you want, all you need to get started is one of their free trial discs. You can't pick up a computer/internet magazine these days which doesn't have one gummed on to the cover. As a result the geek élite tend to dismiss them as high-tech coasters. But for first timers, they're pretty useful. Many new PCs come bundled with a free trial for the Microsoft Network. Some also feature a free trial connection from one of the big internet service providers. If you decide an ISP is what you want, try it out – but don't stick with it if it's not up to scratch. There are over two hundred ISPs currently in business in the UK, so there are plenty to choose from, which, of course can be something of a problem.

The conventional industry wisdom is that this will change soon, that internet service provision will be dominated by a few big companies (the likes of BT, Demon, Pipex Dial and Netcom), mainly because they will be able to offer the kind of fast, reliable, affordable service the mass

Read about it online – ISPA

UK ISPs now have their own trade organisation, the Internet Service Providers Association (aka ISPA UK) which was set up to counter misrepresentation of the net and lay down a code of practice for ISPs in Britain. For a peek at their idea of acceptable ISP behaviour (with respect to user privacy and the like), go to **http:// www.ispa.org.uk**. ▲

< 78 >

consumer market wants. You can see why this should be. Bigger companies can afford to upgrade quickly to take account of a rise in subscribers. They can afford big, fat connections to the net and so are less likely to offer a slow service at peak times.

That said, the number of ISPs in the country keeps rising. Perhaps in the long term the big players will win out, but at the moment there's clearly still space for smaller operations. Perhaps there always will be, especially for well-run local ISPs who think hard about what users in their area really want, or for companies that successfully target a particular group of users or come up with new ideas for services. Of course, if a small ISP does become successful, it is often bought out by bigger players looking to build market share.

Which ISP?

When it comes to picking an ISP, first of all you need to make sure they're only a local telephone call away. These days, that doesn't help to narrow the field down that much. Most of the big national providers offer local-call access across the UK. Perhaps a better way to start is to ask friends who are online what they think of theirs. Then again, perhaps that's not such a good idea. Moaning about your ISP is default behaviour among net users.

It's worth looking at the ISP performance surveys in the specialist net magazines. Often smaller local services and new start-ups do well at first in these sorts of surveys. They don't have many users. They're keen and motivated. However, they can, if they're not careful, become victims of their own success. They get good reviews so more customers come. The

< 79 >

Tips - Net Magazines

Both of the leading UK net magazines – Emap's *Internet* and Future Publishing's *.net* are pretty good places to keep up with ISP performance, new developments online and new net software. Both regularly feature cover discs with demo versions of net programs and copies of the major web browsers. *.net* is a more consumer-oriented title and *Internet* probably aims more for the business market, but both are worth checking. ▲

company is overwhelmed with the new traffic and doesn't have the money yet to upgrade its technology. Connection speeds slow down, people start hearing the engaged tone when they dial in and the previous number-one ISP slips down the charts.

So it always pays to look at the performance over a number of months before making a decision. Some people may feel more comfortable going with a bigger name. After all, the likes of Virgin and BT are unlikely to disappear overnight. However, don't automatically discount the smaller ISPs. Many provide a great service and do a better job of responding to consumer needs than some of the big players. The thing to remember is that ISPs do not offer a uniform service. They're all selling something slightly different in the hope of getting an edge, so do some research.

After you've talked to friends and read the consumer mags, put together a list of ISPs you think might do the job, call them up and ask them about their service. The kind of response you get (how long you

< 80 >

have to wait to speak to someone, how helpful the person on the other end of the line is) might help make the decision for you. However, there are a number of things you should ask about when calling a prospective ISP.

1. Local Calls

Double-check that dialling up your ISP will only involve a local call. Find out where its Points of Presence are. Some small ISPs may set out to service only a small local area and so will only have one Point of Presence. The big ISPs have points of presence all across the country.

2. Charges

Most UK ISPs charge a flat monthly rate for unlimited access – usually something between £10 and £15. Some take a different approach and offer a freephone number and charge hourly connection rates. On the whole, this can add up to more than you'd pay in telephone charges, so think carefully about it. Some ISPs offer lower rates for people who don't think they're going to be online for a great deal of time per month. These are worth a look. But be advised – it's very easy to lose track of time online and if you go over the set amount, you pay extra.

Jargon file – Point of Presence

The place, or rather telephone number, you dial to connect to your ISP. ▲

< 81 >

Find out if you're going to pay a start-up charge. It used to be standard, but some ISPs are dropping it now. Find out if you have to pay a year in advance. You shouldn't have to. Only consider paying several months in advance if some serious discounts are on offer. Check on what sort of payment they accept and how easy it is to cancel an account, whether you have to do it in writing and how much notice you need to give. If there's some confusion here, you can find yourself paying for another month on a service you don't like. Not an ideal situation.

3. Software

Here's what you need to get about online: a web browser, which you use to access the World Wide Web, an email package, a newsreader, which you use to read and post messages to the Usenet Newsgroups, an FTP client which you can use to download and upload files and software and, if you're running Windows 3.x or a pre system 7.5 Mac, a TCP/IP stack.

Tips – Free Access

The ISP market is changing all the time and some companies now offer free access to the net. As this book was going to press, the High Street retailer Dixons launched Freeserve, its free internet service. Sign up with them and you can get on the net for just the cost of an 0845 telephone call. So far the service seems to include email and free web space, so it's definitely worth looking into – more information at **http://www.freeserve.net**.. ▲

< 82 >

Jargon file – Client/Server

Two bits of technical jargon for the price of one: you can't have one without the other. Servers are central computers on which data is stored. Clients are the software programs that access data stored on a server. In a more general sense, client often means any bit of software which accesses information via a network. ▲

A good ISP should supply you with all this. Some smaller outfits try to cut overheads by supplying you with an FTP client and suggesting you download your own stuff from the net. This isn't good enough these days. The absolute minimum you should get from an ISP is a web browser (i.e. a version of either Netscape Navigator or Microsoft's Internet Explorer) which you will need to access the World Wide Web. You can

Jargon file – TCP/IP

As mentioned before, TCP stands for Transmission Control Protocol. IP stands for Internet Protocol. Both 'protocols' (think of them as networking languages) allow your computer to communicate with the internet. A TCP/IP stack is several bits of software in one – TCP/IP software, packet driver software and sockets software – each of which is needed in order to send and receive data across the net. ▲

< 83 >

Jargon file – Plug Ins

Programs that you add to a browser so that it can handle different sorts of files, specifically multimedia files, sound, video and animation. ▲

also use this to send and pick up email, access Usenet and download files. Some ISPs may send you a browser and nothing else. Check that any software sent will be configured for you. Some ISPs also make things easier for beginners by supplying browsers fitted with multimedia plug-ins and offering automatic installation programs which take you through the first connection. Ask about this.

You should get basic software for free. Don't pay for it. If you don't get this, think about trying a different ISP. Many people now also want filtering software to prevent their kids from accessing unsuitable (i.e. pornographic) sites. Some ISPs now supply this kind of thing as part of their introductory package. Ask about it, if it's something you feel you need.

4. Connections

Check that they offer a PPP connection – virtually all of them do. Also check that they do POP3 mail. If they do, it makes it easier if you want to pick up your mail while you're travelling. POP3 is pretty much standard now. Find out which modem speeds they support. When there were two competing types of 56 Kbps modems, some ISPs only supported one. This should have been resolved by now, but it's worth checking.

< 84 >

Jargon file – PPP

PPP stands for Point to Point Protocol, which is used to hook computers up to the net. **POP3**, as in POP3 mail, stands for Post Office Protocol, version 3. This is the protocol that is used when it comes to receiving email. **SMTP** (aka Simple Mail Transfer Protocol) is used to send email. ▲

5. Customer Support

Find out when customer support is available. Office hours are no good if you do most of your net surfing from home. If you're going to be online late into the night you might want to see if it's available 24 hours a day. Make a few test calls to a support line at different times of the day and see how long you have to wait. Check how much it's going to cost to call the support line.

6. Company Background and History

Ask a little bit about the company, when it started, whether it is funded by a bigger company. Ask how many subscribers they have and about their user to modem ratio. Obviously this will have an effect on how often you dial up and get an engaged tone. Look for a user to modem ratio of 15:1 or less.

7. Usernames and Domain Names

Find out if you can pick your own user name. If you can't, find out the kind of thing you're likely to be stuck with. If you're planning to use your

< 85 >

Jargon file – Spam

Net slang for unsolicited email sent in bulk to thousands of users at once, i.e. electronic junk mail. It's also a verb – you can spam someone as well as receive spam. The name comes from the *Monty Python* sketch and is supposed to refer to the way it keeps on coming. Apparently Hormel, makers of real-world Spam, have considered taking action to prevent their product being associated with such a heinous practice. ▲

net connection for business purposes, ask if the ISP can help you with registering the appropriate domain name (i.e. something like **daves-hot-pies.co.uk**) and how much that will cost. See if the ISP offers unlimited email addresses on the same account. This can be useful for families, since it means each family member can have their own personal address.

8. Usenet Groups

There are thousands of Usenet newsgroups. Most providers can't carry them all but will get certain groups if you ask. Some ISPs won't carry certain groups on principle – for example, groups that feature porno-graphic images or those used by paedophiles. Blanket bans on broad categories can be a problem. The alt.sex groups include many non-porno-graphic discussions of gay rights and sexual politics in general but are often censored. The best thing to do is check the ISP's policy on this.

< 86 >

9. Personal Web Pages

Most ISPs now offer free space so that you can put up your own home-page on the World Wide Web. Find out how much free space is on offer (it's usually anything from 2 to 10 Mbs). This is perhaps looking a little far ahead but if you do put up a page and it becomes 'too popular', your ISP can cut it off. Check their policy on this.

10. Mail Services and Spam

Some ISPs now offer various services along with basic email. They will forward mail to another address (for example, your office connection) or page you when you get mail. Find out what they're offering. Check on their policy with regards to junk email or spam. Some ISPs take action to try to stop it before it gets to your mailbox. Others will offer advice and, in some cases, spam-filtering software.

11. Mac Support

PC users are the dominant population online and many ISPs are generally much happier dealing with them rather than Mac users. Some don't even supply Mac software. However, some ISPs make a point of being Mac friendly. At least it narrows down the field if you're a Mac user.

Signing up with an ISP

So you've found an ISP you like. Once you've paid your money, they should send you the software you need and a bundle of information about your account – your username and password, the various dial-up tele-phone numbers, email address, email account user name, mail server

< 87 >

address and much else. You'll need this information to configure your software, though ideally, your ISP should do that for you. Even so, hang on to this information because if you download new software programs from the net, you'll need it to configure them. ▲

• •

Connecting for the first time

Talk to anyone who started out on the net a few years ago and you will undoubtedly hear a few first-time-connection horror stories. An early subscriber to Demon, the UK's first ISP, apparently commented that setting up an account and connecting was 'a bit like giving birth – so difficult that afterwards, you can never quite remember how you did it' (from *net.wars*, Wendy Grossman's enjoyable book about net culture – more about this in Further Reading, page 432).

Back then, if you'd actually bought into all that techno-hype about how you had to get online right now or risk being left behind as everyone else accelerated off up the old information superhighway, experiencing difficulties connecting for the first time was deeply depressing, even vaguely humiliating. It was as if you'd bought a car but then couldn't figure out how to get the key into the ignition. There you were, ready and willing to get with the program. All around you, people seemed to be moving effortlessly forward into the smart new digital future. But you just couldn't hack it.

< 88 >

There were two ways you could react to this. You could either sink into self-pity – write yourself off as an information-age casualty, already surplus to requirements, and sit back and wait for some bright, shiny Cyber Youth patrol to come and take you off to a home for the terminally inept. Or you could get mad and in a digital version of road rage – screen spleen, perhaps – you could take it out on your machine, or the ISP support line staff . . . if you ever managed to get through.

The worst thing about all this was, nine times out of ten, it wasn't your fault. In the early days, internet service providers seemed to set out to make the whole process as difficult as possible. Their connection software often refused to connect to anything but still made a mess of your hard disk in the process. Their 'easy to follow' guides always seemed to be written by someone fluent in C++ but with only a passing acquaintance with English. When you did get through to their telephone support line, you discovered that it was manned by the CEO's idiot kid brother.

More generally, ISPs were so keen to talk up the net, they failed to tell first-timers that it still wasn't 100 per cent reliable, that sometimes you could do everything right and still not get online. The good news is that things are a lot easier now. Many ISPs have learnt from their mistakes and now go out of their way to help out nervous newcomers.

Of course attempting anything for the first time is always a little disconcerting. But don't worry. Over the next few pages, we'll take you through the basics and attempt to anticipate some of the standard problems. The thing to remember about all those connection horror stories is that eventually people sorted out the problems and got online.

< 89 >

Installing your modem

If you buy a new computer, it will more than likely come with a pre-installed modem. If you do need to install your own, it should be a problem-free process. Hook your modem up to your computer, turn it on, then turn on your machine. Often your computer will detect your new modem and then ask you to insert the special installation disc it came with. If that doesn't happen, if you're running Windows 95/98, it's pretty easy to set the installation process going yourself.

Click the **Start** button, then select **Settings**, then **Control Panel**, then double-click on the **Modems** icon. You'll then be walked through the installation process and prompted to insert the disk. Then it's just a question of specifying the modem you're using from a list of possibles. Once that's done, if you need to, you can always click on the **Properties** button to change the settings. The only thing you really need to worry about here is connection speed. Always pick a speed well above that officially listed for your modem, preferably double.

Connection software

To connect to the net, you need your TCP/IP stack. As mentioned before, if your computer runs Windows 95/98, Windows NT or Macintosh System 7.5 (and anything after that), then you already have something suitable. Your ISP's introductory package will most likely be set up to work with the TCP/IP stack already on your machine. When you install it, it will create a connection file that it will then use each time you call up your ISP. However, if you're running Windows 3.x, you will need to install a TCP/IP stack. Your ISP should have sent you what you need –

< 90 >

probably a version of Trumpet Winsock. If you have an older Macintosh, you'll need MacTCP/MacPPP.

Many ISPs now provide introductory packages that walk you through the installation and configuration process and even make the first connection for you, setting up your account automatically. However, even with the best connection packages, you will still have to enter some information yourself – for example, the communications port your modem is connected to and the speed it will connect at.

If you do have to manually configure your own TCP/IP stack, don't worry. Windows 95/98 features an **Internet Setup Wizard** that guides you through it all. Set it going by clicking the **Start** button, then selecting **Programs**, then **Accessories**, then **Internet Tools**, then **Internet Setup Wizard**. Alternatively, double-click on the **My Computer** icon, then **Dial-Up Networking**. Double-click on **Make a New Connection**, then follow the directions. By the end, you will have created a connection file for your ISP. When you want to connect, just double-click on that icon. If you're running Windows 3.x and using something like Trumpet Winsock, you generally have to select the **File** menu, then **Setup**.

In both cases, you will need some of the technical information, addresses and telephone numbers your ISP sent you. As you go along, you may need to enter some of the following:

Domain Name This is your ISP's domain name – something like **yourserviceprovider.co.uk**

< 91 >

Domain Name Server/IP Address Four numbers separated by full stops. This is the computer version of the domain name

Dial Up Telephone Number The number you use to connect to your ISP

Username and Password The name and password you chose or were assigned when you subscribed

Email Address Your own personal Email address – as in **yourname@yourserviceprovider.co.uk**

Email Account Username and Password Relevant if you have a POP3 mail account – and you probably will

Mail Server This is the address of the computer that handles mail at your ISP – something like **mail.yourserviceprovider.co.uk**

Tips - Readme's

Often, the technical information you need for configuring software will be available on the disc your ISP sent. Look for a file called 'readme.txt'. It's a bit of a drag when you want to get on and play but it's generally worth perusing any 'readme' files your provider includes on their disc. They'll contain updates on the software and information they didn't have time to get into their paper manual. ▲

< 92 >

News Server The address of the computer at your ISP that handles Usenet newsgroups – usually something like **news.yourserviceprovider.co.uk**.

This shouldn't be too confusing, but if you do have problems or if the basic information your ISP sent you seems unclear, then call them. It's in their interest to get you online as quickly as possible.

In the past, if you'd been connecting via an online service and then tried to install and use an ISP's connection software, especially something like Trumpet Winsock for Windows 3.x, you could occasionally encounter problems. These were caused by competing versions of the same connection software getting tangled up. As far as I can tell, this isn't usually a problem with Windows 95/98 and many of the online services have sorted out the problem. But if you are using an older machine with Windows 3.x and plan to run accounts with an online service and an ISP at the same time, the safest thing is to call both just to check that there isn't going to be a problem.

Get Online with the Online Services

For worried first-timers, an online service is probably the best bet. With AOL and the rest, you don't need to bother with configuring your TCP/IP stack and the rest of it. All you have to do is put one of their discs in your computer and follow the instructions. If you're using a free trial disc, it should have a number on it. You'll be asked to enter this at some point. You'll also be asked for your credit-card details. Don't worry about this – it's one part of the general security procedures to make sure that you don't keep trying to log on for free with trial discs.

< 93 >

You won't be charged. At least you shouldn't be, unless you decide to sign up at the end of the trial period. However, some of the big online services have had problems with what you might call general billing anomalies. So if you decide after the trial that you don't want to subscribe, check your next credit-card bill just to make sure there haven't been any mix-ups.

After entering a few personal details, the software will usually select a local dial-up number. Then it will automatically connect you to the service. Once you're hooked up, you'll be assigned a username and a password. With some of the online services, you do get a chance to pick your own name, though this can be frustrating. They have such huge numbers of subscribers that you can pretty much guarantee that someone will already have your preferred nickname. If you want to use your Christian name, you

Read about it online – Tech Support Jokes

Humour web sites are packed with jokes about tech support telephone lines, usually written from the perspective of the person taking the call and struggling to figure out what this particular clueless fool is on about. The same stories do the rounds on most sites – the person who thought the mouse was a foot pedal and the CD ROM disk caddy a cup holder, along with the same parodies – for example, the tech support caller who wants to be walked through a visit to the loo. For a typical sample, try Jokes for the Jolly – **http://www.humorspace.com/humor/stories/stechsup.htm**. ▲

< 94 >

may have to resign yourself to being JimMcClel9687 or JaneMcClel5271. This may not seem too much of an indignity but for some it's a symbol of the corporate, impersonal nature of the online services.

Once you've connected properly, you'll see the home-page of the online service. You aren't on the net, not yet, not quite. You're accessing information from one of the online service's computers. If you want to explore the internet proper, look around for the Internet Gateway. On AOL, for example, there's a big button marked **Internet**. Click on that and you will be taken to the Internet Gateway. From here you'll see a screen offering you the chance to get on the web, check out the newsgroups, download software or whatever. If you want to check out the web, click on that button and the AOL version of Microsoft's web browser, Internet Explorer, will start up. You're ready to go.

Get Online with Internet Service Providers – ISPs

Connecting via an ISP really isn't that difficult these days. Many ISPs now produce software that's as easy to use as the stuff provided by the online services. But if you are worried and have a friend who's online, why not tap them for some advice. It's probably better if you can persuade them to come round to help in person. Advising via the telephone is rather tricky and likely to try the patience of even the firmest of friends, so bribe them with a few beers to come round and take you through it.

Your net-literate friends have made their excuses. Perhaps they mentioned something about how friends who attempt to teach other friends to drive don't stay friends for too long. So you're on your own. But don't fret. This will be easy. First step – double-click on the icon on

< 95 >

your desktop for your ISP. If their installation process didn't create one, double-click on the icon for your TCP/IP stack. Alternatively, on Windows 95/98, open up **Dial-up Networking** in the **My Computer** folder, then double-click on the connection file you created for your ISP.

Once your TCP/IP software is running, you'll hear the modem open the telephone line and tap out a number. If your ISP isn't engaged, you'll hear chirruping fax-like noises as your modem establishes a connection. Onscreen, you'll see a dialogue box which tells you what's happening – when your computer is dialling, when it's verifying your password. If you have Windows 3.x and are using a version of Trumpet Winsock, you'll see a low-tech version of the same.

You may be asked to enter your password and username the first time you connect. Some software is completely automated, so if you have already entered that information during configuration, it will just go ahead and log on. If everything goes smoothly, your connection should be established. The dialogue box will tell you everything is fine. Windows 3.x/Trumpet Winsock users may see a bit of jargon onscreen telling them that they are hooked up properly – 'Hello – SLIP/PPP enabled' or some such.

< 96 >

Troubleshooting

Sounds easy, doesn't it? And it should be, as easy as switching on the TV. Unfortunately, though great strides have been made in the last two years, there are still problems.

The dial-up number your ISP gave you is engaged

This is more likely to happen if you're calling during peak time – in the early evening, between seven o'clock and ten o'clock. If they encounter a busy line, many connection software packages will automatically try again a few times. If this doesn't work, wait a while and then have another go. If you find it happening a lot, you may want to call your ISP to ask what's going on.

The first time someone showed me round the net, in 1993, we had to wait around twenty minutes to get through to his service provider. Things have got a lot better since then. According to recent surveys done by the specialist net magazines, around nine out of ten calls to ISPs get through the first time. If your ISP falls below that standard, try someone else.

As mentioned before, you can keep track of the performance of different ISPs by checking out the monthly survey published by *Internet* magazine. Here, ISPs are called at different times of the day and night and given a percentage rating for 'availability'. These ratings can fluctuate quite dramatically. In some surveys of ISPs done in the summer of 1997, BT was one of the top providers. But by the end of the year it had fallen dramatically, with only 70 per cent of calls connecting first time.

< 97 >

You connect but it all seems incredibly slow

Welcome to the net. Unfortunately, that's often the way things are online. No doubt you've heard the gags about the World Wide Wait. Sometimes problems are caused because your provider just has too many subscribers online and hasn't upgraded bandwidth to cope. An efficient ISP should be able to keep things running smoothly as they grow.

If things seem persistently slow, call your ISP and ask if they've been experiencing problems. They will probably say it isn't their fault. Often it's hard to disagree. There may just be heavy traffic online across the net in general, in which case there's nothing you can do about it.

Jargon file - Bandwidth

Network capacity, i.e. the amount of data that can be sent over a net connection. Bandwidth is the scarce resource of the digital age. We have plenty of information, but not enough space on the wires we send it down – hence insults which refer to online incompetents as 'a waste of bandwidth', organisations like the Bandwidth Preservation Society and geek slang in which people who say a lot in a short space are 'high bandwidth' individuals. In the future, bandwidth will be plentiful, say the techno-Utopians – but don't believe it. Networks might be like roads – traffic will always expand to fill the available space. ▲

< 98 >

Many UK net users claim that everything works just fine until the mid afternoon, when 'America wakes up, gets into the office and logs on' and everything online seizes up. You can see why this might be the case. But then again, the East Coast and the West Coast get up at different times, plus students, heavy users in the US, get up later than everybody else and stay up later than the average working stiff. So you do wonder if it's actually some sort of net myth. That said, things often do seem to get very slow online at around 3 or 4 o'clock in the afternoon.

If speed is a problem and you can be flexible, try different times of the day (and night). Alternatively, if you are connecting from home, try the weekend. Recent surveys have suggested that the bulk of UK users connect from the office, so logically there ought to be a fall-off in UK-based traffic on Saturday. However, thanks to BT's new cheap weekend rates, these are becoming increasingly busy. Still, it's worth a go.

Read about it online – Net Traffic

Tracking traffic and conditions on the net – call it info-meteorology – is a growth area, especially in America. Texas-based outfit MIDS run a web page called The Internet Weather Report, which offers maps, graphs and even little animations detailing traffic hotspots and problems on the net round the world **http://www4.mids.org/weather**. One for the techies. ▲

< 99 >

The modem makes all the right noises and you seem to connect fine but when you try to start up your web browser, you can't get anywhere

It may be that you haven't actually established a proper IP connection. Your connection software will usually tell you if that is the case. But if you're really keen, you can check the connection yourself with a program called Ping. Your ISP may give you this as part of the start-up kit. Some versions of Windows 95/98 come with Ping included. You can access it via the Start button. Select **Run** then use the **Browse** button to look for the Ping program.

Start Ping up and type in a domain name (eg **www.guardian unlimited.co.uk**). If you have established a proper connection, this should be converted into an IP address, i.e. a group of four numbers separated by full stops. If that doesn't happen, you have a problem. It could be that your software isn't configured properly. Alternatively, your ISP might be having trouble. Either way, have another look at your TCP/IP software and check the various addresses and names against the information sent by your ISP. Try connecting again. If you still have problems, call your ISP.

< 100 >

Your modem dials up without any apparent hitch, you seem to get through fine, but then nothing happens

This could be because your ISP's computers are down. This doesn't happen as often as it used to but is still not completely unknown. You could try telephoning customer support to find out what's going on but other frustrated users will probably be trying to do the same thing, so you might not get through. ▲

< 101 >

3 GETTING TO GRIPS WITH THE NET

• •

Before you start, a quick word about the way this section is organised. I've started with **The World Wide Web – The Basics,** because that seems to be the most popular part of the net. However, email comes a close second, so you could quite easily go to that part of the section first. If you do start with the Web, it would make sense to move on to **Searching the Web** next, then **FTP and Downloading Files From The Net.** If you start with the portion on email, then it might make sense to go next to **Usenet Newsgroups,** since once you've cracked mail the latter will be a doddle. After that, you will be well prepared to tackle **Online Chat.** In other words, read these sections in whatever order you like. ▲

< 103 >

The World Wide Web

The web is just one portion of the internet (though many people seem to think that the web is the net, end of story). It's the part where you can not only read text, but look at pictures, both static and animated, watch video, listen to music, navigate 3D graphic worlds and much else. More to the point, it's the part that comes with an easy-to-use GUI. For the most part, instead of typing in complicated commands, you can use the mouse to just point and click to wherever you want to go.

The writer David Hudson (the man behind the excellent webzine *Rewired* – **http://www.rewired.com/**) has a nice line on the web – a cross 'between a slick magazine and very slow television' – which catches the web's hybrid nature and its ability to be both exciting and frustrating at the same time. Of course, for many would-be techno-business people, the web is simply 'where the action is'. Its graphic user-friendliness has meant

Jargon file – GUI

Graphical User Interface. Developed in the seventies at the Xerox PARC research lab, brought to ordinary punters in the eighties by Apple, the GUI made computers user-friendly by replacing text commands with a visual interface made up of icons, windows and the whole desktop metaphor. If you want to sound as if you know what you're talking about, pronounce it 'Gooey'. ▲

< 104 >

it has been embraced by entrepreneurs everywhere who think it might offer a quick route to riches. It hasn't yet. Few people are making proper money on the web, but that hasn't stopped the investment bucks flowing in as more and more advertising sites and online shops go up. As a result, some have written the web off as a transnational shopping mall. Certainly it's one of the places to go to see what the much-vaunted global economy actually looks like.

But the web isn't just a commercial thing. It also lets all sorts of ordinary individuals have their say. Seen from one angle, it is McLuhan's global village reconfigured as a virtual mall. But take another view and it looks like an international psychoburbia, a cacophony of competing voices in which the passions, obsessions and pathologies of those ordinary people who live next door to you are all out on show.

Like a lot of things online, the web had its beginnings in the world of academic research and is, believe it or not, a British invention. It was developed by British physicist Tim Berners-Lee, mainly as a way to help researchers at CERN (the European Particle Physics Laboratory in Geneva) access and share resources more efficiently. He came up with an extension of an old idea – hypertext. When you read a hypertext document, certain words or phrases are marked as links. Click on these and you go to another document with a connection to the first – an essay on a related subject or a table of statistics.

Hypertext links connect documents so you can easily move between them, following up specific ideas or trains of thought. Berners-Lee adapted this for computer networks. So a document stored on one computer (or server) could be linked via a network to another on a

< 105 >

Read about it online – Tim Berners-Lee

Tim Berners-Lee is currently working at the Massachusetts Institute of Technology and is also the director of the World Wide Web Consortium, an organisation set up to oversee the web's development and make sure that it retains common standards – amongst other things. The W3C site is a good place to go to catch up on new web developments – **http://www.w3.org/**. Berners-Lee's own page is at **http://www.w3.org/People/Berners-Lee/**. ▲

different computer. Berners-Lee first came up with the idea for the web in 1989. Over the next two years or so, he developed HTML (HyperText Markup Language) which could be used to format and link text documents on a network and wrote the first web browser/editor, the first web server and most of the communications software.

Berners-Lee made his various innovations available online in 1991. Things really took off when the first graphic web browser was released in 1993 (something that angered Berners-Lee, who apparently thought images on web pages trivialised his original idea). Called Mosaic, it was developed at the National Centre for Supercomputing Applications at the University of Illinois (by, among others, Marc Andreessen – who went on to co-found Netscape).

The World Wide Web and Mosaic caught on for several reasons. The point-and-click interface made the net user-friendly. The web was also the first part of the net which looked sort of OK. In addition, it was all avail-

< 106 >

able for free. If Berners-Lee and the programmers responsible for the first Mosaic had set out to make money, it's likely that other companies would have appeared with their browsers or 'new improved' versions of HTML that weren't compatible and everything would have quickly found itself bogged down in a battle over standards. By giving their ideas away, they helped establish a standard everyone could then work with. Faced with the web today, packed as it is with advertising sites, online shops and webzines put up by multinational media conglomerates, it's easy to forget its beginnings in what some people refer to as the internet gift economy. But those roots are important and still exert an influence.

Another reason for the web's success is that HTML is relatively easy to use. After a couple of days of swotting, people could create their own web pages. When the web first got started, many people did just that, not for profit but for fun or to get something off their chest. Personal homepages quickly became a sort of digital folk art. Some were the online equivalent

---

Jargon file – Standard

A format that is approved and accepted by the computer industry as a whole. Standards serve ordinary users because they mean that products – hardware and software – produced by different companies will work with each other. Ordinary users in the past have suffered because of competing standards (cf. Apple Macs vs. Windows). It was hoped that the web would offer a bright, new, universally compatible future. We'll see. ▲

< 107 >

Jargon file – Web Pages, Web Sites & Homepages

Let's get these straight before we go any further. A web page is a document, usually formatted in HTML, which might contain text, images, animations, sound and even video. A web site is a collection of pages put up by an individual, institution or business. A homepage can be (a) the first page your browser shows when it starts; or (b) the first page of a web site. But most non-geeky types now think of a homepage as a personal web site put up by an ordinary net user to reflect their interests and obsessions. ▲

of the slideshows you inflict on neighbours you don't really like – chock full of pictures of kids looking cute. But others were clever, thoughtful and passionate, like a good print magazine. Whilst big companies struggled to 'get' the web, many ordinary users just got on with it.

The rudimentary nature of the technology meant that someone in a bedroom in Brighton could create a web site that was better than something done by a big company. The conventional wisdom is that, as the web has developed to incorporate multimedia, it's become a lot harder for ordinary users to compete with bigger companies. As a result, the argument goes, claims that the democratic nature of the web allowed ordinary people to become media producers now look a little overblown.

However, it's still possible for someone with a good idea and the commitment to see it through to make a splash on the web. Some well-chosen words can still beat flashy graphics and bouncy animations.

< 108 >

Read about it online – Geocities

Geocities now hosts over 1.5 million homepages. Users get help in creating their homepages (everything from advice to site templates they can follow) and can put their site in a community of like-minded users (everyone from science-fiction fans to family-values types can find their digital home). For more information, go to Geocities at **http://www.geocities.com**, Tripod at **http://www.tripod.com** or try the British competitor, Fortune City at **http://www.fortunecity.com**. ▲

Perhaps the attitudes or prejudices of web users (or rather, the journalists in the media who review web pages) is the real problem. As the web has become more slick and commercial, there has been a creeping tendency to see amateur sites and personal homepages as the preserve of cranks.

Sometimes it feels as if personal homepages have been drawn into the general commercialism of the web, with the baby pics taking a backseat to pages that aspire to being little more than digital business cards. Certainly, homepages have become big business for some. Companies like Geocities and Tripod have become successful by creating places where people can set up personal homepages.

As a result, there are more personal homepages than ever, and a lot of them are still pretty worthwhile. Sure, the commercial sites are exciting and useful, but in your rush to get the latest news, download dialogue samples from *Pulp Fiction* or buy the latest Martin Amis novel online, don't forget about the other side of the web. ▲

< 109 >

Software

To access the web, you need a web browser. When browsers first appeared, they were, as the geeks put it, pretty 'cool'. But they were also pretty basic. In the last two years, browsers have grown into multimedia devices capable of handling sound, video and 3D graphics. They've also become multi-purpose net tools – the easy-to-use front end of what marketing types refer to as an integrated internet suite – i.e. a pile of related tools which you use to deal with your email, download software from FTP sites, read newsgroups and much else.

Getting a browser is pretty simple. There are two big players in the browser business – Microsoft and Netscape. Netscape's browser has always been called Navigator – except that now, somewhat confusingly, it's been swallowed up by Communicator, a 'suite of net tools'. Microsoft's browser is Internet Explorer. You can get this in the basic browser version or with all sorts of extra attached programs. Navigator/ Communicator and Internet Explorer were both on Version 4.x when I was writing this book, though new versions were on the way.

Your ISP should supply you with one of these. The sensible thing to do is to try that out for a while. If you really don't like the browser your ISP gave you, go online (either to **http://www.microsoft.com** or **http://www.netscape.com**) and download the one you haven't got. (There's advice on how to do this on page 236.) Alternatively, look for the cover discs given away with the specialist net magazines. If you do decide to get a new browser, be prepared for a lengthy download (I can think of more amusing things to do when you first get online). When you get

< 110 >

Read about it online - Net Diaries

How personal are personal homepages? Very personal, it seems. Lots of people put their daily diaries – which cover everything from when they last had sex to the breakfast cereal they ate this morning – on the web for everyone to read. American critic Mark Dery once suggested that these net journals were both critiques of modern celebrity obsession and part of that obsession. Open Pages – **http://www.aloha.net/~ophelia/OP** – has links to over 400 online journals. Some net diarists are now online celebs thanks to their efforts. Take Justin Hall – **http://www.justin.org/vita/** – whose monster site also has links to other diary pages. ▲

Communicator or Internet Explorer, you'll be offered various options. If you only want to use your browser for the web (and you don't have much disk space), go for the browser-only option. Otherwise, get the full versions, which come with all sorts of useful programs. With Internet Explorer 4.x, you get the option of downloading the Active Desktop – a sort of preview of Windows 98. Don't bother at first. We'll cover Active Desktop later and it's no trouble to acquire it if you don't have it.

Both Microsoft and Netscape regularly pump out upgrades and new versions of their browsers. And both browsers have menu links which take you directly to pages where you can get new versions/upgrades. You could find yourself downloading a new browser every couple of weeks. But there's no need. The best way to handle upgrades is to wait until the

< 111 >

official release – e.g. 5.0 – then get a version after that (5.x or whatever) when they have cleaned up all the bugs they didn't have the time to take out of the official release. Each new offficial release of the big two browsers now tends to come with roughly similar must-have cutting edge features. Version 4 of Communicator and Internet Explorer came with push programs – a new method of information delivery which was going to set the net alight but has so far failed to sizzle even slightly. For more on this go to page 404. According to the early previews that were beginning to surface just as this book went to press, the big idea behind the upcoming fifth version of Netscape's Communicator/Navigator is something called 'smart browsing' – a way of aiding general web navigation and tying users more closely to Netscape's homepage/portal site, Netcenter. For example, you will be able to click on a 'What's Related' button to call up from Netcenter a list of sites similar to the one you're currently visiting. There will also be something called Internet Keywords, an attempt to make web addresses easier to understand. Apparently, you'll also be able to store details of your favourite sites on the Netcenter site, so that you can access them whatever computer you're using. It seems likely that Microsoft will so something similar. 'Smart browsing' sounds potentially useful, but it's hard to tell what will click until you actually get to use a browser.

When it comes to choosing browsers, factors beyond simple usability may influence your choice. If you despise Bill Gates and all his works, you may want to go with Netscape. Alternatively, even if you don't like Internet Explorer that much, you may want to stick with it because it works with all the other Microsoft software you have. Make your deci-

< 112 >

sion, pick a browser and then forget about it and get on with the interesting stuff – i.e. wandering around the web.

Unfortunately things aren't that easy. The sad truth is that picking a browser has become part of what net journalists hype as 'The Browser Wars'. The ongoing battle between Netscape and Microsoft to become the preferred way of accessing the web (and the net) has become one of the grimmer things about life online. It dominates the technology press and, though it is important, there's something phoney about it all. The battle serves mainly to pump up the image of the big two and to squeeze out alternatives. Since it has led to the arrival of incompatible standards – some web pages can't be accessed if you don't have Internet Explorer – it's also unclear whether it has actually benefited ordinary punters.

With around 50 per cent of the market, Netscape is still ahead, though Microsoft is gaining fast. Netscape used to be a lot further ahead.

Read about it online – Non-Browser Specific WWW

Once on the web, you might see signs on a site saying that it is 'best viewed with this or that browser'. This is the result of the likes of Microsoft and Netscape adding their own extensions to HTML rather than waiting for a standard to be approved. It irritates a lot of people and goes against the spirit of the web, which was supposed to be universal. Hence sites like the Campaign for a Non-Browser Specific WWW – not the catchiest title, but the web site is worth a look – **http://www.anybrowser.org/campaign/**. ▲

< 113 >

It was the first company to realise the commercial potential of the web and the first version of its Navigator browser took over the net when it was released for free in 1994. Netscape had the market to itself then, because it took Microsoft a while to 'get' the net (i.e. realise that as computers became ever more connected, the browser might turn into an 'Operating System for the net', capable of supplanting the ubiquitous Windows). It took Microsoft even longer to produce a reasonable version of its Internet Explorer browser. But by the time IE3 came out (1996), it was accepted that Microsoft had caught up, thus reinforcing the general perception that it takes the company three tries to get anything right.

Microsoft began to make up lost ground by giving IE away for free and has apparently pledged that it will continue to do so for ever (Netscape moved quite quickly to charging for Navigator). However, critics argued that the company was also trying to catch up by using its general dominance in computer software. The US government is currently taking action over claims that Microsoft unfairly used its operating system monopoly to win the browser war (for example, by pressurising computer manufacturers into including a copy of Internet Explorer in PCs that ran Windows). It's easy to understand the worries. Few users, particularly first-timers, will go to the trouble of downloading a copy of Navigator when Internet Explorer is there on their desktop.

Microsoft's recent strategy has been to integrate its browser and the Windows operating system ever more tightly, so that you move seamlessly between them. In other words, the operating system will be the browser (and/or vice versa). That's the big idea behind Windows 98. Simplifying

< 114 >

Read about it online – Anti-Microsoft Sites

The web is heaving with them – some silly and sophomoric, some very serious. In the latter category is the page on Microsoft and anti-trust issues maintained by the Consumer Project on Technology – **http://www.essential.org/antitrust/microsoft/ microsoft.html**. The CPT homepage is also worth a look – **http://www.cptech.org**. Not everyone online hates Microsoft, though it sometimes seems that way. The Ayn Rand-ite magazine *Capitalism* has organised a campaign to stop the persecution of Bill Gates – it's at **http://www.moral-defence.org/sign/addpetition.html**. ▲

things slightly, this lets you put a browser-like interface on many of the files and apps on your computer. There are back/forward buttons and an address box you can use to navigate your hard drive. Rather than clicking to select something and double-clicking to open it, you move the cursor over a file to select it and click once to open it – as you do on the web. Whatever you're working on on your computer, it's easy to launch Explorer and move on to the web, then back to your desktop.

The conventional wisdom is that, in the end, this approach will inevitably win the war. As a result, the US government has attempted to intervene. There have been suggestions that Windows PCs should come with Navigator as well as Internet Explorer or that Microsoft should make it as easy to integrate rival browsers into its operating systems as Explorer.

< 115 >

Step back for a minute and think. Do you really want the web 'seamlessly integrated' with the rest of your computer? Do you want it to be unclear when you move from your desktop to the web and back? (Incidentally, once browser and operating system are 'seamlessly integrated', Microsoft's claim that Internet Explorer will always be free becomes meaningless. I imagine the cost will be factored into the price of Windows 98 and succeeding versions.) In the meantime, Netscape has pulled an interesting move, releasing the source code for Navigator 5.0 so that geeks can mess around with it and produce their own version.

Have the browser wars benefited the ordinary punter? It's true that both big browsers are now available for free. But both have become rather bloated as each company adds new features and gimmicks in an attempt to get an edge. And because they rush them out too quickly,

Read about it online – Web Stalker

The digital art world is beginning to get involved in the browser wars. Take the Web Stalker, an alternative browser which recently emerged from what might one day be called the 'interface underground'. Produced by I/O/D (a loose alliance of programmers and artists), Web Stalker may not be the greatest piece of tech in the world but it does show you that there are different visions of the web that are being crowded out by the ongoing war story. For a version of WebStalker and some interesting thoughts on the browser wars, go to
http://www.backspace.org/iod/. ▲

< 116 >

neither is as reliable and stable as it ought to be. And although both companies keeping adding new features that 'differentiate' their product, both big browsers are essentially the same. Certainly, they both push a fairly standard vision of what a browser could and should be.

Some people expect you to take sides in the browser war. Netscape has been celebrated as the plucky little guy that might end Bill Gates' progress to world domination. But there's not really much difference between the big two. Both are big companies keen to turn a profit. Netscape's recent moves to give away the source code to its browser scores them brownie points with geeks and people who work in the computer industry – who are understandably fed up with Microsoft's dominance.

But ordinary punters just want software that works and lets them share their work with friends and colleagues. And Internet Explorer has improved drastically. Even some long-term Netscape users nowadays

---

Tips – Browser Watch

There are several high-profile sites online pushing war stories, updates on new browsers, reviews, comparisons and much else. MecklerMedia's Browserwatch is worth a look **http://www. browserwatch.com**. ClNet's site **http://www.browsers.com** is good on links to what it calls 'rebel browsers' (translation – stuff not made by either Microsoft or Netscape). It does sound a bit more exciting than 'geek toys'. ▲

< 117 >

prefer Internet Explorer 4.x. Try them out and pick the one you like. If you have the disk space, keep copies of both and pick and choose.

If you haven't got the space or memory to run either Microsoft or Netscape, there are smaller browsers you can try. It's perfectly possible to be a conscientious objector in the browser war. For example, you could try Opera, a small but increasingly popular browser produced by a Norwegian software company. You have to pay for it, but it's fast, reliable, does virtually all the things the big browsers do and takes up less than 2 Mb of disk space. The makers say it will work fine with a 386 PC with 8 Mb of RAM. So if you're using an old PC, you know what to do. You can download a version from **http://www.operasoftware.com**. ▲

● ●

Surfing the web for the first time

You don't need to configure your browser before you can get moving – if all you want to do is go on the web. You will need to enter some information if you're planning to use it for email and Usenet newsgroups, but otherwise you can get on the web without any hassle. So, get online, then start your browser (i.e. double-click on its icon on your desktop). When it loads, you'll most likely see either a Microsoft start page (if you're using Explorer) or the Netscape homepage (if you're using Navigator). Alternatively, your ISP may have configured the browser they sent you so that you go to their site. (You can change your browser so it goes first to

< 118 >

Tips – Non-Hypertext Links

There is an outside chance that you may click on something on the page which isn't the standard hypertext link. Many web pages contain email links, so that you can send feedback to the site easily. Click on these and your mail program will start up in a separate window. Obviously, we don't want to get into that, so close the window and try another link. You may also click a link which causes some software to download – if that happens, just hit the **Stop** button on the toolbar and look for another link. ▲

a page of your choice but we'll get to that later.)

Whatever page loads first, you should see text, graphics, pictures and little icons. To the right there will be a scroll bar that lets you move up and down the page. You will see words either highlighted or underlined – these are hypertext links. You may see a little animated icon, perhaps a turning world, one of the great clichés of web design. As you move your cursor over the highlighted words, the arrow will change to a pointing finger, indicating a clickable link. If you click on this, you will move to another document or web page – either on the same computer or on another one on the other side of the world. On many corporate web sites, you'll also see colourful banner ads – usually featuring eye-catching animations. Click on these and you'll go to the site they're advertising.

Move the cursor over a link and click on it. If you haven't picked an email link, another page will load. Find a link on that and click on it.

< 119 >

You'll go to another page. Find a link and click that and another page will come up. You could continue like this. Netheads call it 'surfing', though it's preferable to think of it as online rambling, a kind of serendipitous digital pottering-about which can take you to all sorts of unexpected places. The conventional wisdom is that people did this a lot in the old days of the web, but now they just find the sites they want and go there.

The buttons on the main toolbar are the easiest to use for basic navigation. If a page starts to appear that you don't like the look of, click the **Stop** button. That stops the page from loading. Click the **Back** button and you'll move back to the page you were at previously. Click the **Forward** button and, surprise, surprise, you'll go forward to the page you just left. If you've followed a long set of links and just want to get back to your home/start page, click the **Home** button. As you go back through pages

Read about it online – Surfing

It is one those bits of net slang everyone loves to hate. If you can't stand the term, blame Jean Armour Polly, who is officially accepted as the person who first came up with it – as the title for a piece she wrote about the joys of the net for a library journal back in 1992. Apparently, her inspiration came from a promotional mouse pad from the Apple Library which showed a surfer getting radical with a big tube (or something) and bore the legend 'Information Surfer'. Read all about it at **http://www.well.com/user/polly/about/birth.htm**. ▲

< 120 >

you've visited, you'll see that the links you clicked have changed colour. It's a simple way of helping you keep track.

How about going to a site you select for yourself? Let's try the *Guardian*'s site. For this, you'll need the *Guardian*'s URL (it stands for Uniform Resource Locator) or web address, which is **http://www.guardian unlimited.co.uk**. Web addresses are the sum of a few standard parts. First is the protocol, it stands for HyperText Transfer Protocol and is used to send web pages across a network. Next comes the domain name of the computer – that hosts the site – **www.guardianunlimited.co.uk**. In this case, the computer is a web server – hence the **www** bit. The *Guardian* URL ends there, but URLs can specify a specific document (e.g. **document.html**) and the directories in which it's stored.

Click in the address text box at the top of your browser, just underneath the main tool bar, then delete the address that's there. Type in the *Guardian* URL, then hit **Enter/Return**. Alternatively, in Internet Explorer, select the **File** menu, then **Open,** then write the URL in the text box and click **OK**; in Navigator, select the **File** menu, then **Open Page,** then write the URL in the text box. Check the line **Open location or file in** has a tick next to the **Navigator** box. Then click **Open.**

Mouse Menus

Using the left mouse button to click on a link will bring up that link (or download a file or an image). You can also use the right mouse button to aid your web browsing. Right-click on something on a web page – a link, an image, the page background even – and a "mouse menu" will appear which offers you various options (saving the page, or 'creating a shortcut'

< 121 >

Guardian tip - Browsers

As mentioned before, your browser can do more than access the web. You can use it to access newsgroups, send mail, download files via FTP and much else. If you do, you have to enter addresses prefixed with different protocols. So to access an FTP site, type **ftp://** before the address. To go directly to a Usenet newsgroup, type **news**. before the name of the group. More on this in the relevant sections. ▲

– more on these later). As you attempt more complex operations online, you will find yourself right-clicking and using mouse menus a fair amount. Apple Mac users can't right-click, but they can usually call up mouse menus by holding down the Apple key and clicking the mouse button.

Here's something simple to try: at some point on the web you will inevitably find yourself waiting for a big page to load. You don't have to sit there twiddling your thumbs. You can open up a new browser window and check out another web page while you wait. In fact you can open several, though if you open too many you may end up slowing everything down. Using two or more browser windows at once can be useful if you're looking at a page of useful links. You can keep that page open and explore the links in new windows. In both Navigator and Internet Explorer, right-click on the link you're interested in, then select **Open in a New Window**. Alternatively, in Navigator, select the **File** menu, then **New**, then **Navigator Window**; in Internet Explorer, select the **File** menu, then **New**, then **Window**.

< 122 >

Frames, Image Maps and Forms

As you wander round the web, you'll come across pages with frames, image maps and forms. Frames are used to create different sections within a browser window. You might have a basic document in the main part of the window, with an index to the web site as a whole framed off on the left. Frames came in with Navigator 2.0 (some older/low-tech browsers can't cope with them) and they were misused by some web designers – let's call them framespotters – who turned their pages into a mad patchwork of different boxes, some featuring text, some logos, some ads, some lists, some completely pointless graphic images.

Things have improved (hyperactive webmasters have multimedia and animations to fiddle with now) and frames are now pretty easy to use. To use the example given above, clicking on a link in the index in the left frame will cause a new page to open in the large main frame. Frames can make general navigation a little more complex. For example, on a framed site, the **Back/Forward** buttons will take you back or forward within a frame. If you've moved through a lot of different frames, to move back to the page you visited before the framed site, in Internet Explorer select the **File** menu. Towards the bottom, you'll see a short list of sites you visited previously. Click the one you want. In Navigator, select the **Go** menu and you'll bring up a similar list.

Image maps are large graphic images, different portions of which are links to other documents. As you move the cursor over the image, you'll see the pointing finger appear, indicating the links. Image maps might seem more interesting than your standard list when it comes to presenting a set of links. But in the early days of the web they were often more trouble than

< 123 >

they were worth. They took ages to load and it was often unclear what they were linking to. Things are generally better now, but if you get confused, move the cursor over the map and look for the URL/description that comes up in the bottom-left text box of your browser.

Forms are like forms in real life. Just click in the dialog box and type in the information required, then look for a **Send** button to click. You often have to refine the information you send via drop-down menus. Just click on the arrow pointing down to bring up a menu, select the relevant category, click then move on to the next question. Typically you use forms when you're using a search engine to look for something online, when you're buying something online or when you're trying to get into a site that requires you to register before they let you in. Before you send the information, your browser may flash up a warning about security. If you're not sending important information (e.g. credit card details), don't worry too much about this. ▲

● ●

More complex navigation

The **Back/Forward** buttons are useful enough if you're reading and moving between a few pages. If you build up a longer trail, then want to get back to an early page, you'll need something else. As mentioned above, you can use the **File** menu (or **Go** in Netscape) to bring up a list of sites previously visited. In Internet Explorer, you can get a similar list via the **Back/Forward**

< 124 >

toolbar buttons. There's a little inverted triangle to the side of each. Move your cursor over it and it turns into a button. Click on it and a list of sites appears. Alternatively, just right click on the **Back** button. This works in roughly the same way in Navigator. With both browsers, you can also pull down a list of the URLs you entered in the toolbar address box by clicking on the pull-down menu at the right end of the box.

The above methods don't always work. Say you're on a site and you follow a set of links through it to a page you want, then use the **Back** button to come back to the front page, then follow a new set of links to a different document on the same site. The new trail of links will be recorded over the previous set, so that when you use the **File/Go** menu or the **Back/Forward** menus, you'll only see that latest trail. For a more comprehensive list of all the pages you've visited, you can use the **History** file, which will also let you get back to a site you visited right at the start of a long session.

Your browser keeps a history file of sites you've visited in this particular session (and over previous days). In Internet Explorer, click the **History** button on the toolbar and the History list will open in a separate frame (sometimes called a browser bar) on the left of your main browser window. Look for the site, click on it and it will come up in the main window. To remove the browser bar, click the **History** button again. In Navigator, select the **Communicator** menu, then **History**. A separate window will open, showing the sites you visited. Double-click on the one you want and it will open in the main window.

You can use the history file while you're online. But you can also go offline and use it to access sites you've previously visited – a rudimentary

< 125 >

form of what's known as offline browsing. Both Navigator and Internet Explorer will let you go offline and then access pages you visited in your last session on the web. If your web use is confined to reading certain sites, the **History** file will definitely save you some money. Visit the sites you're interested in, make sure they've downloaded completely, then log off and read them offline via the **History** file. Internet Explorer 4.X is particularly slick here. Disconnect, then click the **History** button, then click on the site you want. A **Dial-up Connection** dialog box will come up – click the **Go Offline** button. The you can move around as you wish within the history file which is laid out by date and sites visited on each day. If you're going to use Navigator to read pages offline, it's best to set it up for work offline. Select the **Edit** menu, then **Preferences**, then **Offline**, then check the box next to **Offline Work Mode**.

You can specify how long you want Internet Explorer to save pages in the history file by selecting the **View** menu, then **Internet Options**. Look for a section on **History** on the **General** dialog box, where you'll be able to change the number in the box next to the line **Days to keep pages in history**, then click **OK**. In Netscape, select the **Edit** menu, then **Preferences**. In the Navigator dialog box, in the **History** section, change the number in the box next to **Pages in history expire after X days**, then click **OK**. The thing to remember here is that the history file is a kind of interface for documents stored in a file known as the cache. If you extend your history file, but don't also allow more disk space for your browser's cache, you won't be able to access some of the earlier entries (there's more on the cache below). If you feel weighed down by the past, in both browsers there's a **Clear History** button in the section where you specify the size of the history file. ▲

< 126 >

Getting to your favourite sites faster

As you get to know the web, you'll find yourself getting to like certain sites. Browsers allow you to keep a list of your favourites, so that you can access them a bit quicker. In Internet Explorer, you can mark a page as a Favourite. If you're on the page you want to mark, click on the **Explorer document** icon in the address box, hold down the button, then drag the icon across the screen and drop it on to the **Favourites** button. Alternatively, select the **Favourites** menu, then **Add to Favourites**, or just right-click in an empty part of the page, then select **Add to Favourites** from the mouse menu. An **Add Favourite** dialog box will come up. Ignore all the stuff about subscribing to the site for the moment and tick the option to just add the page to your Favourites list, then **OK**.

To use your Favourites list, click the **Favourites** button on the toolbar. It will open in a browser bar on the left of the main window. Click on the site you want to go to and (if you're online) it will load in the right-hand window. (If you're offline, Internet Explorer will get the last version of the page you accessed, if it's still in the cache). To remove the browser bar, click the **Favourites** button again. If you don't like the browser bar, you can use the **Favourites** menu to view your list.

Navigator handles all this in a similar way, though there you 'book-mark' your chosen site. If you're at the site, click on the **Page Proxy** icon (the funny little thing next to the address text box) and, as above, drag and drop it on to the **Bookmark** button (on the toolbar to the left of the

< 127 >

Tips – CTheory

As you use your browser you'll find that there are several different ways of doing the same thing. Don't worry about learning all of them. Just get comfortable with one and forget about the others. That way, you'll have some time to read 'The Technology of Uselessness', a reasonably pertinent essay about this kind of thing by the US art collective Critical Art Ensemble – at the webzine CTheory – **http://www.ctheory.com/a-technology_of_useless.html**. ▲

---

address text box). The **Bookmark** menu will open and you can drop the bookmark where you want. Alternatively, click the **Bookmark** button, then select **Add Bookmark** or right-click on an empty space on the page and select **Add Bookmark** from the mouse menu. To access your bookmarks, click the **Bookmark** button and a list will come up. Click on the site you want to go to.

Both Navigator and Internet Explorer will let you bookmark sites without having to access them. Say you see a link on a page that looks good but you're too busy to get it now. Right-click on the link and select **Add Bookmark/Add to Favourites**. Alternatively, click on the link in the normal way, hold down the mouse button and drag the link to the **Bookmarks/Favourites** toolbar button.

Both Navigator and Internet Explorer will automatically check to see if your **Bookmarks/Favourites** have changed since you last visited them. In Navigator, this is pretty simple. Click the **Bookmarks** button, then

< 128 >

select **Edit Bookmarks**. When that window opens, select the **View** menu, then **Update Bookmarks**. You can then choose which sites you want to update. You can also do this with Internet Explorer but it's part of its method for offline browsing and is a little more complicated, so we'll leave it until later. There is little need to update Bookmarks/Favourites, though. Presumably you visit your favourite sites on a regular basis and get a feel for when they change. You don't need to tie up time online getting your browser to check for you. Still, give it a try if you like.

If you build up a big **Favourites/Bookmarks** file, it can be time-consuming finding your way to the entry for the site you want. You can get round this by creating an **Internet Shortcut**. This is an icon on your desktop. Double-click on it and your browser will launch and load that site. The quickest way to create a **Shortcut** is first to access your chosen site. Then resize the browser window so you can see your desktop. Click

---

Tips – Organising Bookmarks

It's pretty easy to build up a big file of Bookmarks/Favourites after a while. So start organising your Bookmarks and filing them into specific folders as soon as possible. In Internet Explorer, select the **Favourites** menu, then **Organise Favourites**. In Navigator, click the **Bookmarks** button, then select **Edit Bookmarks**. Once you've put your bookmarks in folders, Navigator will let you put a particularly useful folder on the your Personal toolbar. Just right-click on it, then select **Set as toolbar folder**. ▲

< 129 >

Tips - Internet Shortcuts

If you've downloaded two browsers so that you can cut between the two, be aware that Internet Shortcuts will only work with the one nominated as your default browser. Unless you tell it not to, the browser that isn't the default will ask you whether you want to make it the default every time you load it. So it's pretty easy to change things around if you need to. ▲

on the **Page Proxy** icon (in Navigator) or the **Internet Explorer document** icon and then drag and drop the icon on to your desktop. Navigator will let you create shortcuts to links you haven't yet visited (though I'm not sure why you would want to) by right-clicking on the link, then selecting **Create Shortcut** from the mouse menu.

Shortcuts are fine, though they can clutter up your desktop. Instead you can put buttons on the toolbar for sites you access regularly. In Internet Explorer, look for the word **Links** on the toolbar to the right of the address text box. There's a little ridge by the word. Click on this, hold down the button and slide it to the left to reveal the links bar (and hide the address box). Alternatively, move it down and the whole **Links** bar will be displayed below the address text box. You'll see various buttons which will take you quickly to various Microsoft sites (e.g. Best of the Web, Product News). Then go to your chosen site and drag and drop the **Internet Explorer document** icon on to the **Links** bar. A button will be created. Click on that in future and you'll go directly to that site. In

< 130 >

Navigator, check that your **Personal Toolbar** is visible (via the **View** menu). This is a toolbar of quick links to Netscape pages listing new or cool sites. To add buttons for sites of your choice, access the site, then drag and drop the **Page Proxy** icon on to the **Personal Toolbar**.

Once you've mastered Favourites/Bookmarks, shortcuts and all the rest of it, typing in web addresses may seem like an awful lot of hard work. Actually, you don't have to type in the full **http** version to get where you want to go. You can drop that and the **www** part. For example, if you want to go to the *Guardian* site, just type **guardianunlimited.co.uk** into the relevant text box. With sites that end with **.com**, you can drop that too and just enter the basic name – e.g. **microsoft**, and you'll go directly to the

---

Read about it online – Real Names

If you have trouble writing out URLs without making mistakes, there are several companies that feel your pain (and hope to make money out of it). Real Names have created a piece of nifty technology which will let you just type a brand name into a browser and go directly to the site in question – for more information and a test run, go to **http://www.realnames.com/**. When Real Names was launched, someone at the press demo thought it would be a good idea to use a Disney site. So they typed Bambi into the Real Names-enabled browser, but instead of going to the cutesy deer's special area on the Disney site, they accessed a porn site. Apparently, the technology works a lot better now. ▲

< 131 >

site. Internet Explorer has a function called AutoComplete which watches while you type in URLs, guesses what they are, based on sites and pages previously accessed, then tries to fill them in before you. This could be useful if you have to type in particularly lengthy URLs, but it's potentially irritating too. You can disable it by selecting the **View** menu, then **Internet Options**, then the **Advanced** tab, and then remove the tick next to **Use AutoComplete** (in the **Browsing** section).

Troubleshooting

Sometimes you won't be able to get to a particular site. Your browser will usually tell you what the problem is and flash up some sort of error message. Here are a few problems you may encounter.

Your browser says it is unable to locate the server or that the server doesn't have a DNS entry

Check that you entered the URL correctly. Check for spelling and remember that URLs are case sensitive. If that's all fine, try again. If you still can't get through and get the same error message, it may be that the server at the site is down or that the site has closed down and vanished from the web (not unknown).

A message comes up saying that the "Connection was refused by Host"

Don't take it personally. The problem here is that the site you're trying to access is probably very busy. Try again and if you get the same message, leave it until the site is likely to be less busy.

< 132 >

Read about it online – Spelling Mistakes

We're always hearing that the net is home to innovative minds looking for new and clever ways to make money. So perhaps it shouldn't be surprising that companies have figured out a way to profit from your spelling mistakes. They have registered common spelling mistakes or typos close to some of the biggest sites online, and put pages up at these destinations which feature some advertising and then direct you to the page you wanted. Try typing **http://www.yaho.co.uk** into your browser to see what happens. Alternatively, go to **http://www.typo.net** to see what such companies think they are up to (they're free online spell checkers, apparently). ▲

You seem to get through to the site but a page comes up saying File Not Found

It may be that the site has been reorganised and that the page you're looking for has been moved. You can usually find your way to the document by working back through the site URL. For example, if you can't get anywhere with the URL – **http://www.hipsite.com/index/television/simpsons.html**, it may be that the document **simpsons.html** is now in a different directory. Click in the address text box, delete **/index/television/simpsons.html**, leave **http://www.hipsite.com** intact and hit the **Enter/Return** key. This will take you to the front page of **hipsite.com.** From there, look around for links that might take you to the page you're looking for.

< 133 >

You get an error message saying that the Document contains no data

Most URLs end with a web document – in the example above, the document is **simpsons.html**. Usually with URLs that don't end with an **.html** or **.htm** document, the browser will hunt around for a default document – something like **index.html** – which it can display. If there isn't one, it can get confused and show the above error message. The best bet is to go to the front page of the site (by taking the directory path out of the URL, as in the previous example) and hunt around for a link to the page you want.

You get into the site you want but things move very slowly and the page seems to seize up

Again, a problem caused by excess traffic on a site. Sometimes all you can do is wait – and keep track of progress by checking the Status bar in the bottom left of the browser, which will tell you roughly how much of the page has loaded. Sometimes you can get somewhere by hitting the **Stop** button, then the **Reload** button (in Navigator) or the **Refresh** button (in Internet Explorer). Your browser will try to get the page again and this time you might be able to get through.

You're on a page, you click a link and nothing happens or the wrong page comes up

This is probably down to dodgy programming on the site. Broken links are less common nowadays, but they're still around. The average web site usually offers several different routes to its various sections. So look around for an alternative link to the page you want.

< 134 >

Customising your Browser

When you get your browser, it will be set to do certain things by default – for example, load your ISP's site as the homepage. You can personalise your browser and speed up your web surfing by making a few changes. The first thing you might want to alter is your browser's homepage. In Internet Explorer, select the **View** menu, then **Internet Options**. In the **General** dialog box, in the **Home page** section, enter the URL you want in the **Address** box. The **Use Blank** button means your browser will show a blank page as its homepage, which will make it load quicker. In Navigator, select the **Edit** menu, then **Preferences**. In the **Navigator** dialog box, you can choose a blank page or, in the **Homepage** section, enter your chosen URL in the **Location** box.

The last year has seen big business focus on homepages as a way to make money online. Online services (AOL – **http://www.aol.com**), software companies (Netscape – **http://www.netscape.com** and Microsoft – **http://www.microsoft.com**) and search sites and directories (Yahoo – **http://www.yahoo.com**) all believe that there are some serious advertising

Tips – Bookmarks

In Navigator, you can also use your bookmarks as a homepage. They're stored in a page called **bookmark.htm**. So in the **Navigator** dialog box, click the **Browse** button to look for this file – it should be in the **Default** folder within the **Program** folder in **Communicator**, then click **Open**. ▲

< 135 >

bucks in being the page you see when you start your browser. Consequently, they've set out to create so-called 'portals', user-friendly sites which offer free email, search engines, online shopping and homepage areas and hence 'can supply all your net needs on one page'. Give these sites a look, but remember that though they're hyped as 'gateways to the net', the business plan behind them is built on the theory that they'll wind up as 'destinations' – i.e. you won't go through the gateway that much but will stay on the site in question and hence see all the strategically targeted ads.

If you do stay, you'll also end up sampling a limited version of the net. When you're on a portal, you can only access the news/shopping/search sites the portal has deals with. Remember that it's very easy to assemble a portal via your favourites/Bookmarks. If you find news/community/ shopping sites you like, bookmark them and then you can get to them quickly without having to go to someone else's portal. Though portals are currently seen as the 'online future', it's worth remembering that two years ago people said the same thing about push – a new method of information delivery which used the net to send news and sports scores to you at regular intervals. It was supposed to take over but now people look vaguely embarrassed when it's mentioned. The web business is still very fad driven and portals may turn out to be merely the latest gimmick.

Another simple way to speed up your surfing is to tell your browser not to bother with the visual or multimedia elements of a webpage. In Internet Explorer, select the **View** menu, then **Internet Options**, then **Advanced**. In the **Multimedia** section, remove the ticks in the boxes next to **Show picture**, **Play animations**, **Play videos** and

< 136 >

Play sounds. In Navigator, select the **Edit** menu, then **Preferences**, then **Advanced**, then remove the tick next to **Automatically load images**. When pages come up you'll see a small icon where the image should be and possibly a caption describing the image. If you want to see a particular image, click on it and it will load. Alternatively, in Navigator, select the **View** menu, then **Show Images** and all the pictures on a particular page will load.

You can also mess around with the general look and feel of your browser. Both Navigator and Internet Explorer let you change colours and fonts. In Internet Explorer, select the **View** menu, then **Internet Options**, then click the **Colours** and **Fonts** buttons at the bottom of the

---

Tips – Auto-hide

Internet Explorer handles the whole 'how many toolbars can I hide without being unable to get anywhere?' thing nicely. Basically, you can keep all the buttons showing to help you with navigation. Then when you get to the page you want, hit the **Full Screen** button on the toolbar and Internet Explorer will expand the page to fill the screen. It keeps a small toolbar of icon buttons at the top. Right-click on this and select **Auto-hide** and this will disappear too, reappearing when you move the cursor to the top of the screen. The same thing goes for the desktop toolbar at the bottom. When you've finished checking out the glory of wide-angle graphics, click the **Full Screen** button again to bring back your toolbars. ▲

< 137 >

General dialog box. In Navigator, select the **Edit** menu, then **Preferences**, then either **Fonts** or **Colours**. You can also remove some of the toolbars so that you can see more of the web page you're accessing. To try out the various toolbar options, in Internet Explorer and Navigator, select the **View** menu. Try out various permutations here to see what you're comfortable with (i.e. which of the scores of buttons and menus you actually need when you're wandering round the web). You can also drag and drop the toolbars around if you feel you need to change the way they are stacked up. Navigator can even be set to show text-only toolbar buttons – select the **Edit** menu, then **Preferences**, then **Appearance**, then under **Show toolbar as,** tick **Text only**.

Actually, there's nothing to stop you removing all the toolbars. Navigator makes this easy – just click on the little raised tags at the left end of each toolbar. Then click them again to make them reappear. If you do hide all the toolbars, you can use keyboard commands to navigate. People who are comfortable with the keyboard often find this quicker and easier than using the mouse. Here's a quick list of useful keyboard commands (or shortcuts):

INTERNET EXPLORER

Alt + Left Arrow	Move back one page
Alt + Right Arrow	Move forward one page
Ctrl + Tab	Move forward within frames
Shift + Ctrl + Tab	Move back within frames
Alt + A + A	Add the current page to your favourites list
Esc	Stop loading a page

< 138 >

Ctrl + I	Load the images on a page
Ctrl + O	Open a new location or file
Ctrl + N	Open a new browser window
Ctrl + R	Refresh the current page
Ctrl + S	Save the current page
Ctrl + P	Print the current page
Ctrl + F	Find something on the current page

NETSCAPE NAVIGATOR

Ctrl + Left Arrow	Move back one page
Ctrl + Right Arrow	Move forward one page
Ctrl + A	Bookmark the current page
Ctrl + I	Load the images on a page
Ctrl + O	Open a new location or file
Esc	Stop loading a page
Ctrl + N	Open a new browser window
Ctrl + R	Reload the current page
Ctrl + S	Save the current page
Ctrl + P	Print the current page
Ctrl + F	Find something on the current page

There are more keyboard shortcuts you could use. Check in your browser's help file for details.

< 139 >

The Cache and Saving Documents and Images from the Web

Every page you access on the web is saved by your browser in a temporary file known as a cache. (In its bid to seem different even when it's the same, Internet Explorer calls the cache its 'Temporary Internet Files'.) The idea is to speed up your browsing and do a little towards saving the net's limited resources. So whenever you direct your browser to a site, it will first check in its cache to see if it already has the relevant page. The most obvious way this is used is when you click the **Back** or **Forward** button. Rather than go to the trouble of heading off to get the page all over again, your browser gets it from the cache.

You can improve your browsing speed by changing some of the cache settings. In Internet Explorer, select the **View** menu, then **Internet Options**, then the **General** tab. In the **Temporary Internet Files** section, click the **Settings** button. You can then specify how much disk space you want the cache to use via a small slider control. The bigger you make the cache, the more pages it can store to call on during revisits. On the other hand, you don't want to overload your hard disk, so don't go mad.

You can also change how often the browser checks for new versions of pages, rather than retrieving the ones stored in the cache, via the **Check for newer versions of stored pages** section. You have three options. Ignore **Every visit to the page**. This will make your browsing incredibly slow, since the browser won't use the cache at all. **Never** is also probably one to avoid, since this means that the browser will always get the version from the cache – so you might miss changes on the site in question. The one to go for is **Every time you start Internet Explorer**. This means that

< 140 >

your browser will check the page if you haven't yet visited it in the current session on the web, but if you have, it will get the stored version from the cache. If you do choose **Never**, you can find out if the current page has been updated by clicking the **Refresh** button, which will make Internet Explorer go and get the latest version of the page.

Navigator basically handles all this in roughly the same way. Select the **Edit** menu, then **Preferences**, then **Cache** to call up the relevant dialog box. With Navigator you have to type in the amount of space for both the **Memory Cache** and **Disk Cache**. This is obviously a little trickier than in Internet Explorer, since you need to know how much space you have to play around with. It's probably not a good idea to go for less than the default. With the line **Document in cache is compared to document on the network**, make sure that **Once per session** is ticked.

Once you've specified the size of the cache, your browser will fill it up, then as you add new pages it will dump the old files. However, this process can slow down your browsing. You may see everything slow down onscreen and hear your computer rattling away as it sorts out the browser cache and gets rid of old files. To avoid this and to free up disk space, in Internet Explorer click the **Empty Folder** button in the **Temporary Internet Files** section; in Navigator, click both the **Clear Memory Cache** and **Clear Disk Cache** buttons in the **Cache** dialog box.

Since it automatically saves copies of pages you visit, the cache is a potentially useful resource. Rather than going to the trouble of saving individual pages, you could go and check them out in the cache. That's the theory, anyway. Both browsers make it easy to get to the files in the cache. In Internet Explorer, select the **View** menu, then **Internet Options**,

< 141 >

Tips - Proxy Serves

If you get particularly obsessed with speeding up your browsing, it might be worth investigating Web proxy servers. These are local servers which keep copies of the most popular sites. You can set your browser to get those copies rather than going out on to the net proper. Some ISPs have their own web proxies, so ask about it. To set Navigator to use a proxy, select the **Edit** menu, then **Preferences**, then **Advanced**, then **Proxies**. Mark the box next to **Manual proxy configuration** then click the **View** button, then enter the details of the proxy – your ISP should supply these. In Internet Explorer, select the **View** menu, then **Internet Options**, then **Connection**, then click the box next to **Access the Internet using a proxy server**, then enter the details in the relevant text boxes. ▲

then **General**, then click the **Settings** button, then the **View Files** button. In Navigator, select the **File** menu, then **Open Page**, then click the **Choose File** button to look for the **Cache** (it's in the **Users** sub-directory of the **Netscape** folder).

Once you get there, you'll see that it's rather difficult finding the page you want because of the computerese of Netscape's file-labelling system. Internet Explorer handles this a little better – it shows the name of the file and the URL it came from. But it's still not a patch on the **History** file, which is the thing to use if you want to check back on pages you've previously visited. Of course, then you have to remember when you visited

< 142 >

them. So if you find a page you know you'll want to refer back to, it might be easier to go ahead and save it anyway. That way, you will know what it's called and where it is.

To save a web page, in both browsers select the **File** menu, then **Save As**. Then pick a name and a location on your disk for the saved file. You can choose to save the page as an HTML document or as text. If you choose the former, when you open it again (with an application that can handle HTML, like your browser), it will retain the basic formatting it had on the web (but not the images). If you choose text, all you get is the text and some basic formatting. If you're saving a page with frames, make sure you click in the frame you're interested in before you start the saving process.

You can save a link without actually going to it. Right-click on the link, then choose the **Save Target As** (in Internet Explorer) or **Save Link**

Tips – Web Pages

Rather than save web pages that seem particularly useful, you can always print them out for future reference. Use the **Print** button on the toolbar in Navigator or select the **File** menu, then **Print** in Internet Explorer. On the **Print** dialog box, in the **Print range** section, make sure **All** is ticked. If you want to see whether the page is going to look something like it does on screen, select the **File** menu, then **Print Preview** in both browsers. If you like what you see, click the **Print** button. Make sure you have plenty of paper. Web pages seem a lot shorter on screen than they are in real life. ▲

< 143 >

As (in Navigator) from the mouse menu. Your browser will get the page at the end of the link and you can then choose the format, name and location as above. You can save images from web pages by right-clicking on the image, then choosing **Save Image As** (in Navigator) or **Save Picture As** (in Internet Explorer) from the mouse menu. Some web pages feature sound and video files and you can save these. However, since you'll often need special plug-in programs to play these, it's best to use those to save these sorts of multimedia files. There's more on this on page 299.

Next Step?

By now, you should be comfortable with your browser and the web. The next step is to learn how to find your way to new sites. For that, go to the next section on search engines. It may have occurred to you that, with things like the cache and the **History** file, your browser is saving a lot of information about you which could tell someone else what you've been up to online. For more on this and on browsing and privacy, go to page 366.

• •

Searching the web

Neo-Luddite critics often moan that the net is just a vast, disorganised mess, that even when there is useful information online it's impossible to get to it. If all the search engines and online directories disappeared overnight, they might have a point. As it is, as usual, they're getting rather melodramatic. The truth is that modern net search tools now make it easy

< 144 >

to find information. Like a lot of things online, they could be a lot better. But if you take the time to learn how to use them, they work well enough. In fact, you really can't get by without them.

That's why companies in the net/web search industry are among the most successful of net businesses. The market leaders (for example, the leading online directory, Yahoo) have experienced phenomenal growth over the last few years and are among the best-known online brands. Although venture capitalists have become more cautious about funding net businesses, they still queue up to throw money at start-up companies with new ideas for searching and ordering the web. The big search sites are among the busiest on the web and some even turn a profit (a relative novelty in the net business).

Online search tools were around before the web caught on. The first really popular net search engine, Archie, appeared in 1990. Archie helped people locate files online. They had to know the exact file name first, but using Archie they could quickly locate an FTP site where it was stored and then go there and download it. Once the web emerged, web search engines soon followed – even in the web's infancy (in 1993), it became clear that logging its various sites was going to be beyond mere human capabilities.

The first web search engine was something called the World Wide Web Wanderer. Strictly speaking, it didn't start out as a search engine – it was designed to keep track of the web's growth. However, it did work in roughly the same way as the big modern search engines. It consisted of a 'bot' – an autonomous, automated software program, which went out on to the net and performed a particular task (in this case counting web

< 145 >

Tips – Gopher

If you feel like trying out another archaic online search tool, you could mess around with Gopher. This was/is a sort of web-like (but very un-visual) way of finding text files. Basically you click links to track down the file you want. Before the web turned up, it was going to be the next big thing. Now gopherspace is the equivalent of an online ghost town. However, it is still used by academics and it can still be useful. You can try it out via your browser. Try Gopher Jewels at **gopher://cwis.usc.edu/11/Other_Gophers_and_Information_Resources/ Gophers_by_Subject/Gopher_Jewels**. ▲

servers) then reported back with its findings. After a while, the Wanderer was tweaked so it collected URLs too. These were then added to a database, called the Wandex.

The Wanderer showed how web search engines might work. The first to make a big impact was called the WebCrawler. It was developed by students and staff at the University of Washington Computer Science department and was released in April 1994. The WebCrawler is still around today (though it's not one of the better engines). It made such a big impact because it was the first search engine that could do a full text search on the web. Within a year, a whole series of now familiar names – Lycos, Infoseek, OpenText – appeared touting roughly similar technologies and the search business was born.

< 146 >

Search Sites on the Web

In theory, there are two distinct types of search site – search engines and directories. Both let you search through vast databases of links to different web sites. They differ in the search methods they offer and how they assemble their databases of links. As mentioned before, search engines rely on autonomous software programs (aka bots, spiders or crawlers) which roam the web (and other places on the net) collecting details about different pages – the URL, the title, the keywords chosen by the creator of the page as a summary of its content, known as meta tags, and usually these days, the whole text of a page. A database is created from the bot's findings. Users can then search this database and turn up links to different sites, grouped in order of relevance.

Directories offer collections of links, arranged into different categories and themes. The directories employ people to do their searches and assemble their lists of sites. But some also use bots. They also accept submissions sent in by the webmasters responsible for particular sites. You can use a search engine to search a directory's links. But you can also drill down through different directories looking for the sites you want. Directories may deliver less information than search engines, which can turn up thousands of sites which are apparently relevant to your enquiry. They generally make up for this in the quality of the information they deliver – i.e. the search results usually have something to do with the original enquiry, not always the case with search engines. Aside from general directories, there are lots of specialist sites which index links in a particular field.

In fact, the distinction between search engines and directories is so blurred nowadays as to be pretty useless. There are still a few 'pure'

< 147 >

Tips – Themed Search Engines

New contenders in the search business are trying to find a gap in the market by offering search engines devoted to specific themes. These target online resources devoted to a particular theme – for example, Exes **http://www.exes.com/** is a travel search engine. For more links to specific search engines, try ClNet's Search.com – **http://www.search.com/**. ▲

---

search engines out there, but most also come with a directory of some sort as well. In general, a search engine isn't enough to cut it in the search business these days. Anyone can knock one of those up. You have to figure out ways to 'add value'. As a result, search sites now feature all sorts of other services from free email to chat rooms. The people behind companies like Yahoo don't even like to use the word 'search' any more; they refer to themselves as a 'media company'. Other search companies prefer to say they're in 'knowledge management'.

The upshot is, rather than talk about search engines and directories, you should perhaps just refer to them all as search sites. The best known are:

AltaVista **http://www.altavista.com**
Hotbot **http://www.hotbot.com/**
Infoseek **http://www.infoseek.com**
Excite **http://www.excite.com**

< 148 >

Kore legs

http://www.cranfield.
ac.uk/ccc/spark/
Pxcate etc

Events 1999

http://www.bletchleypark
.org.uk/diary 99.htm
(Atz winter).

Lycos **http://www.lycos.com**
WebCrawler **http://www.webcrawler.com**
Yahoo **http://www.yahoo.co.uk**

Using a Search Engine

Superficially, search engines look pretty easy to use. Just enter your subject in the text box, click the button and in a matter of moments you'll be on the way to a set of sites that are exactly what you're looking for. That's the theory. The reality is a results screen which tells you that the search engine has found several hundred thousand pages which contain the terms you entered. And if you start clicking the links to some of these pages, you will discover pretty quickly that many have little or no connection to the subject you're interested in.

This doesn't seem to trouble journalists who, in the past, have shown remarkable stupidity when using search engines, quoting huge search engine results (6 million pages found!) as proof that the micro-trend they're discussing is socially significant. Here's one example. Recently, a men's magazine ran a story about support groups for men who felt they were . . . ahem, under-endowed. The writer noted that a net search for pages titled 'small penis' yielded 1.5 million entries. The implication was that each of these represented a web page specifically devoted to this subject.

Whilst people do let it all hang out online, it seems highly unlikely that there are quite that many men willing to open their hearts (and flies) to the world. As a reader pointed out in the next month's letters page, the journalist responsible for the piece probably hadn't used the search engine properly and had merely carried out a general search for all the

< 149 >

pages containing the words 'small' and 'penis'. Such a search would have turned up pages that featured both words together, but would also have found pages with only one of the words and pages that featured both but not in combination. As you can imagine, there are lot of pages on the web that contain the word 'small' somewhere. There are probably even more with 'penis'.

The lesson here is not that you shouldn't bother with men's mags but that if you want to avoid what I suppose we could call the 'small penis' problem, learn to use a search engine properly. Whichever one you pick, read the help file first so you know how to refine your search – in other words, how to make your search terms more specific so that the engine in question at least has a fighting chance of turning up something appropriate.

Take AltaVista, which is currently the most popular of the search engines. It gives you the choice of either a **Simple Search** or an **Advanced Query**. With the former, the first thing you can do is to specify where you want to search (the web or Usenet) and in what language, by using the drop-down menus above the main text box. When you enter search terms, using several can help you focus your search – for example, **cats pets homes** might yield more relevant results than just **cats** on its own. You can make your search more specific by using various characters. A + sign before a word means that that word must be included in the search. A - sign means that a word must not be included. So **+cats +breeders** should turn up sites devoted to breeding cats; **+cats -musicals** should make sure you turn up sites devoted to pets and avoid accidental exposure to Andrew Lloyd Webber.

< 150 >

It doesn't matter how you order search terms. **Cats siamese** and **siamese cats** will bring the same results. To make the previous example work, you should really use capitals (AltaVista does searches for words as they appear and does recognises cases) and quotation marks. The latter are a way of searching for a particular phrase. Words inside quotation marks should appear together on a document. So for the previous search, you should enter **"Siamese cats"**. (You can also use hyphens to search for phrases – for example, **Siamese-cats**.)

You can use the * sign as a 'wildcard'. Tack the asterisk on to the end of a word and AltaVista will search for other similarly spelled words that contain up to five additional letters. So **breed*** will look for breed, breeders and breeding. Some search terms don't need to be refined that much to yield good results. Entering proper names will usually turn up the person you're after.

Aside from refining your search terms, you can also constrain your searches to specific areas. For example, to restrict your search to the titles

---

Tips – Be a Web Voyeur

If you're having trouble with your search, why not amuse yourself for a while with the WebCrawler search ticker **http://webcrawler.com/ SearchTicker.html**. It lets you sneak a peek at other people's searches by flashing up keywords currently being searched for in their databases. ▲

< 151 >

of documents, put **title:** before the words you're searching for. For example, **title:** 'World Wide Waste of Time' will search for a web page called **World Wide Waste of Time**. Use **anchor:** to restrict your search to the words found in links. To search for a web address, use **url:** followed by the word you want to find in the web address. To restrict your search to a country, use **host:*** then the domain name for the country in question – for example, **host:*uk**. Use **image:** then the name of the image to search for images. You'll find more about this in AltaVista's help file.

When you've sorted out your search terms, click the **Search** button. After a while, AltaVista will take you to a results screen which will probably tell you that it has found tens of thousands of pages that fit your search. It ranks the pages found in terms of relevance and shows you links to the top ten (along with a short description of what's on the page). Relevance is determined in a fairly straightforward way. If all the search terms appear on a page, it comes higher than if only one or two appear. If a unique term (e.g. a proper name) appears on a page, then it will move up the rankings. Usually, you can find what you're after in the first twenty or thirty links turned up by AltaVista.

AltaVista's Simple Search will often be enough. If you're very keen, you can try an **Advanced Query**. For this, you need to construct your search terms using something called Boolean logic. It sounds slightly forbidding but what it basically means is that you don't use + or - to refine search terms but words – AND, OR, NOT and NEAR – which are known as Boolean operators. These work in roughly the same way as + or -. Using AND (you can write it in lower case if you want) means that the engine will search for all the words in a search. OR means it will search

< 152 >

for either. NOT is used to exclude certain terms but it can't be used on its own. So you have to write **cats AND NOT musicals**. NEAR can be used to search for words or phrases that occur within ten words of each other in a document. AltaVista suggests that this is useful when you're doing a search on names (for example, **John NEAR Kennedy**), which might occur in a document in various forms.

Advanced searches let you look for documents modified within a specific time frame – just enter the required dates in the appropriate boxes. They also let you specify your own ranking words, which will determine the order in which your results are listed. To use the example AltaVista gives, with a search on **COBOL AND programming,** you can use **advanced** or **experienced** as ranking terms so that those pages will come first in the results page. If you are going to use **Advanced Query**, you have to enter a ranking term.

Read about it online – Meta tags

You can spend plenty of time refining your search and still turn up completely irrelevant pages. Often it's not your fault. Unscrupulous web designers deliberately mislead search engines by assigning inaccurate keywords or meta tags to a page. For example, one site used its meta tags to suggest it was useful for parents worried about child care. In fact, it was a site that sold kids' clothes and was trying to divert more people its way. ▲

< 153 >

The other search engines work in roughly the same way, though each has it own quirks, so read those help pages. Each search engine has its own strengths. AltaVista is the market leader and is very powerful. However, HotBot has been winning awards recently and is reputed to update its database most frequently. Infoseek is thought by some to be the most user-friendly. You could try Search Engine Watch if you're really keen – **http://www.searchenginewatch.com/**. Hosted by MecklerMedia, this has a search-engine status report which regularly ranks the big names, lots of general search tips and a good explanation of how search engines work.

Navigator and Internet Explorer both have **Search** toolbar buttons which provide quick links to search sites. Navigator's takes you to Netscape's search page which has links to all the big sites. Microsoft's opens a browser bar on the left of the main window with links to Infoseek, Yahoo and various UK directories. If you use one of these, your search results will appear in the browser bar. Click on the links shown

Read about it online – Search UK

If you feel like backing the Brit contender, you could always give Search UK a whirl **http://www.searchuk.com/**. For some reason, its searchbot is called SuperEwe. Search site designers tend to go for spidery imagery or canine metaphors (you know, sniffing out the info). Sheep aren't widely known for their searching skills, but presumably Search UK know what they're doing. ▲

< 154 >

Tips – Trading Names

You don't always have to turn to a search engine. In some cases, a little thought will get you to the site you're after. If you're searching for a business site, their trading name will probably be the domain name. So if you're looking for the site for Dave's Hot Pies, try something like **http://www.daves-hot-pies.co.uk**. If you don't get any joy, try substituting the **.com** top-level domain. This often gets you to the site you're after pretty quickly. ▲

and the site comes up in the main window (while the search results remain in the browser bar). Both browsers will also let you use a random search engine without going to the site. In Navigator or Internet Explorer, just enter the terms you want to search in the address box (if you only enter one word, put + before it), then hit return. The results from a random search site will appear in the main browser window.

In the spring of 1998, the NEC Research Institute at Princeton published a fairly sceptical report about search engines. It claimed that even the best search engine (HotBot) only managed to cover 34 per cent of an estimated 320 million pages of information available online. People have argued about the report and its conclusions. But it's hard to disagree with one of its recommendations – that if you really want to make sure you search more of the web, you should use one of the MetaSearch sites, which allow you to combine the results from several of the major engines. Of course, merely covering more sites doesn't necessarily guarantee end

< 155 >

results will automatically be better, but it's certainly worth trying a site like MetaCrawler **http://www.metacrawler.com/** – if nothing else, it means you only have to learn one set of search guidelines.

Using an Online Directory

Those who shrivel at the thought of something called a 'Boolean search' will probably get on a lot better with online directories. Yes, they do tend to have their own site search engine, and yes, there are a few guidelines to follow if you want to get the best out of them. But you don't have to sit there messing around with + and - signs. You can just click through various directories and sub-directories in search of the subject you want (and the links to the sites that cover it).

Take the opening page of Yahoo. Here you'll see fourteen or so general headings – Arts and Humanities, Business and Economy, Education, News and Media, Reference, Society and Culture and many others. Under each general heading is a selection of sub-headings. So under Society and Culture, you see People, Environment, Royalty and Religion. Each of these headings and sub-headings is a clickable link. Click one and you move to that area of the directory, where you'll be presented with more links.

As an example, let's look for Yahoo's list of web search tools. Look for the **Computers and Internet** heading. Underneath you'll see several sub-headings – **Internet, WWW, Software, Multimedia**. Click on **WWW**. That will take you to the general **World Wide Web** section. At the top you'll see links which take you to UK or Ireland-only sites in the general category. Below is another set of general categories to do with the web, from **ActiveX** and **Announcement Services** to **Web-based Entertainment**. By some of these

< 156 >

categories, you may notice the @ sign. This indicates that this section cross-references with another general category. So if you click **ActiveX@**, it will take you to the **Computers and Internet: Software** section.

Actually, if you want to be specific, the exact location of this section is shown at the top in a list of all the directories it is nested within – **Top: Computers and Internet: Software: Operating Systems: Microsoft Windows: Windows 95/98: Technical: ActiveX**. This kind of directory chain appears at the top of every page in Yahoo. If you follow a wrong turn, you can just click the previous term in the chain to go back or click **Top** to go the Yahoo homepage. Alternatively, click the **Back** button. Do that here and go back to the **WWW** section and click **Searching the Web**.

This takes you to a page which features more categories – from **All-in-One Search Pages** to **Web Directories**. Beside each heading is a number which tells you how many links are in that section. Click **Indices to Web Documents** and you'll be taken to a page which features more categories (**Best of the Web** to **What's New**) along with a huge general list of links to different types of web index sites. At the top of each page, incidentally, there's a search engine which lets you search the whole web, UK sites or just sites in the particular category you're investigating.

Good online directories are like well-designed libraries. In real-world libraries, you often arrive at a shelf stacked with scores of titles relating to a field you're researching. Unless you know beforehand what title you're looking for, the only way to find out if a book is suitable is to take it down and browse. Similarly, when you're faced with a list of 30 or so links to sites offering to tell you 'What's New on the Web', a list which only gives you the title, you don't have much choice but to click the links

< 157 >

and have a look. And that can be a bit hit and miss. Yahoo is great at cataloguing sites, but it isn't in the business of quality control.

Some directories attempt to offer a bit more information. A slightly different, more personal approach is offered by The Mining Company **http://www.miningco.com/** in which guides put together lists of sites in a particular area and write regular features on the subject. At the last count, the site employed around 600 guides covering around 11,000 subject areas. It's worth a look, as are several British directories which claim to do a better job of classifying home-grown content than the UK version of Yahoo. Try UKPlus **http://www.ukplus.co.uk** or Global Online Directory aka GOD **http://www.god.co.uk/**. The best known of the UK directories is probably Yell **http://www.yell.co.uk**, the web site for the Yellow Pages, which has a directory covering 20,000 UK sites, the Electronic Yellow Pages (a searchable directory of UK businesses) and various other search services.

If Yahoo seems too big and baggy, you could try one of the specialist directories. Many of these are laid out in the same way as Yahoo but confine themselves to specific subjects and hence usually have the space and time to deliver a bit more information about the sites they list. As you might expect, Yahoo is good place to go to find specialist directories (there's a section in the **Searching the Web** category we were looking at earlier). You'll find that there are online directories covering pretty much everything you can think of. Here's a few to be going on with:

The Media UK Internet Directory – http://www.mediauk.com/directory/
A useful collection of links to British TV and radio stations, magazines and newspapers and much else besides

< 158 >

Seniors Search – **http://www.seniorssearch.com/**

The Internet directory for the over-fifties, laid out like Yahoo but with categories like 'Just for Grandparents' and 'Seniors Personal Homepages'. There's a UK area too

WWWomen – **http://www.wwwomen.com/**

Bills itself as the 'premier search directory for women online'. Again, set out like Yahoo but with categories like 'Women in Business' and 'Personal Time for Women'

Disinformation – **http://www.disinfo.com/**

Designed to be the search service of choice for people looking for the 'hidden information' that 'falls through the cracks of the corporate-owned media conglomerates'. Categories include Propaganda, Revolutionaries, Censorship, Counterculture, Counterintelligence and Newspeak. Hunting around in Counterculture, I found a set of links relating to the Darwinian scientist Richard Dawkins. He'd probably not be keen to be next to sections on Conspiracy Theory and Crop Circles, but the links were good.

Listings, Awards and Web Rings

One of the first things people used to do when they got on the web in the early days was make a list of the sites they found, then group them under a heading – cool sites, new sites, underground links or some such. Presumably it was a way of helping them get to grips with the growth of the web. Maybe there wasn't much else to do on the web back then. More to the point, perhaps they weren't quite sure what to put on a web page.

< 159 >

So they just created helpful lists of links, which soon became lists of links to lists of links, and so on.

The first What's New page came out of the National Centre for Supercomputing Applications – the place where Mosaic, the first big web browser, was developed. It was maintained by Marc Andreessen (one of the Mosaic team) and was essentially his bookmark file. It started up in the summer of 1993. By December, Andreessen was complaining that maintaining the list was a full-time job and left shortly afterwards to start Netscape. I guess he had bigger fish to fry, but lots of other people saw that they might be able to get ahead online by compiling lists which told people which sites were cool, new or even useless. There are an awful lot of these listings sites around now. They're not exactly a serious search tool, but they can be fun and they can point you towards sites you might otherwise never find.

The Links toolbar on Navigator has buttons which will take you quickly to Netscape's What's New and What's Cool pages. In Internet Explorer, the Links bar has a button which takes you to Microsoft's Best

Read about it online – NCSA

The NCSA What's New page is now defunct but preserved for posterity at **http://www.ncsa.uiuc.edu/SDG/Software/Mosiac/Docs/ archive-whats-new-0596.html** (don't you just love those long URLs?). If nothing else, it lets you see how excited people got about the web back then. ▲

< 160 >

of the Web section on its Start page. As ever, Yahoo provides an exhaustive set of links to listings sites – look in the **Searching the Web** directory as before. What's New and What's Cool sites are the most common sorts of online listings. But they can be about anything – take the self-explanatory Geek Site of the Day **http://www.queue.org/scott/gsotd**. You would have thought that this was one site which would never run out of material, but it's now defunct, though you can still browse it. Some listings are undoubtedly clever. If the people who put together the big directory sites are like online librarians, then the linkmeisters behind listings are more like editors. The best ones take a particular angle and show you something about the web you hadn't seen before.

Take Steve Baldwin's excellent Ghost Sites of the Web **http://www.disobey.com/ghostsites/**, a site of links to other sites which are still online but no longer breathing; in other words, they haven't been updated in ages, but live on, a relic of earlier web times. Listings are also a great source of what you might call the online trash aesthetic. For every linkmeister dutifully logging his cool sites of the day, there's another one totting up the web's worst pages (and adding sniggering captions to the links). Mirsky's Worst of the Web was the big daddy of all this. It's gone now – Mirsky gave up updating it when he realised he'd never be able to make any money from it. But there are a few remains on his new site **http://mirsky.com/wow/**. Plenty of other eager net trash aficionados have picked up the torch. For a similar but more forgiving site, try the Useless Pages **http://www.go2net.com/internet/useless/**, which specialise in highlighting all the supremely pointless sites on the web.

< 161 >

Listings sites with pretensions tend to move into the online awards business. As you move around the web, you see sites sporting lots of little logos that proclaim that they are in someone's top 5 per cent of sites or that they are Dave's Animated Site of the Week. The first awards site to become really popular was the Cool Site of the Day, which turned its creator, Glenn Davis, into something of a net celebrity. (He now runs a new awards site called Project Cool – **http://www.projectcool.com/**.) Dreaming of microfame (or of the ad dollars a site with his traffic could garner), amateur web users and gamey corporations followed Davis's example and set up various awards sites.

Like all awards scams, they generally share the same secret purpose. It's often not so much about recognising excellence; it's about showing that you, the judicious authority handing out the gongs, know what you're talking about (and might be available for online consultancy, if the price is right). A lot of web awards sites are harmless fun. Many are pointless and have come in for some serious ridicule. But a few carry some authority and are genuinely useful. If you're interested in web design, it's worth looking at High Five **http://www.highfive.com/**, which hands out awards for the best designed web pages. For a general list of awards sites, try Yahoo (there's a **Best of the Web** category in the **WWW** section. Alternatively, go to **http://www.thecorporation.com/**, one of the many awards parodies, where you can download various joke award icons (e.g. Sell Out Site of the Year) to put on your homepage.

For more fuzzy but occasionally useful searching, you could try web rings. These are loose collectives of sites (often personal homepages put up by fans) all devoted to the same basic subject. Once they might have

< 162 >

been deemed to be in direct competition with each other. But someone somewhere rather cleverly figured out that, as the web got bigger and more corporate, small pages might make more impact and draw more traffic by sticking together. In a web ring, sites are connected so that you can move from one to the other by clicking the Next Site link at the bottom of a page. Alternatively, the starting-point of the ring usually offers a link to a master list of all the sites involved.

There are web rings devoted to all sorts of subjects – from Afro-American issues **http://www.halcon.com/ halcon/1ring.html** to the *Tomb Raider* computer game **http://members.tripod.com/~zeeman4/index.html**. These rings can get very big (there are almost 800 sites in the Afro-American web ring) and you might find yourself browsing more than searching. And they're a bit hit and miss. Some amateur/fan sites seem deranged, but others are brilliant mini-archives of useful material. So web rings are definitely worth investigating. For general links, once again, look in Yahoo. Alternatively try WebRing **http://www.webring.org/**, a web ring directory which lets you search web rings or find the one you want, Yahoo-style, by going through various subdirectories.

Research Online

Most search sites are good for moving you on to other locations. But what about research sites proper, sites that are destinations in their own right and offer searchable databases of information? There are plenty of these online – look under the Reference category on Yahoo. As you might expect, you can research all sorts of things online, from films at the Internet Movie Database – **http://uk.imdb.com**, to job ads at Jobsite UK –

< 163 >

Tips – Research Sites

Here are a few research sites worth trying. Ask Jeeves **http:// www.askjeeves.com/** is actually more of a research toy. You can enter natural language questions – for example, 'Where can I get a cheap computer?' and Jeeves will do his best to find a site that supplies an answer. For more serious enquiries, try the excellent Research-It – **http://www.itools.com/research-it/research-it.html** – a self-styled 'one-stop reference desk' which lets you search dictionaries, a thesaurus, collections of quotations, maps and much else, all from the same page. Finally, an awards-laden British business search site you shouldn't miss is Scoot – **http://www.scoot.co.uk/**. ▲

http://www.jobsite.co.uk/, and technical terminology at the PC Webopaedia – **http://www.pcwebopedia.com/.** However, it's no surprise that one of the areas in which the net is strongest is searchable archives devoted to itself. Try the Usenet newsgroup archives at Deja News **http://www. dejanews.com** and Reference.com **http://www.reference.com/.** The latter also lets you rummage through an archive of public mailing lists. Both are surprisingly useful general research tools.

< 164 >

Future Directions

Though it sometimes seems as if the same few big names get all the attention, the search engine business is anything but stable. There are various new ideas currently being tried out by small companies. Given the main search sites' 'size matters' mentality, it's not surprising that they're focusing more on ways of making online searches deliver not quantity but quality, in the form of better-organised, more relevant results. Northern Light Technologies' search site **http://www.nlsearch.com/** claims it only indexes top-quality content, some of which you won't find elsewhere, and lets you organise results into different categories. The catch? You have to pay for some of it.

If you don't like the sound of that, try GoTo.com **http://www.goto.com** where companies will pay to be ranked higher in the search results. Another interesting idea which might find its way on to the web soon is Rankdex **http://rankdex.com/** which doesn't index sites by the keywords/metatags which webmasters choose. Instead it uses the anchor text from other sites that link to the site in question – in other words it relies on how other users describe the site, a clever way of producing more relevant searching.

Further off on the horizon, companies (Perpsecta Inc – **http://www. perspecta.com/** – and ThemeMedia – **http://www.thememedia.com/**) are working on visualisation – presenting information in a 3D visual form that can be searched more intuitively. If you've read William Gibson's science-fiction novels, you'll remember that he imagines cyberspace as just such a 3D environment, a sort of cityscape/Rubik's cube in which people move about by literally shifting around blocks of information. The

< 165 >

companies involved are targeting the business world so it will be a long while before something like this finds its way to the net.

Perhaps the most interesting future developments involve the use of intelligent agents and collaborative filters. The former are basically bots which do your bidding. They are supposed to find out what you're interested in and then go out and locate it for you online. Collaborative filters rely on pooling recommendations from individual users then cross-referencing them. So if one user like movies X and Y and you like movie X too, the filter would suggest that you might also like movie Y. Firefly (yet another company recently bought by Microsoft) used to be the market leaders in collaborative filtering but now concentrate more on protecting consumer privacy online **http://www.firefly.net**. If you want to play around with a collaborative filter, try LikeMinds' MovieCritic **http://www.moviecritic.com**.

Next Step?

Now you're on top of search sites, you could take a break from the web for a while and learn about online communication in the next section on email. If you want to learn more about the web, go to page 236 and the chapter on **FTP and Downloading Files**. If you want to continue learning about searching the web/net, there's more on intelligent agents in the chapter on shopping online (page 314) and in the **Power User** section (page 393). ▲

< 166 >

Email and Mailing Lists

When I got online, the first thing I did was send some email to a friend who'd been connected for a while. It wasn't much of a message – the epistolary equivalent of those telephone calls you used to get from people where the first thing they said was, 'Hey, I'm calling on my mobile'. But he wrote back. And when his reply appeared, I'll admit that I was blown away. Back then, the web was only just getting started and email was one of the more immediate things you could do when you got online. That's my excuse, anyway. Today the web has become the thing most people go for when they first get online. But lots of people still think email is the net's killer app (as techno-pundits put it). Even those who make a profession out of net-bashing usually make an exception for email, which they 'really couldn't live without'.

Jargon file – Killer App

As in 'killer application' – the piece of software that works well enough to convince people they need to spend lots of money on the hardware needed to run it. So, according to some accounts, the spreadsheet was the killer app which sold the business world on computers. ▲

< 167 >

Jargon file – ARPANET

ARPA stands for Advanced Research Projects Agency, essentially the Pentagon's R&D department during the cold war So, as you might expect, the ARPANET was the network it set up to test out new computer communications technology. ▲

Email has been around almost as long as the net. When ARPANET (a trial network that was essentially the beginning of the net) was set up in 1969, it was supposed to enable the sharing of scarce computing resources. But the researchers who used it soon began to send messages across the trial network, first about official business, then about office gossip, then about the science-fiction novels they were reading.

Today, every major business and institution has an email contact address. TV and radio programmes, newspapers and magazines can't do without them. Email regularly features in Hollywood films, though for obvious reasons it always looks a lot flashier and more exciting than the thing you get on your desktop. The epistolary novel has been updated to take email into account, courtesy of Stephanie D. Fletcher, whose *E-mail – A Love Story* is, ahem, of historical interest but not actually worth reading. (If you want to see how dense with meaning and how distinctive email can be, look at the online correspondence in *Before I Say Goodbye*, the collected columns of the late Ruth Picardie.) The precise meaning of email is argued over by lawyers and US Presidents Reagan, Bush and Clinton have even been to court to prevent White House email being made available to the public.

< 168 >

Read about it online – Email fiction

To sample an experiment in using email for fictional purposes, go to the site run by net celeb Carl Steadman and try *Two Solitudes*. Subscribe and over the next few days you'll be sent a series of emails in which two people play out an email romance – look for the link on **http://www.freedonia.com/**. ▲

It's not hard to see why email caught on. For the cost of a local telephone call, you can send messages to someone on the other side of the world in a matter of minutes. It's easy to save email and keep track of your correspondence. It's cheaper than faxing someone and you don't have to worry about paper and ink. You can also send more than plain text – attaching image and sound files to mail is simple. For no extra cost you can send mail to lots of people at the same time, building up informal mailing lists where you can thrash out political problems or discuss last night's TV. You can also subscribe to more formal mailing lists devoted to particular subjects and receive regular updates and news. The arrival of HTML mail means that web pages can be delivered directly to you. You can also sends your friends mail that resembles web pages, with flashy graphics, images and hyperlinks.

Email's attraction isn't just to do with speed and ease of use. Perhaps because it sits somewhere between speech and writing, because it's like a letter with the immediacy of a telephone call, it seems to encourage directness and intimacy. People get to the point quicker in email and sometimes

< 169 >

Jargon file – HTML Mail

Email that doesn't come in the form of plain text but is formatted using Hyper Text Markup Language, the computer code used to create web pages. ▲

seem more open and accessible. Email can also be less potentially painful or embarrassing than face-to-face contact, which might be one reason why it's apparently finding favour as a way to ask people out on a first date. Incidentally, email is also being used by some to dump boy or girlfriends. When it is, this hugely intimate form of communication can seem paradoxically impersonal; the absence of face-to-face accountability makes it all the harder to bear for the person on the receiving end.

Perhaps because it's less of an intrusion than a telephone call (generally, you can't just phone up your boss to tell him what you think), email seems to break down barriers and cut across hierarchies, especially in offices and the business world in general, where it has helped some to communicate more effectively. Telephoning someone on the other side of the world always involved negotiating time zones and inflated call charges. Email means you don't have to lose sleep (especially over your bank balance) to stay in touch with friends and business colleagues abroad. ▲

< 170 >

What software do you need?

Your internet service provider may supply you with email software when you sign up. One of the most popular mail programs is Eudora, which is available for both PC and Mac. There are two versions – Light, which is free and fine for most people's purposes and Pro, which has lots of snazzy extra features which you may or may not use and is free for the first thirty days. After that you have to pay. If your ISP doesn't give you a copy of Eudora, the Light version is often on the cover discs given away by the net magazines. You can also download Eudora from the web at **http://www.eudora.com/**. For information on downloading software, go to page 236.

You don't need a separate program for your email. Web browsers come with useful mail clients – one reason why your ISP might not send you separate software. In the past, these were never quite as good as Eudora. But the latest versions (4.x) of the browsers by Netscape and Microsoft offer much improved mail packages (called Messenger and Outlook Express, respectively). If you don't want to clutter your computer with programs, browser mail could be the best option. If you're connecting to the net via an online service like AOL, mail software is part of their general package.

If you have lots of disk space, there's nothing to stop you running several mail programs, but you will have to nominate one as your default, so that when you click an email link on a web page (for example, to send mail to the person responsible for the page), the computer knows which

< 171 >

program to start up. All very simple, or it ought to be. However, rather irritatingly, Netscape have made it very difficult for you to use their Navigator browser and have Microsoft's Outlook Express as your default mailer. It requires some technical fiddling. For similar reasons, Microsoft don't go out of their way to make it easy for you to use the Explorer browser with Netscape's Messenger mail software. This might be a reason to use Eudora, which will neatly install itself as the default mailer for either browser.

Configuring Your Mail Software

If you're going to use the mail program that came with the browser/internet suite supplied by your ISP, you may find that it was configured during the general installation process. Similarly, if you're using an online service, everything will be sorted out during the main installation. However, if you're installing something from scratch, you will need to enter a few personal details before you can send any mail.

You may have to enter any and all of the following:

Your name: As in Jim McClellan

Your email address: Your ISP will have given you this when you signed on – something like **yourname@yourserviceprovider.co.uk**

Your return email address: Usually the same as above, though you can enter something different if you're going to be picking up replies at another location (e.g. work)

< 172 >

Your user name (also known as the account name): This is the first part of your email address – i.e. **jim.mcclellan**

Outgoing Mail Server (SMTP): The computer at your ISP that handles the mail you send to other people. This will usually be something like **mail.yourserviceprovider.co.uk**

Incoming Mail Server (POP3): The computer on which the mail sent resides. Again, this will be something like **mail.yourserviceprovider.co.uk**

Password: The password your ISP gave you when you signed up.

If you do have to configure Netscape Messenger, select **Edit,** then **Preferences.** Then click on **Identity** and **Mail Server** in turn to enter the relevant information. If you're going to use Microsoft's Outlook Express, the first time you start it up the **Internet Connection Wizard** should take you through configuration. It starts by asking you to pick a name for the email account you're going to create, then will prompt you to enter some of the information listed above. If you need to change any of this account information (you might change ISPs and email address), select the **Tools** menu, then **Accounts.** Pick your account, then click on **Properties.** ▲

< 173 >

Your first message

If you've got friends who are online, now's the time to bug them with those 'Hey, I just got on the net' messages. (If you really want to wind them up, you should call them up repeatedly to see whether they actually got your mail.) If you don't have any friends who are online (or want to avoid irritating those that are), you could always send a message to yourself. Alternatively, why not send a message to the *Guardian*.

We've set up a program which will automatically send out replies to all mail sent to the *Guardian* at the address given in this book. It may be a touch impersonal but at least you can check quickly and easily whether your first mail reached its destination. And you'll also receive a bit of news about what's happening online at the *Guardian*.

Open your mail program and click the **New Message/Compose Message** button. A window will open which is split into two parts. The bottom part is where you write your message. The top part is where you enter details about the address to which you're sending your mail. Click in the **To:** field to move the cursor there, then enter the address – **guidetest@guardian.co.uk** – making sure that you don't capitalise anything (net addresses are case sensitive). Don't add an extra period at the end – however they may appear in books or the papers, email addresses do not end in full stops. If all this looks rather confusing, go back to page 32 for more information.

Your own address may already be in the **From:** field. In the **Subject:** field, enter a brief description of what your message is about – My First Message or some such. When you come to file mail sent to you, you'll

< 174 >

realise how useful the **Subject:** field is and you'll curse people who don't bother entering anything there. Ignore the other fields in this window for the moment. Once you've filled out the address information and the subject line, click in the bottom part and write your mail. What you put here is up to you – you might want to tell us whether you think this book is any use. On second thoughts, perhaps you should just say what sort of day you're having.

Email style

At school, you may have been given advice on how to lay out a letter. None of that really applies to email. When it comes to layout, you don't need to start by writing your address in the top right-hand corner. When people get your email, before they open it, their mailbox will show them who sent it and what it's about (if you enter something in the **Subject:** field). Some people don't bother opening their mail with a 'Dear Jim' and just get straight to the message.

Email purists also don't sign off with a 'Yours, Dave' or whatever, but instead include a personal 'signature file', aka 'sig file'. This usually contains your contact details – name, email address, perhaps snail mail address and telephone number(s) – all the stuff you might put at the top right-hand corner of a piece of snail mail, plus a jokey/deep quotation that shows what an interesting/deep/sexy individual you are. A few years ago, 'So long and thanks for all the fish' from Douglas Adams' *Hitchhiker's Guide to the Galaxy* was a popular sig file choice, so popular that it has now been officially outlawed, along with all quotations from *Monty Python*, *Blackadder* and *Shooting Stars*. Some sad folk also

< 175 >

Jargon file - Snail Mail

Snide net slang for old-fashioned mail that comes in envelopes, is delivered by the Post Office and takes a lot longer than email to arrive. Actually, in the past, some well-known UK ISPs have had problems with mail at particularly busy times of the year and some unlucky users found themselves waiting two weeks and longer for their email. ▲

include ASCII art – those 'clever' little pictures made up with keyboard characters.

Your mail package will let you compose a signature file and save it. When you write mail, you will automatically be able to paste it in at the end of the message. Many let you have alternative signature files – one for business correspondence and one for personal letters. You specify which to include when you write your mail, via a menu on the toolbar at the top of the **New Message** composition window.

In terms of general style, brevity and directness are key. People are paying to download your mail, so the idea is not to add to their bills, in however minuscule a way. Perhaps because it hovers somewhere between speech and writing, email tends to be more informal and slangy than snail mail. In theory, you don't need to take quite as much care with your grammar and upper and lower cases. You don't need to go back over your messages and make sure everything is just so. Of course, sending illiterate pieces of doggerel isn't good email style either and won't make

< 176 >

Tips - Email conventions

The thing to remember about email style conventions is that you don't have to follow them rigidly. Don't be intimidated by people who babble on about netiquette and insist that email should look a certain way and should end with a sig file. If you don't want to turn out something conversational, if you want your email to be like your snail mail, fine. The only principle you should stick to is to keep things brief wherever possible. ▲

that good an impression. Both Messenger and Outlook Express have spell checker programs which will automatically go over messages before you send them.

TLAs and Smileys

There are a few distinctive elements of email/online style you should know about – probably so that you can ignore them. You can compress messages even further by using TLAs, as in Three-Letter Acronyms. This includes things like WRT – with regards to; IMO – in my opinion; LOL; OTOH – on the other hand; RTFM – read the f- manual. (OK, so they don't always have three letters.) Most of these can be understood quickly, without resorting to some kind of TLA dictionary. That's the theory, anyway. Interestingly enough, they've started to spread to print prose. The journalism written by the American novelist David Foster Wallace is packed with WRTs.

< 177 >

The TLAs above are all capitalised, though people tend to write them in lower case. In fact, email, and online communication in general, often seems to be a lower-case medium. Capitals are reserved for emphasis. Writing something in capitals is the online equivalent of shouting. You'll notice that most junk mail features capitalised 'subject' headings – MAKE MONEY FAST!!! You should shy away from it, unless you really need to make a point. It can look rather rude and people do get the hump. It may sound daft if you've never been on the net, but a splurge of capitals in an online message does feel hectoring and confrontational.

When you're writing your email (or chatting or posting to a Usenet newsgroup), you can also use emoticons, aka smileys. These are little sideways-on faces constructed from keyboard characters, which are used to indicate emotion – :-) means happy; :-(indicates sadness, and ;-) is supposed to signal irony. The prevailing theory about this is that sometimes it can be hard to tell what a person mailing or chatting to you online means exactly, or it can be hard to grasp their tone, especially if they're trying to be funny or sarcastic, mainly because you're not face to face and hence can't pick up on the physical/facial cues they're giving. Hence smileys.

Read about it online – TLAs

For a pretty comprehensive list of smileys and TLAs (and a useful glossary of general net jargon), try Netlingo at **http://www.netlingo.com**. ▲

< 178 >

Of course, most people over the age of fourteen don't feel the need to pepper their ordinary paper letters with little faces to help the recipient understand when they're being ironic. And I can't remember the last time I got some mail with a smiley in it. So it may be that smileys are just a product of the novelty/strangeness of email. They can be useful, though there is sometimes something slightly bogus about them, especially the irony smiley which some people use as an all-purpose get-out clause. As the science-fiction writer Bruce Sterling once pointed out, writing 'you, sir, are a complete asshole', then following it up with **;-)** to show that, hey, you didn't really mean it, is probably not going to go down that well with the recipient of your message.

HTML or Plain Text Mail?

Email used to be plain ASCII text. But now we have HTML mail, which means letters with pictures, links and more. Most new mail programs – e.g. Messenger and Outlook Express – automatically use HTML mail for email unless you tell them otherwise. Some older mail programs may have difficulties with this. It's not that big a deal. If you send HTML mail to someone whose software can't handle it, it will appear in their inbox as text plus an attached HTML file. However, to save on aggro, you can always check that the person you're mailing can receive HTML mail. If they can't, choose to send just plain text. (This is generally the best option when sending messages to mailing lists.) With Messenger, when you're writing a new message, click on the **Message Sending Options** button in the bottom-left corner of the **Address** window. Then look for the drop-down **Format** menu on the left which will let you pick text or HTML or

< 179 >

Tips – Cut and Paste

You can always write your mail in your word-processing package, then cut and paste it to the **New Message** window. But all that clever formatting you spent hours on won't come out, especially if your mail software is set to send plain text. You could always attach particularly flashy documents. ▲

---

both. Similarly, with Outlook Express, when you're writing mail, just select the **Format** menu then either **Plain Text** or **Rich Text** (HTML).

For the moment, you should concentrate on sending a simple message. However, thanks to HTML, you can produce very flashy email, complete with different fonts and colours, much like the kind of thing you can do with a modern word-processing program. Once you're used to email, try the options available via the **Format** menu. In Outlook Express, select the **Format** menu, then **Apply Stationery** and you'll be able to use various standard templates for your email – party invites with coloured balloons, snow scene Christmas cards and the like. If you sign up with an online service like AOL, you'll also be able to send flashily formatted messages to people on the same service. ▲

< 180 >

Sending your first message

You're happy with your message. Click on your mailer's **Send** button. Your connection software should now kick into gear. You can now choose to go online and send the mail straight away. Alternatively, you can stay offline. Your mail will be transferred to your **Outbox** or **Unsent Mail** folder, depending on which mail program you're using. You can then write more messages and stack them up in the **Outbox** to send all at once. Alternatively, you can wait and send them later. If you close your mail program without sending your mail, you may get a brief reminder asking whether you want to send it now. With unsent or queued mail, most mail software will send it automatically the next time you check your own mail. Alternatively, with Messenger, you can select the **File** menu, then **Send Unsent Mail**.

Tips – Reading Mail Offline

Perhaps this sounds a bit obvious, but whenever possible work on your mail (i.e. read and write it) offline. Once you've downloaded mail sent to you, disconnect and then read it. Some programs log off automatically. But if you have one that doesn't, don't get your mail and start reading it, forget you're still connected and then write the reply online. It's easy to do and then you end up paying BT or whoever for all that time puzzling over the *mot juste* or the right smiley. ▲

< 181 >

Let's say you choose to send your mail straight away. You'll have to enter your password, then the mail software will send your mail and check to see if you have any messages as well. There might be something from your ISP welcoming you aboard.

Most mail software is set up by default to save a copy of mail you send, usually in the **Outbox** or in the **Sent Items** folder. Some older programs used to automatically send you a Carbon Coby (aka CC) of any messages you sent. Either way, it's a good method of keeping track of mail. However, if you don't want to save your mail, in Messenger select the **Edit** menu, then **Preferences**, then **Messages**. Then remove the tick in the box next to **Automatically copy outgoing messages to a folder** (by clicking in it). In Outlook Express, select the **Tools** menu, then **Options**, then click the **Send** tab, then click in the box next to **Save copy of sent messages in the Sent Items folder** to remove the tick.

After you've sent your mail to **guidetest@guardian.co.uk**, go and make yourself a cup of tea. With luck, if everything's working, you should get a reply from us in the next couple of hours – perhaps quicker, though don't hold me to that.

Troubleshooting

Email is one of the more glitch-free parts of the net. Occasionally, mail might be bounced back to you unsent. Usually, the problem is caused by errors in the address. Remember that email addresses are case sensitive. Also, don't add spaces or extra periods. If you've checked everything and it appears OK, it may be that the person you're sending it to has changed address. If that isn't the case, the problem may be

< 182 >

at the ISP where your intended recipient has his or her mailbox – their computers may be down – in which case, try sending your message later. ▲

• •

Getting your mail

Email sent to you sits in your mailbox on your ISP's mail server until you go and get it. If you want to see if you have any email, in Messenger, click the **Get Message** button; in Outlook Express, click **Send and Receive**. You'll connect to the net and your messages will be downloaded. Log off. A window should open showing the new mail in your **Inbox**. If not, click on your **Inbox** icon or button. For each piece of new mail, you'll see a line of information, telling you who sent it and when and what it's about. Double-click on that and the message will open in a new window.

Most people prefer to check their mail manually. However, you can get your mailer to pick it up automatically at regular intervals – every hour or so, or whatever you decide. This is mainly of use if you (a) get an awful lot of mail and (b) are online all the time because it doesn't cost that much where you live or because someone else is paying your bills. If that sounds like you, in Messenger, select the **Edit** menu, then **Preferences**, then **Mail Server**, then click the **More Options** button, then tick/change the line **Check for mail every X minutes**; in Outlook Express, select the **Tools** menu, then **Options**, then click the **General** tab. Make sure there is

< 183 >

a tick in the box next to **Check for new messages every X minutes** and change the figure to suit your requirements.

By default, most mail programs will clear out your mailbox on a regular basis. If they didn't, your mailbox could eventually fill up and new mail might be bounced. To ensure that won't happen, in Messenger, select the **Edit** menu, then **Preferences**, then **Mail Server**, then check that there is <u>no</u> tick in the box beside **Leave messages on server after retrieval**. In Outlook Express, select the **Tools** menu, then **Accounts**. Then highlight your account, click the **Properties** button, then the **Advanced** tab. In the Delivery section, check that the box next to **Leave a copy of messages on server** is empty.

When you're reading your mail, before you get to the message proper you may encounter a lot of technical-looking information known as the 'header'. This gives details of when the message was sent and by whom, the path it took on its way to you and other bits and pieces. You don't really need to see all of this and by default most mailers remove or trim down the headers. However, the header can sometimes be a useful starting-point, if you're on the receiving end of junk email or abusive messages and want to find out more about where they're coming from. To display the full header if you need to, in Messenger, click on the message, select the **View** menu, then **Headers**, then **All**; in Outlook Express, open the mail you're interested in, select the **File** menu, then **Properties**, then click the **Details** tab. ▲

< 184 >

Replying to your mail

A friend has emailed you and you want to reply. You don't need to open a **New Message** window, then write his or her address in the relevant section. You can just click on the **Reply To** button. This will open a **New Message** window with your friend's address already filled in. In the **Subject:** field, it will say 'Re: whatever your friend entered in the Subject line in the mail they sent you'. When replying to mail, it can be helpful to quote from the previous message – especially if you're writing to someone who gets lots of mail and thus may lose track of their correspondence. If you use the **Reply To** button on some mailers, when the message window opens it will display the past message – indented with what are known as 'quote tags', as in:

>Jim

>blah blah blah

>Wally

You can then edit this, selecting the bits you want to keep, then adding your own contributions, as in:

On the 10th March, Wally wrote

< 185 >

>blah blah blah

See what you mean, Wally.

Jim

The end result simulates a kind of conversation and helps to keep track of ideas over several messages (as a result, it's indispensable when it comes to posting messages to Usenet newsgroups – more on this on page 225).

When replying to email, conventional wisdom says you should reply quickly, if only to confirm you received the message. I was once berated by a famous author I was interviewing by email when I took a few days to reply to one of his messages. 'Bad email etiquette, Jim' he wrote in a mildly tetchy mail asking why I hadn't replied yet. 'If you're going to take that long to reply we might as well use regular mail'. This was stretching it a bit, since he lives on the other side of the Atlantic. But you see his point.

Tips - Editing Replies

Make sure that you edit down the previous message so that only the appropriate bits are included. Don't just automatically send people back a complete copy of their previous mail when replying. Obviously it's not such a problem if the first mail was a few lines. Several thousand words is something else entirely. ▲

< 186 >

Sometimes, if a reply doesn't appear for a while, you start to wonder whether your mail actually reached its destination. Then again, just because email goes a lot faster, it doesn't automatically mean you have to. One of the few bad things about email is the way it often carries a kind of implicit pressure to be more productive, the way it can feel as if it is bullying you to get cracking, speed things up, write back NOW!

Carbon Copies and Forwarding

One of the good things about email (though it is open to abuse, as you will unfortunately discover) is that it is very easy to send the same message to large groups of people. One way to do this quickly is to use the carbon copy (CC) option. Open a new message window. In the top section, underneath the **To:**, **From:** and **Subject:** fields, you should see **Cc** and **Bcc** (blind carbon copy) options. You can use these to send your mail to other people as well as the main addressee. Just type their email addresses in the relevant field, leaving a space after each new address. If you use the **Cc** option, recipients will be able to see who else got your message. If you use **Bcc**, they won't know who else got a copy. To add **Cc** and **Bcc** addresses in Messenger, just click the **To:** button in the **Address** window.

It's also easy to forward mail. Once a message is open, just click the **Forward** button and a new message window will open with the old message in quote tags. You can then enter the address of the person you want to forward it to and add any comments. Some mail packages also let you redirect messages to someone else. Click the **Redirect** button and a window will open containing the message you want to send on, this time without the > tags.

< 187 >

Address Books and Email Directories

If someone sends you mail, you can add their contact details to an address book for future reference – helpful if you find it difficult to remember email addresses or type them out without making mistakes. In Outlook Express, click the **Address book** button; in Messenger, select the **Message** menu, then **Add to address book**. The email address and name will be added by your software. You can then add other relevant details – address and telephone number. Outlook Express and Messenger also give you the option of specifying whether the person in question can receive HTML mail, which is useful. When you want to send a new message, open the address book, look for the relevant entry, then click the **To:** button. A new message window will open with the relevant address entered.

You can also search online directories for email addresses. Both Outlook Express and Messenger are set up to allow you to search various directories – Big Foot, Four11, WhoWhere, Switchboard, Infospace. These are a bit hit and miss. Some rely on submissions from users who want people to be able to find them. Others use software which trawls the net, in particular Usenet newsgroups, for addresses. They all have a definite American bias. Big Foot is probably the best for British users, though there's not much in it. All of them will turn up plenty of results – especially if you do a simple search on a name. Of course, you then have to figure out which, if any, might belong to the person you're trying to contact.

Once you're online, in Outlook Express, click the **Address Book** button, then **Find**. A **Find People** dialog box will come up. Click the **Look**

< 188 >

in drop-down window to pick a directory to search, then enter the name of the person you're searching for and click the **Find Now** button. In Messenger, get online, then select the **Edit** menu, then **Search Directory**. In the **Search** dialog box, use the **Search for items** drop-down menu to specify a directory, enter the name you want to search for, then click the **Search** button.

Email and Attachments

You can send more than just text using email. It's possible to attach all sorts of different files to your messages – everything from images and sounds to video and programs. However, there is a size limit for email messages of 64 Kb – generally fine for most text messages, but not for images, programs and the like. In addition, most files you might want to send are binary (8 bit), whilst email is all 7 bit ASCII text. So before files can be sent, they have to be converted into ASCII. Then they'll be converted back to their proper form by the person who gets your mail. In theory.

Attaching files to email has been made easy by modern mail software. In Outlook Express or Messenger, just click the **Attach** button on the toolbar (the one with the paperclip on it), then find the file you want to send in your directory, then click on **Attach**. However, problems are caused by people not checking whether recipients of their mail have software that can cope with the type of attachments they're sending.

A few years ago, most PC mail programs converted attachments using something called UUencode. Newer mail programs use something called MIME which is becoming the standard. Mac mail programs also used

< 189 >

Tips - Mailing URLs

If you're using Messenger, you can attach a web page to mail you're sending to a friend. Get online, then write your mail. Click the **Attach** button, then select **Web Page**. Write the web page URL or address in the **Please Specify a location to attach** dialog box, then click OK, then send the mail. Messenger will then go and get the page and attach it to your mail. This can be a fun way to tell people about a good page you've found. But check they can receive HTML mail and think about the size of some of the pages before you send. It might be better just to send the URL. You can also do this via Internet Explorer. If you're browsing and find a page that might interest a friend, select the **File** menu, then **Send**, then choose whether to send the page or the link. Then Outlook Express (or whatever your default mailer is) will open and you can write your mail and send it. ▲

something called Bin Hex. Modern mail programs can cope with all of these. However, many people don't religiously upgrade their software. Especially with something like email, they're happy chugging along with the mail program they've always used. Until they get a chunk of indecipherable gibberish in their mailbox.

So before you send an attachment to someone, find out what conversion method their mail program uses. If they use a newer mailer, there should be no problem. If they have an older program, you'll have to use UUencode. To use UUencode for attachments in Messenger, click the

< 190 >

Message Sending Options button in the bottom-left corner of the **Address** section of the **Composition** window, then click in the box next to **UUencode instead of MIME for attachments**; in Outlook Express, select the **Tools** menu, then **Options**, then the **Send** tab. The **Mail sending format** will be set to HTML. Click the box by **Plain text** to change it, then click **Settings**. You can then specify either MIME or UUencode.

If you use an online service rather than an ISP, attaching files to messages to members of the same service is no problem. However, in the past, you did encounter trouble, especially when receiving attachments from friends elsewhere on the net. Most of the online services have sorted things out now and can handle MIME files but you could always double-check if you're sending to a friend on one of the online services.

When it comes to receiving mail with attachments, Messenger will usually display attached images as part of the main message. If you want to save images displayed like this, right-click on them, then pick **Save Image As** from the menu. If Messenger can't display an attached file, it will show a link to it. Click on that to open it. If you have an application

---

Tips – Viruses

Always virus-check Microsoft Word documents that are sent to you as attachments. They can be host to various macro-viruses. These are more irritating than dangerous, but they're still a pain. Even if the document was sent by a friend, check it. Often people pass these on without knowing. ▲

< 191 >

on your computer that can run the file, it will start up. If not, you can save it to your disk. Alternatively, there should be a paperclip icon at the top of your mail. Click that to display the attachment as an icon in a separate window below the main message. Right-click this to either save it or open it. Incidentally, if you want Messenger to show all attachments as links, select the **View** menu, then **Attachments,** then click **As Links.**

Outlook Express is set by default to show picture attachments in the body of the message. To change this, select the **Tools** menu, then **Options,** then the **Read** tab and remove the tick in the box by **Automatically show picture attachments in message.** If the attachment isn't an image, there should be a paperclip icon at the top of the message when you open it. Click that. The file's name will appear. Click that and you'll be asked if you want to open it or save it.

Tips – Compressing Files

If you are going to send a large file via email, to speed things up, you might want to think about compressing it. The best way is with a program called WinZip (evaluation copies are available for download from **http://www.winzip.com/**). Check that the person you're mailing can deal with zipped files. For more on downloading files and using WinZip, go to page 236. Incidentally, if you are using an older mail program that has trouble with MIME, UUencode or BinHex and you have a PC, you can use WinZip to convert all these file types and more. ▲

< 192 >

You can attach large files to email but sometimes you have to break them up into parts. (What qualifies as large? 1 MB per message, including attached files, is the usual limit.) Your mail program may break up a large file and send the parts, but check in the **Help** file for details. For example, if you want to set Outlook Express to break up a large message, select the **Tools** menu, then click **Accounts**. Then click the **News** tab, the **Properties** button, then the **Advanced** tab. In the **Posting** section, you can tell Outlook Express to break up messages above a certain size. Then when you try to attach a large file, it will kick into gear.

When it comes to receiving attached multi-part files, check your mail software's **Help** files to see how it handles them. If you try to open one part of a multi-part attachment, some programs will automatically open the rest and put them together. With others, you have to mark the various parts before your software can deal with them. For example, in Outlook Express, click on all the parts (press **control**, then click on each header), then select the **Tools** menu, then select **Combine and Decode**.

Managing your email

Obviously, it's up to you how hard you work at filing your mail. There are people who let months of mail pile up in their **Inbox** without doing anything about it. It's easily done. Email doesn't exactly clutter up your office the same way as the stuff that comes on paper. But it can get out of control. Anyway, it's very easy to organise and file email.

First, try to read messages as soon as you get them and reply quickly. Messages in your **Inbox** will most likely be sorted according to the date they were received. If it helps you get through them quicker, you can order

< 193 >

them in another way – by sender, subject, etc. In Messenger or Outlook Express, select the **View** menu, then **Sort** or **Sort By**. Be ruthless when it comes to deleting messages you don't need. It's easy to save your mail, but often you don't need to. If you do want to keep mail, file it when you've read it. You can set up specific folders for mail from different people, organisations, mailing lists or subjects, then transfer it easily as you read it. To create new folders, select the **File** menu, then **Folder** or **New Folder**. To file a piece of mail in Outlook Express, select a message, then select the **Edit** menu, then **Move to Folder**. In Messenger, click the **File** button on the toolbar.

You can create filters which automatically direct incoming mail into specific folders rather than the **Inbox**. Here you have to tell your mail software to look out for messages that carry certain keywords in the subject line or come from a particular person or place. In Messenger, select the **Edit** menu, then **Mail Filters**. In Outlook Express, select the **Tools** Menu, then **Inbox Assistant**.

In each of these, click on the **New** button to create a filter. From here you have to specify what you want your software to look for and what it should do with a message that fits the parameters you set. Say you get a lot of mail from a particular business colleague. You can put his or her email address in the **Sender** category, then arrange to transfer it to a special mailbox/folder. Alternatively, if they never say anything interesting, you could get it diverted straight to the trash. Outlook Express can even be set up so it won't even bother to download certain messages from your ISP's mail server. Actually, there are now many filter programs specifically designed to block junk mail, which generally work better

< 194 >

Tips - Filters

Filtering messages directly to specific files may make you feel as if you've dealt with them, so you might not actually read them for a while. Cue a huge email backlog. For some people, it may be better to read stuff as it comes in, then file it manually. On the other hand, filters may do the job for you. ▲

---

than the filters in your standard mail package. For more on this, go to page 379.

Free Mail, Redirection and Other Mail Services

You already have an email address/account. But do you want another – for free? Of course you do. Start up your web browser and go to one of the web sites run by companies like Hot Mail (now owned by Microsoft). In a matter of minutes you can set up an email account (with your own password). You can then use your web browser to read and send mail.

Web mail is currently very popular, something computer industry analysts failed to predict, though perhaps you can't blame them. Most people online already have an email address. In general, ISPs don't offer the option of not having an email address and paying a little less. So why bother with an extra one? Never underestimate the hypnotic power of that word 'free'. Nevertheless, a web-based email address offers a few tangible advantages. First, it makes it very easy to get your mail whilst travelling. All you need is a computer with a connection to the web. You

< 195 >

don't need separate email software any more – you can use your web browser.

You can change your ISP without having to inform friends and colleagues of your new email address. You can create multiple email addresses on the same net connection – for example, for family members. You can 'maintain your independence' from work or college, according to one Free Mail site. Translation: if you have an official mailbox at work and if that's your only connection to the net, you can set up something for your personal mail on the web. It's also true that if you have an account at home that you share but you want to keep some mail private, a web mailbox is a good option. Then the mail you want to keep private won't be sitting around on your machine at home, waiting to be discovered.

All this sounds fine and dandy. However, not all of these benefits stand up to scrutiny. Take the basic attraction – that Hot Mail and others offer a 'free' service. Clearly they don't charge up front. What they do is sell advertising space, so you have to look at ads while you get your mail. Sometimes your mail may also contain ads. Given the way web mail works, you'll inevitably end up composing your mail online – which obviously means a bigger telephone bill. As you may already have discovered, the web can be slow, which means getting your mail will be slow too, perhaps considerably slower than downloading it from an ISP. And sometimes servers can be down, which means you won't be able to get your mail at all.

Given that the big browsers come with mail software attached, the advantages of being able to deal with everything via the browser are minimal. Many ISPs now allow you to create multiple email aliases on the

< 196 >

one basic account, so that other family members can have their own addresses. Some free web mail services give users the chance to send mail anonymously and claim this as a benefit. There's more on why you might want to do this and how on page 371. However, there has been some abuse of web mail in this respect and some of the bigger players (e.g. Hot Mail) will not now let people send messages anonymously.

If you use web mail for personal purposes at work, your mail will remain private, but if the boss is keeping tabs on your time online, he or she will know that you keep making repeat visits to the Hot Mail site and might wonder why. On the subject of privacy, you hand over a certain amount of personal information in return for your free mail account and you can't always be certain how that information will be used in the future, or if it will be adequately protected.

So what you're left with is a separate address where you can receive mail you might not want to show up in your standard mailbox and the ability to change ISPs without hassle and to pick up mail while on the move. These are considerable benefits, so you should definitely have a look at the free mail sites. Here are a few worth checking:

Hot Mail – **http://www.hotmail.com**
iName – **http://www.iname.com**
Rocket Mail – **http://www.rocketmail.com**
MailCity – **http://www.mailcity.com**
Net@ddress – **http://www.netaddress.com**

< 197 >

Read about it online – Electronic Postcards

To amuse or irritate your friends, why not try the Activegrams web mail service and send them a deeply naff animated greetings card? Choose from a variety of cards to suit all occasions and locations at **http://www.activegrams.com/**. For a more useful email service you can access via the web, try Remind-U-Mail. Here you create a kind of personal calendar filled with important dates (e.g. your mum's birthday). Then you'll get an email reminder so that you don't forget it. It's free, so you have no excuse – **http://calendar.stwing.upenn.edu/**. ▲

A good free email service has become one of those things you have to have if you're putting together a so-called portal site. These are the huge, user-friendly, service-packed pages put together by the likes of Microsoft, AOL, Netscape and the net directory Yahoo which they hope ordinary punters will choose as their browser homepage (the page that loads first when you start up your browser). If all this sounds a bit confusing, perhaps you should come back to this after reading the section on the web (starting page 135).

Some web-based mail services are designed not to replace your ISP mail account but to work in tandem with it. Take Big Foot (**http://www.bigfoot.co.uk**), who do one of the better email directories and will also let you create what it calls an email address for life – **jim.mcclellan@bigfoot.com** or some such. This is what you give out to people. Mail arriving at this address is then redirected to your ISP mail account. Once again, this reduces hassle when it comes to changing ISPs.

< 198 >

Other companies (e.g. iName) give you the opportunity to pick a name which sounds a bit better than the thing your ISP lumbered you with (in certain cases, charging you for it). Once again, this address is the one you give out and mail is redirected to your ISP mail account.

Bigfoot also offers a variety of other useful services. It's very good when it comes to blocking junk mail and spam. When you go on holiday, it has a facility which can be set up to send out messages automatically to people who mail you, telling them you are away until a certain date. Many ISPs will do the same and if you think email is going to be particularly important to you, check to see what special services are on offer. For example, Virgin will also redirect mail to another address for you and send notification about new mail to your pager (which could be useful for business people on the move). ▲

• •

Mailing lists

Mailing lists are one of my favourite things about the net. At their best, they offer quick and painless access to (usually) high-quality information about a particular subject. When they're open to contributions from all subscribers, the discussions that are generated are more focused, productive and friendly than the free-flowing anonymous brawls you often find in Usenet newsgroups.

There are thousands of mailing lists online. Some are one-way only. You subscribe and everything from product information to news bulletins

< 199 >

Tips – Mailing Lists

For access to all sorts of high-quality commercial mailing lists, try Netscape's InBox Direct (look for the link on Netscape's main page – **http://www.netscape.com/**). Hot Mail offer a similar service, called Web Courier – go to **http://www.hotmail.com/**. ▲

is sent to you on a regular basis. Many webzines run mailing lists which update you about content and even send web pages direct to your mailbox. Plenty of excellent electronic zines exist only as mailing lists.

With two-way lists, the content of the list is generated by the subscribers. You send a message about something on a particular topic or event. It goes to everyone on the list. Then someone might respond and over time – hours or days, depending on how active the list is – a discussion builds up. Some of these can be pretty serious affairs where people try to thrash out theories and ideas. Others are more relaxed and the ostensible subject of a list – a local pop group, gardening, whatever – often takes a back seat to general chatter.

Two-way lists can either be moderated or completely open. The former are controlled by a moderator who tries to keep discussions on track, and weeds out posts that are off-topic or deliberately abusive. The latter are completely open. Everything anyone sends in to the list goes out to everyone else, which can lead to huge amounts of mail. Moderated lists seem preferable – so long as the moderator is accountable for the decisions he or she might make. Moderated lists appear to be much smoother.

< 200 >

Read about it online – List Directories

The web is the best place to go for information about different lists, and there are thousands you could join. Try the excellent Liszt – **http://www.liszt.com/** or Publicly Accessible Mailing Lists at **http://www.neosoft.com/internet/paml/** or Reference.com – **http://www.reference.com** – a more general search site with information on mailing lists. ▲

People fall out less. And though there's often less traffic, it seems to add up to more.

Subscribing to a list is easy. The general information about the list which you find at a site like Liszt.com will tell you what to do. You send mail – usually with something like 'subscribe' in the body of the message – to the computer where the list is based. You will then receive mail notifying you that you have been put on the list. Save this message. It will contain important details about how to post to the list and how to cancel your subscription. One thing to look out for: lists have two addresses – one to which you send messages intended for the list proper and one for administrative queries. Don't get the two mixed up. Otherwise you may end up sending mail about how your attempt to cancel your subscription was unsuccessful to everyone on the list. More than likely, they will not be too pleased.

Online mailing lists are usually automated. The two most popular list software programs are Listserv and Majordomo. They basically do the same sort of things but respond to slightly different commands and

< 201 >

Tips - Access

Remember that most lists are public forums. They're easily accessible and easily searched. In other words, the things you write might be found by someone using the net to check you out. So you might want to watch what you say. ▲

requests. The main difference is that Listserv is a connected system, which means that if you don't know which computer houses a list you want to join, you can send your subscription request to any Listserv computer. (Of course, you still have to know the name of the list, in which case you're likely to know the proper address.) With Majordomo lists, you need to know where the computer hosting the list is.

It's pretty easy to join a list. Dealing with the number of messages it can generate might prove problematic, however. If you're going on holiday, sign off from high-volume lists before you go. Don't stay on the list and then use one of those services that automatically send people a little note saying you're on holiday: if you're on a high-volume list, in your absence you will end up sending your reply to every message – and you may make the list unworkable. If you find yourself on a high-volume list which is interesting but a bit overwhelming, check with the administrator to find out if there's a weekly digest of the list you can get instead. To avoid messages from a high-volume list clogging up your **Inbox**, set up a mail filter to divert it to its own box. Set the filter to look for the list address or the list name, which is usually in the **Subject** line of messages.

< 202 >

How Not To Be A Slave To Your Email

Email is a wonderful thing but it will take over your life if you don't keep it under control. When you first get online, you may find yourself checking for new email every half an hour and feeling floored and friendless when you don't have any. Then suddenly there's too much of the stuff. You find yourself thinking back to the good old days when you got to work or came home in the evening, started up your computer and just got on with what you wanted to do. Now you start up your computer, get online and there are fifty emails fighting for your attention. Worse still, the important ones are often hidden under a mini-mountain of junk mail. There are things you can do to deal with spam but none of them are perfect. In the end, you have to learn to live with it.

Read about it online – Email Genres

For an antidote to all those who go on about how wonderful and productive email is, go to the webzine Suck and read Thinking Outside the Mailbox by Polly Esther, aka Heather Havrilevsky. A jokey run-down of email genres (the Long Lost Friend email, the Virtual Boss email, the Playing Hookey email), this contains the interesting theory that the After Work Plans email is a revolutionary act because it turns what used to be a two-minute conversation into an endless, time-wasting round of emails as you try to fix a time and a place – **http://www.suck.com/daily/97/01/10**. ▲

< 203 >

Spam may turn out to be the least of your problems. As mentioned before, one of the potentially great things about email is the sense of intimacy it can generate. But this can cut both ways. In other words, it's remarkably easy to annoy people with email without really meaning to. Some people argue that this may be something to do with the fact that it's often hard to catch the exact tone of certain messages. You may think you're being cleverly ironic, but the plain text in the mailbox of your soon-to-be-former friend might end up looking pretty insulting. So what you need is a little smiley to let someone know exactly what you did or didn't mean.

There's another school of thought that says that all the smileys in the world won't help. These people believe that, by filtering out the distractions and diversions of the real world, people get to the point in email, say what they really mean and that's why there are so many bust-ups. People don't agree on things. In the real world, they cover things up and try to get along. But in email, they can't cover things up. The truth is that though email is great for creating and maintaining friendships and romantic relationships, it can also be pretty good at wrecking them.

Aside from arguments over semantics, there's the potential for accidents email opens up. Netiquette says you have to deal with those fifty messages in your **Inbox** quickly or people might get the hump. So you do, but in a rush you send mail to the wrong people. On one mailing list I subscribe to, a message appeared from one list member which was clearly intended for a friend. It was a previous post from one of the more deranged members of the list, plus a few comments on what a wacko this bloke was. Common knowledge on the list, but something that was left unsaid. Consequently, the poor guy had to issue a public apology.

< 204 >

Things get worse in the office. Never, ever assume that email in a business environment is either private or your property. The fact is, the boss probably thinks that he owns all electronic communications made on his computers and that he has a perfect right to read them and the law backs him up. So if you have to send a friend memos about what a fool he is or about a juicy job offer from a competitor, do it on paper. At least you can eat that if the going gets rough. Email will sit on the system in all sorts of places. It's really difficult to delete it completely. And you may end up thinking the boss is the least of your troubles if your steamy emails to the marketing manager in the cubicle down the corridor are discovered and sent to all and sundry by your office colleagues.

So email can cause a few problems. Here are a few survival tips that might help. Be sensible about the mailing lists you subscribe to. Don't take on more than you can handle. If you're up till two in the morning trying to stay on top of your lists, you're on too many. Remember that email in the office environment is not private and could be saved and used against you. And although you're supposed to answer email quickly, think before you press **Send**.

Next Step

Now you've mastered email, Usenet newsgroups will be a doddle. So you could go straight to the next section. Alternatively, if you're worried about email and privacy, or dealing with spam, go to page 366. ▲

< 205 >

Usenet Newsgroups

When people try to explain Usenet newsgroups to first-timers, they usually reach for some sort of helpfully recognisable real-world image. They talk about Usenet as the world's biggest conversation, one that ranges across national boundaries and takes in everything from who killed JFK to how to cook a curry. Others talk it up as a kind of transnational think tank, a global groupmind, a place where experts collaborate on solving problems, where you can find the answer to just about any question you might want to ask. Others less enamoured of the whole thing call it the world's biggest slanging match or dismiss it as a multinational rumour mill, where the daftest kind of disinformation can gain currency.

Let me add my own real-world analogy to all this. Another way to get your head round Usenet might be to think of it as a virtual equivalent of Speaker's Corner in London. It's similarly rowdy and anarchic. Log on and you'll find people standing on their digital soapboxes, holding forth. There are plenty of hecklers who take over the soapbox to have their say. There are also loads of people who don't say anything but are just there to take in the show.

However, in the virtual Speaker's Corner that is Usenet there's space for 25,000 different soapboxes, all devoted to different topics and themes. And if you get on the wrong soapbox, people get cross. Every now and

< 206 >

then someone gets up on a soapbox and says 'Testing, testing, testing'. Then all the other speakers get really mad and yell at him or her for so long that they lose track of what they were talking about. If that didn't make things chaotic enough, every few minutes all the speakers are simultaneously pushed off their soapboxes by people holding up big advertisements for get-rich-quick schemes or porn shops. Then a bunch of people show up to chuck blankets over the get-rich-quick/porn people and push them off the soapbox, so that the original speakers can start up again.

Actually, all this goes to show is how limited real-world metaphors are when it comes to explaining what happens on the net. Let's try something more basic. Usenet is a kind of text-based global bulletin board. It consists of around 25,000 different newsgroups. The name itself is misleading. Groups can cover pretty much everything – not just the latest stories placed in the papers by political spin doctors.

With most groups, people log on to read and respond to previous messages, known as posts or articles. Some groups are one-way affairs, for announcements only. Others are primarily for exchanging files (which could be anything from images to software). People often talk about the anarchic nature of Usenet and it's true that most groups are pretty free and easy. But a few are strictly moderated. Usually this is not primarily from a desire to censor discussions but to make sure that, for example, a group devoted to cooking doesn't keep circulating recipes that have appeared before. There are also fairly rigid conventions governing everything from how to post messages to how to create new groups, so rigid in the latter case that some Usenet users created a much more open set of newsgroups in protest (known as the alt groups).

< 207 >

Usenet isn't the same thing as the internet. It's better to think of it as one of the many kinds of communications traffic carried by the net. Your ISP keeps a database of newsgroup postings on its news server, a computer running the Usenet news transfer protocol. Your ISP's news server is connected to others and a steady flow of postings to the newsgroups is passed between them. You connect to the news server to access the various groups and read the latest postings.

When you send a post to a particular group, it goes to your ISP's news server and is then passed on to others. As a result it can sometimes take a while before everyone on Usenet gets to see your wittily phrased deconstruction of Jerry Seinfeld's haircut. If they don't access Usenet on a regular basis, they may miss it altogether. There's so much traffic (i.e. so many messages) generated on Usenet that ISPs clear out their databases fairly frequently.

Usenet was created in 1979 by some American computer science graduates. Their idea was that, via a computer network, the geeks of America (and the world) could bring their collective brainpower to bear on the multiple bugs and quirks of the Unix operating system and gradually make it better. This original, idealistic vision survives in many newsgroups, where people do attempt to collaborate and help each other out.

Jargon file – Unix

The computer operating system of choice for hackers and geeks, who spend hours tinkering with its various versions. ▲

< 208 >

But as Usenet has spread to the mainstream, it's become clear that plenty of people don't want to be 'constructive', or use technology in such a benign way. Either that, or they have their own, rather odd idea of what being constructive means (for example, putting together lengthy theories to show how the spread of cashpoint machines is hastening the advent of a United Nations take over of America). Plenty of people get completely caught up in the newsgroups but the bulk of users (90 per cent according to some estimates) are lurkers. Drifting round Usenet can be one of the more diverting modern spectator sports. If nothing else, it alerts you to the incredible variety of things people can find to argue about.

Usenet is one of the more controversial areas of the net, mainly because a large chunk of it is driven by uncensored human desire. Yes, there are groups where pornography is exchanged. Unlike web sites, where people are trying to make money, the stuff in Usenet is often given away for free and is easy to download if you're using the latest software. There are also newsgroups devoted to child pornography and paedophilia. It's more than likely that your ISP won't carry these. In the last few years, British ISPs have come under police pressure not to carry newsgroups that contain illegal material and most have complied. As for

Jargon file – Lurkers

Net slang for those who hang around in newsgroups (and chat rooms), read what other people have to say but don't actually post anything themselves. ▲

< 209 >

Read about it online – Wendy Grossman

She wrote an award-winning account of the online scrap over Scientology which formed the start of an excellent book called *net.wars* – an account of the various battles being fought on the borders between cyberspace and the real world. The whole book is available online and it's a great source of information on the history and culture of Usenet and the net in general – **http://www.nyupress.nyu.edu/netwars.html**. ▲

newsgroup porn, be aware that it is there (especially if you have children who use your net connection), but don't get it out of proportion. For more on dealing with it, go to page 360. Incidentally, Usenet controversies don't begin and end with porn. The newsgroups have been the scene of some ferocious online spats, like the battle between the Church of Scientology and its critics taking place in **alt.religion.scientology**.

People are always saying Usenet isn't as good as it used to be. They were saying it when I first got online at the start of 1994, mainly because the newsgroups were being visited by more people like me – non-techie types – and that inevitably caused a few growing pains. People are saying it even more now, not without reason this time. Newsgroups have been hit by a plague of bulk junk messages (aka spam) touting get-rich-quick schemes and pornographic web sites amongst other things. As a result, some groups have become unworkable. Some gloomier net users have concluded from this that Usenet is doomed. Obviously spam is to blame, but people are also going

< 210 >

elsewhere for the kind of conversation and community they once got from the newsgroups – for example, mailing lists and the web.

You can see why people get down. But they shouldn't be too quick to write off the newsgroups. Usenet users have developed some ways of dealing with spam – a few volunteers spend hours of their own time sending out 'cancel messages' which remove unwanted spam. In the spring of 1998, these spam cancellers went on strike to force ISPs to take more action to tackle spam. Despite predictions of infocalypse, Usenet didn't collapse. What the cancel strike did reveal is that most spam goes to newsgroups devoted to sexual subjects. However, some people still think spam has made Usenet unworkable and have put together something called Usenet II.

People often talk about the net in general as a new interactive public realm where free expression rules and everyone can have their say. This is often wishful thinking. Many don't have the time to learn how to put up a web page. However, pretty much everyone who gets online can figure out

Read about it online – Usenet II

According to its creators, Usenet II was set up 'to create a structure where the traditional Usenet model of co-operation and trust can be made to work in the internet of the 21st Century'. This means lots of moderators and rules (no crossposting articles to more than three newsgroups, no binaries – e.g. pictures – text postings only) and much else. Read about it on their web site – **http://www.usenet2.org/**. ▲

< 211 >

how to send a message to a newsgroup. As a result, Usenet is one of the things that lives up to the rhetoric . . . sort of. It also shows you the consequences of that rhetoric. If you want to see what a people-driven info-anarchy actually looks like, check out Usenet. It can be both heart-warming and kind of scary. It isn't always pretty, but it is interesting. ▲

● ●

Choosing a newsreader

To access the newsgroups, read what people are saying and stick your own oar in, you need a newsreader. As with email software, you can either go with the newsreader that came with your browser/internet suite or a separate program. Microsoft's email package Outlook Express is also a newsreader and is pretty good. Netscape Communicator contains a newsreader called Collabra, which is also fine.

For an alternative to the big two, PC owners should try the excellent Agent. There's a free version, called, not surprisingly, Free Agent. Again, Free Agent is regularly included on the cover discs given away by the net magazines. Alternatively, download it from **http://www.forteinc.com/ getfa/getfa.htm**. Mac users could try Newswatcher (download it from **http://www.best.com/~smfr/mtnw/**). Online services like AOL have their own newsreader as part of their general package of software.

To make things go smoothly, whatever newsreader you choose should be able to search the list of newsgroups, read offline and filter messages – i.e. block messages from particularly irritating people. It's also helpful if

< 212 >

it can handle postings in HTML – messages which resemble web pages and feature graphics and links. Most new newsreaders can. On this basis, there isn't much to choose between Outlook Express and Collabra. If you have an older computer and aren't using Netscape Communicator or Internet Explorer 4.X because you don't have the disk space, try a stand-alone newsreader like Agent. Older versions of the standard browsers come with newsreaders as part of the package, but they lack some of the more useful features.

Finally, if you do install several newsreaders, you will need to nominate one as your default newsreader. This will be the one that starts up if you click a link on a web page to a particular newsgroup. As with email software, there can be problems if you want to browse with Netscape and use Microsoft for the newsgroups, or vice versa. If you're using Outlook Express, there can sometimes be problems if you don't also make it your default email program.

Configuring Your Newsreader

This is very similar to configuring your email software. You need to enter details about yourself and the address of your ISP's news server – the computer that maintains a database of newsgroups. The first time you use Outlook Express, the **Internet Connection Wizard** should start up and take you through the configuration process – which Microsoft refers to as creating a newsgroup account. Your news server address is usually something like **news.yourisp.co.uk**. You may be asked whether your ISP requires you to enter a password to access the newsgroups. Check with them but if they haven't mentioned it, you can probably assume you won't have to.

< 213 >

Once you've finished, you may be asked if you want to download a list of available newsgroups. Click **Yes** and then go off and make a cup of tea, as this will take a while.

If the **Internet Connection Wizard** doesn't start up, or if you want to change something, select the **Tools** menu, then **Accounts**, then the **News** tab. To create a new newsgroup account, click on the **Add** button, then **News** and the **Internet Connection Wizard** should start up. To change something you've already entered, make sure the relevant account is high-lighted, then click the **Properties** button. You'll then be able to access and alter any information you previously entered.

To configure Netscape's Collabra, start it up. You should see a Netscape **Message Centre** window. Select the **Edit** menu and then **Preferences**. Select **Mail and Groups**. Click **Identity** to enter your name and your email address. Click **Groups Server**, then click in the **Discussion groups (news) server** text box to enter the address of your ISP's news server. Next, get online, then click the **Subscribe** button. If this is the first time you've used Collabra, it will automatically download a complete list of newsgroups available from your ISP's news server. ▲

Tips – Going Offline

Once you've got a list of groups, log off. It's easy to forget you're connected and start searching for groups you want. However, like reading and writing email, that's best done offline. You don't want to pay BT any more than absolutely necessary. ▲

< 214 >

Getting started

You've downloaded the complete list of newsgroups and are ready to get involved in that big global conversation. First, you need to find the groups that match your interests – not an easy task given that there are tens of thousands. Though it may not look like it at first, there is an order to the newsgroup list – an address system of sorts, though it refers to subject matter, not actual locations.

Groups are ordered into a number of hierarchies – fairly wide-ranging thematic categories – followed by more specific detail about what the group discusses. For example, **uk.politics.censorship** would, as you might expect, be devoted to discussing the politics of censorship in the UK only. There are plenty of hierarchies – some easy to decipher, others rather mystifying. Many refer to discussions specific to a particular country, some to a specific university or company. Here are a few of the more popular ones.

alt As in alternative – the place for discussions with a non-conformist/anarchic/funky flavour

biz You can send your commercial messages here

comp Discussions about everything to do with computers

microsoft Get your product support advice here

< 215 >

misc Catch-all category for stuff that doesn't seem to fit in elsewhere

news Home to announcements about Usenet, debates on what's wrong with it, how to fix it, make it better in the future, etc.

rec Recreation, as in sports, hobbies and the like

sci Science

soc For socio-cultural discussion (and a bit of religion as well)

talk The place to argue out more controversial issues – gun control, for example, though that particular debate seems to occur pretty much everywhere on Usenet

uk Devoted to UK-specific discussions

Of these hierarchies, the **alt** groups are far and away the most popular and also the most controversial, mainly because they're not subjected to quite the same controls as the other groups. The **alt** hierarchy was essentially started as a protest. Frustrated by the rigid nature of the system by which new groups were created and approved, angered by the fact that a proposed **rec.drugs** group was blocked by the Usenet powers-that-be, even though it had passed the vote of users that all new groups have to undergo, a few net users created the **alt** hierarchy on their own computers in 1987.

< 216 >

alt.drugs came into being and a year later, when the proposed **soc.sex** was also blocked despite succeeding in the general vote, **alt.sex** also got started. In contrast to the formal procedures for creating new newsgroups, **alt** groups can be created by anyone whenever they want. What this means is that many groups are actually gags and wind-ups, there for the sake of the name and not thriving communities, though many journalists don't realise this and take some of those groups listing bizarre sexual practices rather more seriously than they should.

When it comes to finding a newsgroup, you could flick through the general list, which if nothing else will give you a good idea of the variety of discussions going on. However, most newsreaders let you search the list. In Outlook Express, click the **Read News** icon, then the **Newsgroup** button on the toolbar. Your list of newsgroups will come up. At the top you'll see a text box underneath **Display newsgroups which contain**. Click in here and write a simple key word – comics, drugs, *The Simpsons*, whatever. In the main window you will see a list of the groups covering that subject.

In Collabra, click the **Subscribe** button, then the **Search for a Group** tab, then enter keywords in the relevant text box. Incidentally, on its main list, Collabra tends to bundle newsgroups in a particular hierarchy together. Scrolling down the list, you may see the **alt** hierarchy, with a number in brackets beside it (something approaching 5,500) indicating the number of groups it contains. Click the little plus sign on the left by the **alt** folder to view the whole list.

You may find the same subject coming up in different hierarchies. One **sci** group might discuss the science of genetics, for example, whilst in a

< 217 >

talk forum people might be thrashing out the political implications of gene trademarking and the like. Sometimes the same subject gets chewed over in groups which don't look that different – you might find an **alt** group and a **soc** group devoted to drugs, for example. Check out each group to see which one suits you best. Finding the right newsgroup is a hit-and-miss affair. This isn't the fault of the labelling system, which is admirably specific. It's more that each group has a flavour of its own, its own history and culture, which determines how it treats a particular subject.

Your ISP might not provide access to all the available newsgroups. In part, this may be due to space. There are so many newsgroups, you can't blame ISPs for attempting to ease the strain on their bandwidth. So it may be that some specialist or foreign-language groups aren't available. If you want access to those groups, ask your ISP. They will usually oblige. If they don't, consider changing to another ISP.

Of course, another reason why groups may not be available is that your ISP has taken the decision to censor its newsfeed. It may not carry some groups because they contain illegal material (i.e. child porn or pirated software) and/or because they don't fit with its image/marketing strategy. Some ISPs and online services specifically target the family market and as a result don't allow access to whole chunks of Usenet which they think may carry porn and the like. Hence, they block all the **alt.sex** groups or whole chunks of **alt.binaries** (one of the places people exchange images).

There are problems with this kind of blanket censorship. For example, some of the **alt.sex** groups are devoted to worthy nattering about sexuality and aren't particularly salacious or pornographic. However, your ISP gets

< 218 >

Tips – Finding Newsgroups

You run a search on the newsgroup list and there doesn't seem to be a group devoted to Namibian woodworking technique. That doesn't mean there isn't one in existence, just that your ISP doesn't carry it. Get on the web, go to **http://www.jammed.com/~newzbot/** and you can search for such a group. It could be that someone before you has recognised the need for a Namibian woodwork group and is trying to start one. To find out if that's the case, look in **news.announce.newgroups** to see which new groups are being proposed and to vote on whether they should be accepted. ▲

to decide which newsgroups it carries. If it's an issue, choose an ISP that doesn't censor the groups so rigorously – up until recently, Demon carried the most uncensored feed of newsgroups in the UK. However, with the internet, there's always a way round censorship. You can always try a publicly accessible news server. Again, try **http://www.jammed.com/newzbot/** for information. ▲

< 219 >

Subscribing to and reading newsgroups

You've located a few suitable newsgroups. Now you need to subscribe to them. In Outlook Express, go to your list of groups and click the one you want, then click the **Subscribe** button. Alternatively, double-click the group you want. A little newspaper icon will appear by it to show that you've subscribed. In Collabra, click the **Subscribe** button, to get your list of groups, then either click the group you want, then click the **Subscribe** button or just click on the dot in the **Subscribe** column. This will change to a tick to show you have subscribed.

The most sensible way to consume Usenet is offline. Once you've subscribed to a few groups, you should go online, get the latest messages from those groups, log off and then read them. In Outlook Express, in the folder list in the separate window on the left of the browser, you should see a list of the newsgroups you have subscribed to. Connect to your ISP, then click on one of these groups. Outlook Express will now download the headers from the newest messages. It should be set to download 300 headers by default, usually enough to get a feel for most groups. You can change it to a higher or lower figure. Select the **Tools** menu, then **Options**, then click the **Read** tab and change the line **Download 300 headers at a time**. Once you've got the headers, if you're keen to save every last penny, log off.

In the top part of the right window, you should see a list of headers. Some will have a + sign next to them. Click on this and you'll see the rest

< 220 >

Jargon file - Headers

In this context, headers are the basic details about the message: what it's about, who sent it and when. They are not the message itself. You'll need to go back online to get that. ▲

of the thread (i.e. the various replies) that this particular message has generated. Scroll through them and you'll be able to see what's being discussed and by whom. The next step is to mark the messages you're interested in so that Outlook Express can download them. Select the **Tools** menu, then **Mark for Retrieval**. You're given various options. You can download individual messages, a thread, or the whole lot. If you're accessing a newsgroup that deals mainly in images, you might want to think twice before downloading everything. You could be in for a lengthy download. Once you've made your choice, if you logged off before, get back online. Select the **Tools** menu again, then **Download This Newsgroup**. A dialog box will come up asking if you want to download all the marked messages. Click **Yes**.

Once your messages have been downloaded, you can log off and enjoy the witty badinage and thoughtful discussion that is Usenet's stock-in-trade . . . Of course, you can do all this online if you're not worried about your telephone bills. It's certainly less fiddly. Download the headers from a group, then just click on a message which interests you. It will be downloaded and you can read it in the window below the list of headers.

< 221 >

Tips - Newsgroups

When you're just starting out, try the **news.announce.newusers** and **news.announce.important** groups. The former is a good place for general introductory information about Usenet. The latter is the place to go for important news and developments – all newsgroup users should make a point of checking in here. It's also worthwhile keeping abreast of what's happening in the UK hierarchy, so make a point of checking out the **uk.net.news.announce** group. ▲

If you want to read newsgroups while online, Collabra works in roughly the same way. In the Netscape **Message Centre** window, under your news server's name you will see a list of the newsgroups you've subscribed to. Double-click the one you want to read. A dialog box may come up telling you how many messages are in that group and asking you if you want to download all the headers and if not, how many. Collabra is usually set by default to ask you before it downloads more than 300 messages or message headers. To change this, select the **Edit** menu, then **Preferences**. In **Mail and Groups**, select **Groups Server** and change the figure in the line **Ask me before downloading more than 300 messages**. Once you've decided how many message headers to download, the Netscape **Discussion** window will open, showing a list of the messages in that particular group in the top part of the window. Click on a message on the list and its contents will appear in the bottom part of the window. Double-click on the header and the message will open in a new window.

< 222 >

To read newsgroups offline with Collabra, in the **Message Centre** window, select the **File** menu, then **Go Offline**. A dialog box will appear. Click in the box marked **Download Discussion Groups**, then click **Select Items for Download**. Your list of subscribed newsgroups will come up. Click the dot next to the newsgroup, which will then turn into a tick. Click **OK**. You'll go back to the first dialog box. Click **Go Offline**. Your newsreader will download the messages. Then you can log off and start reading.

When it comes to reading newsgroups, remember it can take a while to get into some of the discussions. When they respond to a previous message, as with email, people quote relevant sections of that message using the quote tags (>). Again, the theory is that it makes it easier to keep track of the discussion. Stick with a group over a few days and it should start to make sense.

After a while you may realise that some people in the group are complete timewasters. To preserve your sanity and good temper, you can create a bozo filter/kill file – i.e. you can set your newsreader up to filter their messages so that they are deleted before you see them. It has to be said that, in general, this is one area in which standalone newsreaders have the edge. However, Outlook Express will let you filter the newsgroups. Select the **Tools** menu, then **Newsgroup filters**, then click the **Add** button. Then specify the group you want to filter. You can choose to filter messages from a particular person or about a particular subject (gun control, say).

To keep track of discussions, you need to check your groups on a reasonably regular basis, depending on how active they are. To save on

< 223 >

bandwidth, messages tend to be removed after a few days, though the headers remain. Indeed, the first time you download some groups, you may find you have downloaded a pile of headers but can't actually get the messages they refer to.

You can sort the messages in a group according to date or sender. Don't bother with that unless you're trying to keep track of a particular person. The best way to view newsgroups is by thread – most newsreaders have that as the default option. If you want to change it, in Collabra, in the **Discussion** window, select the **View** menu, then **Sort**. In Outlook Express, select the **View** menu, then **Sort By**. To find a particular message, in Collabra, in the **Discussion** Window, select the **Edit** menu, then **Search Messages**. In Outlook Express, select the **Edit** menu, then **Find Message**. If you're using Collabra, as you open a message and read it, it will be marked as read. In the **Discussion** window, unread messages have a little

Tips - ROT13

Every now and then you may encounter a newsgroup posting which looks even more like gibberish than usual. It's more than likely been 'rotated' – encrypted using ROT13, which replaces each letter with the one thirteen steps ahead of it in the alphabet. People use ROT13 if they're sending a posting that some people might think is offensive. To decode ROT13 postings, in Collabra, select the **View** menu, then **Unscramble**; in Outlook Express, select the **Edit** menu, then **Unscramble**. ▲

< 224 >

green diamond next to them. After you've read them, it changes to a little dot. In the **Message Centre** window, it will show how many messages in a particular group you still have to read.

After a while, you may be ready to have your say. But before you do, you need learn a bit about newsgroup style and netiquette.

Newsgroup Style and Netiquette

When it comes to general style, the advice given for writing email applies to newsgroup postings. If you didn't read that section, go back to page 174. Newsgroup netiquette is similar but more complicated than its email counterpart. They might look like chaotic free-for-alls, but newsgroups are very big on manners and conventions. And if you do something wrong or ask a silly question you will inevitably be flamed by someone.

Actually, if you're starting out on Usenet, it's more than likely that whatever you do, someone will find a reason to flame you. One of the drearier things about Usenet is that it is packed with the sort of sad fools you could call 'netlier than thou'. They want to prove themselves part of the online old school. The best way to do this is to beat up (virtually speaking) the new kid on the block – aka the 'newbie'. In the end, you just have to put up with this. However, you can make sure you don't present too obvious a target.

First, read the newsgroup for a while before you send a message. Find out what gets discussed and how, who the group's top dogs are, who can say what to whom, that sort of thing. You will then have a good chance of posting something people will find relevant. Each group will have an FAQ – a file of Frequently Asked Questions, which details what the group

< 225 >

discusses and how. The latest versions are usually posted to the group in question on a regular basis. Read the FAQ for any group you're interested in. That way, you will have a chance of avoiding sending in messages or questions which people will dismiss as obvious or already dealt with. The web is a good place to get FAQs. Try **http://www.lib.ox.ac.uk/internet/news/**.

Don't post a message to an ongoing thread about something completely different – i.e. don't change the subject. If what you've got to say goes off at a tangent, start a new thread. Most importantly, don't spam. In other words, don't send advertising, commercial messages or junk mail to a newsgroup or a group of newsgroups, even if it seems relevant. It is OK to do some discreet personal advertising – i.e. include references to a personal homepage in your sig file, which, by the by, should be kept small. And some groups run the equivalent of small ads offering items for sale. But research this and be careful. Don't post the subject line **Mountain bike is for sale in Croydon** to an international group. However competitive your price, it won't be much use to Joe Sixpack in Idaho. Find the right **uk** group instead.

That might seem like enough dos and don'ts. But there are more. Don't post private email to a newsgroup without getting permission. Generally you're OK re-posting material that has appeared in a news-group already: it's deemed to be in the public domain. But before you do, check its copyright status anyway. It's beginning to be accepted that posting a message to a newsgroup is equivalent to publishing it, which means you shouldn't post illegal or libellous material. On a more down-to-earth level, if you're discussing films or books, specifically how they end, indicate this in the subject line of your posting (i.e. put the word

< 226 >

> ### Tips – Newsgroup Netiquette
>
> You'll get used to seeing messages which quote a long previous message, or selection of messages, then add something like, 'Couldn't agree more'. Don't do this! If you want to show that you agree with something, send private mail to the person who wrote the original message. If you've got nothing new to add to a newsgroup thread apart from 'me too', then don't bother. ▲

'Spoiler' in there somewhere). And don't criticise spelling or grammar. There is nothing that upsets people more and it generally leads to inane, tit-for-tat arguments. There's enough of those on Usenet already. You don't need to start any more.

Knowing all this is obviously useful. But the most important thing is just to think a bit before you post. Remember that there are people on the other side of the screen. Online communication is a paradoxical thing.

> ### Read about it online – Netiquette Guide
>
> Boning up on newsgroup netiquette is a full-time job. There certainly isn't the space to go into it all here. But you can find a lengthy guide to Usenet netiquette, as well as some amusing parodies and lots of other useful information on the UK Usenet homepages at **http://www.usenet.org.uk**. ▲

< 227 >

Tips - Flames

If you do feel like arguing, trading insults and generally winding people up – if that's why you were interested in Usenet in the first place – try the **alt.flame** groups. There are plenty devoted to trading abuse on all sorts of topics. ▲

It can seem both impersonal, as if it doesn't quite matter, and peculiarly intimate at the same time. As a result, it can become rather hurtful. So – and I'm sorry to sound like some sort of cheery teacher – try to be constructive. Some people in Usenet do spout the most incredible rubbish. But it is possible to point this out to them without adding a series of ever more baroque insults. Before you get involved in a flame war, think about the rest of the group. Sometimes it's amusing to watch two people slugging it out. But mostly it's a bore. ▲

Posting messages

So you now know enough not to upset those sensitive souls in your newsgroup of choice. You've read a message you want to reply to. It's pretty simple, virtually the same as replying to someone who's sent you email. Click the **Reply** button and a new window opens, with the address filled out and the previous message quoted. Trim that down and add your

< 228 >

response. Then, when you're happy, click the **Post** button on the toolbar. It's considered good form to send a private reply to the original poster as well as a public one to the newsgroup. That way, they get your reply quickly (sometimes it can take a while for messages sent to newsgroups to appear) and can keep track of the replies they've generated without trawling through the newsgroup itself.

Collabra lets you send both in one go. When you click the **Reply** button, a menu of options appears – pick **Reply to Sender and Group**. With Outlook Express, things aren't quite so neat. **Reply to Group** and **Reply to Author** are separate options. Messages to newsgroups are often crossposted, which means that they're sent to a variety of groups that share some interest in a general subject. When you reply to a crossposting, your message will be sent to all the groups the previous message was crossposted to. You'll see them entered in the address field.

To post an original message, in Collabra click the **New Message** button; in Outlook Express, click the **Compose Message** button. Put a pithy/succinct description in the subject line and then write your

Tips - Crossposting

Think before you crosspost. And don't crosspost or direct follow-ups to groups you don't know. If you're not sure it fits in with the discussions there, don't bother. It's a very good way to annoy people. Remember, they have your email address and they will let you know how they feel. ▲

< 229 >

Tips – Cancelling Messages

You got steamed up and sent a message you now regret. You can do something to retrieve the situation by sending out a cancel message. This will remove the posting (although it takes time and if someone downloads the message before your cancel message reaches the group, there's nothing you can do). In Outlook Express, highlight the message you posted, then select the **Compose** menu, then **Cancel Message**. In Collabra, select the offending message, then select the **Edit** menu, then **Cancel Message**. ▲

thoughts in the text box at the bottom, then click the **Post** button. If you think it might be relevant to other groups and want to crosspost it to them, put their names in the address field. Collabra also lets you put in a **Followup-To** address which will direct replies to another group. If you feel this might be a useful thing to do, in the **Composition** window, click the **Group** button in the address box – a menu comes up. Pick **Followup-To** and then you'll be able to enter the group you want.

If all this sounds a bit daunting, you might want to try a test post first. The bigger British ISPs (like Demon and Virgin) have their own test groups where beginners can find their feet. There's also an **alt.test** group you can try. But whatever you do, don't send a test post to a regular news-group, another sure-fire way to upset people.

< 230 >

Getting answers from newsgroups

Newsgroups are, so people tell you, packed with experts ready and waiting to give up their time to help you. All you have to do is ask. On one level, this is true. But there is a correct way of asking. It's good form, if you have a question, to specify in your original postings that people should answer with private email and that you will post a summary of responses. That way, the newsgroup doesn't become clogged with people sending the same answer. When it comes to posting a summary, trim down the answers you received and avoid repetition.

Incidentally, students shouldn't assume that all those experts in the newsgroups are just dying to help out with their dissertations. In other words, don't send a questionnaire on a particular subject to a series of groups. This annoys newsgroup users (understandably) and you probably won't get any useful replies. An alternative might be to hang out in relevant newsgroups, figure out the more active/knowledgeable members and send them private email asking if they have time to answer a few questions. Then send your questionnaire.

If you're looking for answers, your best bet may be to tap the archived collective wisdom of Usenet via the Deja News web site **http://www. dejanews.com**. Here you can search several years of postings to Usenet. It's more than likely that someone in a newsgroup somewhere has kicked around the query that's troubling you, so give it a shot. You can also access the newsgroups via Deja News.

Archiving may have got them started, but the company has grown by putting a nice friendly web interface on the present state of play in newsgroups. Apparently millions of net users now prefer to get their

< 231 >

newsgroups via Deja News. It offers the kind of services familiar from portal sites – some personalisation, a free email account and the like. It's worth a look. However, you should remember that the web can be slow – slower than downloading messages from your ISP's server. Other companies are attempting to do something similar, offering snazzy web interfaces to Usenet which let users collaborate to filter out spam and idiots – try Talkway **http://www.talkway.com** and Realize **http://www. realize.com** for more information.

Attachments and HTML

Newsgroup postings can come with attached binary files, just like email, and there are plenty of newsgroups whose purpose is exchanging files, not ideas. These files could be anything from images and sound samples to shareware games and programs. But mostly they're images, often pornographic. Groups devoted to exchanging pornography (e.g. many of the **alt.binaries** groups) do account for a sizeable amount of newsgroup traffic. You should be aware of this, especially if your kids are using Usenet. But don't assume that's all there is to newsgroups that swap files.

In the past, dealing with files attached to Usenet postings could be tricky, but the latest newsreaders make the whole thing easy. They work in exactly the same way as email attachments. If you skipped the email section, go back to page 167 for general advice. UUencode has been the standard way to convert attachments on Usenet for a while. However, MIME is becoming more popular. Outlook Express and Collabra can handle both, but if you're using an older newsreader you may experience some problems. A group FAQ might have advice on how to convert

< 232 >

attachments posted to the group. Alternatively, you could hang out in the group for a while and see what everyone else does.

Outlook Express is set by default to encode newsgroup attachments with UUencode. Collabra uses MIME as the default for attachments. There's advice on how to change them if you need to in the email section on page 189. In some groups, you may encounter large attachments split into several messages. If you try to open one part, some newsreaders will automatically find the other parts for you, download them and put them together. With others, you have to download the various parts before your newsreader can deal with them. Check in the help file for details. For example, in Outlook Express, click on all the parts of the message (press the **Ctrl** key, then click on each header), then select the **Tools** menu, then **Combine and Decode**.

In the dim and distant past of the net (three or four years ago), Usenet newsgroups mainly involved text postings and UUencoded attachments. Now the new generation of newsreaders let you send postings that are formatted in HTML and hence look a bit like web pages (i.e. they have links, flashy graphics and embedded images). Both Outlook Express and Collabra can handle HTML. When you're composing a reply or a new message to a newsgroup, you can format it in HTML.

However, before you send off your dazzlingly colourful posting to your newsgroup, think about whether it's appropriate. Many groups prefer plain text. Again, see what seems to be acceptable in the group in question. For information on how to change the format of your newsgroup postings from HTML to text or vice versa, go to page 179 in the email section. One thing to look out for is that if you decide to configure

< 233 >

Tips – Viruses

People sometimes worry unnecessarily about viruses and the net. However, you should worry about software or games that you download from a newsgroup. Always run a virus check on it. ▲

Collabra to send postings to newsgroups in plain text, it will mean that Messenger will send all your email in text as well. So if you want to send text to a newsgroup, it might be best to specify it on a message-by-message basis. In the **Composition** window, click the **Message Sending Format** button in the bottom left of the **Address** window and then look for the **Format** drop-down menu in the bottom right.

Coping with newsgroups

The net makes a lot of things in life easier. However, newsgroups are one of the few things online that still require some effort and commitment if you're going to get anything out of them. You do have to spend some time with them. You have to get to know your newsgroup colleagues. In certain groups, you have to wade through megabytes of spam. But if you do take the time, it can be very rewarding, on an emotional and intellectual level. You may even get so caught up that you want to start your own newsgroup. For information on that, go to page 418.

If you want to get the most out of the newsgroups, there are a few things you should do. In the end, you should probably move on to a good standalone newsreader, one which comes with a good set of bozo filters.

< 234 >

You should learn how to use these (along with the **cancel message** function). Find out as much as you can about Usenet culture. The UK Usenet homepage mentioned before is a good starting point. Make frequent use of the Deja News archive – it really is a terrific research resource. Aside from revealing the huge range of subjects covered by the newsgroups, Deja News also makes you aware that postings to Usenet are public. Potentially, millions of people can read what you say there. Your postings will be archived and at some time in the future may be searched by other people with an interest in you. So the basic message is, once again, to think before you post. This doesn't just mean taking time out before flaming. It means thinking about who might end up reading what you write. You could just write what you want but cover up your identity – by removing your return email details from any messages you send to newsgroups and not giving your real name. Many people now do this anyway, in an attempt to avoid spam. Those responsible for junk email build up their lists of victims via programs which randomly suck up all email addresses posted on Usenet. So keeping your email address to yourself could help. But it also stops you from tapping into the full potential of the newsgroups.

Where to next?

If you're worried about privacy and the newsgroups, go to page 372. Alternatively, now you've got the hang of Usenet, you're probably ready for the real-time rough and tumble of online chat, so go to page 264. ▲

< 235 >

FTP and Downloading Files from the Net

FTP is one of those bits of online jargon that the acronymically challenged love to hate. Those letters stand for File Transfer Protocol, something which enables you to shift files around a network – either upload them to another computer or download them on to your hard drive. Now I admit that, even uncompressed into something resembling English, FTP still sounds forbiddingly technical. But if you've already been on the web for a while before reading this chapter, chances are you've already used it without knowing it.

A few years back, there were specific FTP programs and FTP sites – online libraries packed with all sorts of files you could download. You started up your FTP program, visited the site, hunted in directories for the file you wanted and downloaded it. You can still do all that, but FTP has migrated on to the web. These days, you're more likely to use your browser to download files via a web site. And it doesn't feel like a complicated technical operation. It feels just like clicking on another link.

At the end of it, you have something potentially useful/entertaining sitting on your hard drive – a piece of software, a sound file, a short video clip, even a text version of a classic novel. So don't be put off by the rather clumsy name. (It never sounds quite right as a verb – 'You effteepee-ed

< 236 >

version 2.0 the other day?') Before long, you'll be back to doing it without thinking. And you'll be doing it a lot, because there is an awful lot of interesting material waiting to be downloaded from the net – much of it available for free. ▲

• •

How free is free software

You may have heard someone describe the internet as a gift economy. It's a nice idea, though it does seem to mean rather different things to different people. For some, it seems to mean that you can download lots of stuff from the net without having to pay for it. On one level, that's true. There is plenty of 'free' stuff online: Shakespeare plays, amateur artwork, customised levels from computer games like Doom and all sorts of software – screensavers, personal organisers and pretty much everything you need for the net. And, if you agree to discount telephone charges, it is all free.

However, more often than not, items on the net loudly trumpeted as 'free' come with some kind of cost. Frustrated artists give away their art online in the hope that someone somewhere will pay them a bit of attention. As it turns out, multinational corporations aren't all that different. The first version of Microsoft's Internet Explorer web browser was given away for free because it was the only way Bill Gates and co. could hope to get people to use their software and so start to catch up with Netscape,

< 237 >

who by that time had begun to charge for their then-dominant web browser Navigator.

The first incarnation of IE may have been free but you definitely paid some kind of price when you actually used it (in terms of stress, irritation and general frustration). Internet Explorer has got an awful lot better and is still free, but now its hidden cost (as more people understandably give it a go) is an online world in which Microsoft is the dominant force and alternative ideas are squeezed out. However, Gates and his crew are only doing what everyone else does. Giving away product has become a standard business strategy in the computer software industry. The idea is that you give away stuff now in the hope of getting something back later. Many software developers also give away versions of their products online to build market share and buzz. They hope that you'll get attached to their product and ultimately pay for a version with more features or for upgrades or add-ons.

So 'free stuff' sometimes has a price. As a result, some idealistic programmers suggest that we shouldn't really think about money when we hear the word 'free'. According to Richard Stallman, the founder of the Free Software Foundation, free software is really 'a matter of freedom not price – the freedom to modify the software, redistribute the software and release improved versions of the software'. The idea here is that free software is open, that its source code – the stuff that makes it run – is freely available and can be modified.

That's a big attraction for other programmers. If they find a problem with a free program, they can then mess around with the code, come up with a solution and pass their new, improved version on to other users. As a result, say enthusiasts, where it has a chance to flourish, this kind of

< 238 >

Read about it online – Free Software Foundation

You can read an interestingly hardcore definition of what counts as
free software (and what doesn't) at the Free Software Foundation's
web site at **http://www.fsf.org/**. A good place to start is the essay on
'words to avoid', and 'Categories of Free Software' in the Philosophy
section. ▲

free software ends up being better and more reliable than commercial
alternatives. After all, there's an army of programmers around the world
beavering away on its problems and sharing their conclusions via the net.

Idealistic programmers like this (hackers in the old sense of the
word) have a more high-minded interpretation of the internet gift
economy. Their idea is that you give away your time and the fruits of

Jargon file – Hackers

In the press this has come to mean computer criminal, something
which hugely upsets old-school hackers. Originally, hacker meant
someone who loved programming and messing around with
computers, someone able to make the old machines do all sorts of
thing that weren't in the manual. People who identify with this like
to dismiss younger hackers who get into headline-grabbing mischief
as 'crackers'. ▲

< 239 >

Jargon file - Patch

A small chunk of code designed to fix a bug in a larger program. ▲

your intellectual labour. But you don't lose out, because you benefit from the efforts of numerous other idealists who also do their bit. In the end, nobody gets 'paid' for their contribution but everybody gets by.

Obviously, this is a world away from the *modus operandi* of a company like Microsoft. It keeps a close guard on the source code of something like Windows 95/98 because it sees it as the rock on which its empire is founded. If you have a problem, you're supposed to call the Microsoft support line. Then they'll sort it out for you, perhaps issue a patch and ultimately charge you all over again for a new version of the program in which all the old bugs have been fixed (and a whole set of new ones have been introduced).

It's easy to be snide. And the idealistic vision of the internet gift economy does sound great. But the truth is that ordinary punters generally prefer the commercial way of doing things. They don't have the ability or the desire to go fooling around with source code. As a result,

Read about it online - Apache Project

You can read about the Apache Project, its aims and history (and download the programs) at **www.apache.org**. ▲

< 240 >

Read about it online - Freebies

You don't care about all this idealistic stuff about freedom and software. You just want to get your hands on the free stuff now. Try The Free Site ('home of the web's best freebies', apparently) at **http://www.thefreesite.com/**. ▲

free software is more of a techie pursuit and currently has more of an impact on the back end programs that keep the net running – for example, one of the more popular programs for running web servers is a piece of free software called Apache.

That said, the Free Software movement (some now prefer to talk about the Open Source movement – the word 'free' comes with too much baggage) may soon start to have a more tangible effect on the way ordinary users access the web. Looking for a way to stay ahead of Microsoft, influenced by ideas generated by the movement, Netscape decided to make the source code of its Navigator browser available for free in the spring of 1998. Programmers can now produce their own versions of the browser. If what the free-software champions say is true, this might lead to a more interesting, useful and trim browser in the future. To bring all this down to a more basic level, when you download something that calls itself 'free software' it's as well to be aware of what it is you're actually getting. Here are three basic types of free software you're most likely to find yourself downloading.

< 241 >

Read about it online – Eric Raymond

Eric Raymond – The people at Netscape were particularly influenced by 'The Cathedral and the Bazaar', an essay arguing the case for free/open software by Eric Raymond. You can check it out at his homepage – **http://earthspace.net/~esr/writings/cathedral-bazaar** – which contains lots of good stuff. For more on this, look at the Open Source page **http://www.opensource.org**. For more on Linux, the free/open operating system that has Microsoft worried, try **http://www.linux.org** or **http://www.uk.linux.org**. ▲

Freeware

You don't have to pay anything for this, though sometimes the creators ask for a kind of forfeit – the people behind the free version of the mail program Eudora ask you to send them a postcard of where you live, hence it's known as postcardware. There are fully fledged freeware programs but often many commercial software companies release free patches. The people at the Free Software Foundation don't like this word – they prefer 'free software' which means not software that comes at zero price but software that comes with certain freedoms – i.e. the ability to monkey around with the code.

Shareware

One of the more misunderstood terms in computer culture. Shareware is actually a 'try before you buy' thing. The idea is that you try out an evaluation copy of a program for a given period. Once the trial period is over,

< 242 >

Read about it online - Freeware

This doesn't have to be computer software. The SF author and critic Bruce Sterling made his book about hackers, *The Hacker Crackdown*, freely available online. If they wished, people could download the complete text. Sterling called it 'literary freeware'. He argued that since no one would actually take the time to download the whole book and risk eyestrain by reading it all from the screen, his giveaway worked as a kind of ad for the print version. Certainly, it's meant that the book is everywhere online. For a web version, go to **http://www.mit.edu/hacker/hacker.html**. ▲

if you want to keep using the software you have to register it and pay something. Some pieces of shareware are set to 'time out': you can't use them after a certain point. Others continue to work just fine but with a few features disabled, so you could keep using them. The makers can't force you to pay up if you continue to use their program. Rather, they rely on you being honest. So, if you like a program, you really should pay your shareware fees. Plus, shareware is a clever way of keeping software prices down. It bypasses the regular commercial channels and all their built-in overheads. And it only works if everyone plays the game.

Beta Versions

These are test versions of software currently in development and due for eventual commercial release. Betas let you see what's coming, but you also have to put up with occasional bugs and crashes. Some betas time

< 243 >

out after a given period. Companies don't charge for them, but neither do they offer technical support. Some run competitions in which you can pick up rewards for identifying bugs. Though they can be buggy, often betas run just fine and it can be tempting to stick with them rather than fork out for the official version. When Netscape started charging for its Navigator web browser, a lot of net users got by without paying by using Navigator betas. ▲

• •

Getting Started

You don't really need a separate program for FTP, especially if you're just starting out. Your web browser will do the job more than adequately, especially if you have Internet Explorer 4.X or Netscape Communicator. If you find that FTP is the thing for you, you may eventually want to get a proper FTP client. They're sometimes a bit quicker and have some nifty features. If you don't have the disk space to run the big browsers, it's worth looking at standalone FTP programs. For PC owners, there's CuteFTP **http://www.cuteftp.com**, FTP Explorer **http://www.ftpx.com** – somewhat bizarrely, this page plays a version of the *Doctor Who* theme tune when you arrive or WS_FTP **http://www. ipswitch.com**. The most popular Mac FTP client is Fetch **http://www. dartmouth.edu/pages/softdev/fetch.html**.

If you're going to use your browser, you can get moving straight away. But before you do, it's worth spending some time sorting out your

< 244 >

computer so you know where to put all those files. If they're not there already, create directories or folders on your hard drive called **Download** and **Program Files**. When you download a file, stick it in the **Download** directory or folder. We'll deal with the others shortly. ▲

• •

Downloading files from the web with your browser

We'll start with this because the web is where you're likely to do most of your downloading. Start your browser and go to the WinZip web site **http://www.winzip.com**. If you missed out the section on the web and came straight here, go back to page 103 for details on entering web addresses. To save space and speed up download times, files online are often 'compressed' into a smaller form – known as archives. Before you can use them, you need to decompress them. WinZip is the leading compression/decompression program for the PC. You can't really get by without it and you can download an evaluation copy from the web site. Mac users could go to the Aladdin Systems web site **http://www.aladdinsys.com** where they can get versions of Stuffit/Stuffit Expander, programs which will decompress/compress Macintosh files.

Once the page comes up, click on the **Download Evaluation Version** link. The Download page contains links to details of new WinZip

< 245 >

Tips - Shakespeare

You don't want software, you want culture? Why not get some
e-Shakespeare from the SUN site at Imperial College
http://sunsite.doc.ic.ac.uk/media/literary/authors/shakespeare.
Click on the comedies directory and you'll be able to download the
complete text of the play that most sums up how you feel about the
net – *A Comedy Of Errors* perhaps, or *Much Ado About Nothing* or
As You Like It or maybe even *All's Well That Ends Well*. ▲

features, FAQs and installation instructions. Check these out if you like,
then look for the link to the appropriate program for your machine
(Windows 95/98/NT or Windows 3.1). Click on that and the download
process will start. A dialog box will come up asking whether you want to
open the file or save it. Pick the latter. You'll then be asked to specify
where you want to save the file. Pick the **Download** directory you created,
then click **Save**. The program will begin downloading. Once it's done, yet
another dialog box will appear telling you so. Click **OK**. Incidentally, if
you find yourself stuck in the middle of a slow download, you don't have
to wait around doing nothing. You can open a new browser window and
get on the web, or start to download something else. In both browsers,
select the **File** menu, then **New**. ▲

< 246 >

Downloading files from an FTP site with a browser

Accessing FTP sites with a browser is similar to accessing web pages. You key in an address, click a button and go. FTP addresses are roughly similar to web site addresses. (If you skipped the section on the web, go to page 103.) The differences are that they don't begin with **www** but with **ftp**, when you enter them you start with **ftp://** rather than **http://** (although with some browsers you don't have to bother with that) and if they are for a specific file they can be rather long, since they specify all the directories and subdirectories it is stored in. One example might be **ftp://ftp.gamesdomain.co.uk/pub/patches/**. Tap that into your browser and it will take you yo FTP sites run by Games Domain, specifically to a directory of patches, little add on programs which will tweak well known computer games to make them run faster or look more gory.

Tips - Games Domain

While you're at the Games Domain site, it's worth looking at the FAQ section. This contains text files which tell you how to get to the end of pretty much every game going. So if you're stuck down a blind alley with Lara Croft or if you want to be able to beat your kids just once, check it out. ▲

< 247 >

FTP sites are a little more complicated to deal with than web sites. Some sites are private and to access them you have to enter your username and password. Sites that are open to the public are accessed via what's known as anonymous FTP. You still have to enter some details but you don't have to give your real name. When asked for your username, enter anonymous, and for your password, enter your email address. You can enter a fake address and still get in, but it's not good form. If you're using a browser, it will take care of anonymous FTP automatically.

FTP sites give you a glimpse of what the web was like before the arrival of all those animated corporate logos and flashy graphics we know and love: grey backgrounds, spidery text and long, vaguely impenetrable lists of links to files – it's enough to make an old geek get a little watery-eyed. When you first go in, you should see something called the **Root Directory** – basically a welcome message, general information about the site and a list of the main directories. Some anonymous sites allow you access to everything. Others restrict some of their contents. The files that are open to all-comers are usually in a directory called **pub**. On most sites, the **pub** directory will contain the files of most interest to general users.

Click on a directory name and you'll see the contents of the directory – perhaps a series of sub-directories, which you click to open until you track down the file you want. Beside a particular file you may see details of when it was uploaded on to the site and how big it is. If you follow a set of links and can't find what you want, retrace your steps with the **Back** button. Alternatively, look for a link which says **Up to a higher level** directory, which is usually at the top of the page. On some sites you may see the following links – ".." and "..". Click on the former and you will go

< 248 >

back to the root directory. Click the latter and you'll go up a directory level. If this sounds complicated, rest assured it becomes easy after a while, rather like moving around in the files and directories on your own hard drive.

When you first access an FTP site, look around for a text file called **Index** or **ReadMe**. This will tell you how the site is structured and where everything is. Sometimes you might have the exact address for a file, in which case you can go to it directly. Often though, it's a better bet to rummage around a site and see what's there. When you find a file you want to download, click on it and the download process will start. Direct the file to your **Download** directory as before. ▲

● ●

Downloading files with an FTP program

These days FTP programs all come with user-friendly interfaces which make downloading/uploading look and feel like shifting files around your own computer. To show how to use them and what they can do, I've chosen CuteFTP 2.0, but the others are just as good and work in a roughly similar way. When you install CuteFTP, you're asked to enter your email address – and that's all there is to configuring an FTP program. When you start up the program, the first thing you see is something called **FTP Site Manager**. This lets you enter and save details of certain sites, whether you're accessing them via anonymous FTP, what

< 249 >

passwords are needed, etc. When you want to go somewhere, you just click on the site name, then click the **Connect** button.

In CuteFTP, the **FTP Site Manager** comes with a variety of sites pre-entered (e.g. Microsoft, Netscape and other places to get useful bits of net software). You can add your own sites to the **FTP Site Manager**. Click the **Add** button. An **Add Host** dialog box will come up. Enter a name for the site you want to access in the **Site Label** text box and its address in the **Host Address** box. With FTP programs, you need to indicate how you plan to log in via the **Login type** box. Usually, it will be **Anonymous.** If you choose **Normal,** then you need to enter your **User name** and **Password** in the appropriate boxes.

With some programs, especially older ones, you also have to specify the file type you want to download. Software, images, sound and video are all binary files, so if that's what you're after, make sure you specify that. With modern FTP programs you don't have to worry. In CuteFTP, the **Add Host** dialog box has a section marked **Transfer Type,** with options for **Text, Image** and **AutoDetect.** The latter is the default and means that the program will figure out what file type you're downloading and take the appropriate action. If you want, you can also specify which directory on your own computer should be opened by CuteFTP when you access this site. In the **Initial Local Directory,** enter your **Download** directory (e.g. **C:\Download**). This means that you will be able to download to that directory a little bit faster.

If you don't want to bother with the **FTP Site Manager,** you can just enter the details of a site you want to access via **Quick Connect:** there's a button on the toolbar (the one with the lightning bolt). Alternatively,

< 250 >

select the **FTP** menu, then **Quick Connect**. The **Quick Connect** dialog box will come up. To try this out, let's go to the FTP site maintained by Aladdin Systems and get a copy of Stuffit Expander. (Incidentally, lots of software companies maintain FTP sites as well as web sites and if you know what you're looking for, it sometimes seems a bit quicker getting programs from an FTP site rather than the web.)

Enter **ftp.aladdinsys.com** in the **Host Address** box and in **Login type** mark **Anonymous** and enter **C:\Download** in the **Initial Local Directory** box. Then click **OK**. When you connect to the site, CuteFTP will display an introductory message. Click **OK** after you've read them. Then you'll see a window split into two, with a **Status Bar** across the top which will tell you what's happening with your connection. The left window shows the contents of your hard drive or the directory you specified in **Initial Local Directory**. The right window shows what's on the FTP site.

CuteFTP (and other FTP programs) make FTP sites look and feel like the directories on your computer. Double-click on the directories in the right window to view their contents. To move back, double-click the arrow at the top of the window. When you find the file you want, double-click on it to download it. Alternatively, you can drag and drop it on to your chosen directory in the left window, or you can click on the **Download** button on the toolbar. So at the Aladdin Systems FTP site, double-click on the **pub** directory to open it. CuteFTP is set by default to get any index files automatically. Any index that is downloaded will appear once it's done, in the **Download** directory in the left window. Click on it, then click the **View** button on the toolbar (it has a magnifying glass on it). The file should open in **Notepad**. Reading that should help you find the file you want. Stuffit

< 251 >

Tips – Mr Cool

If you become keen on acquiring software via the net but become frustrated by the occasional lengthy downloads, it might be worth getting your files via email or even via Net Services' Mr Cool program. Basically, if you start a download and realise it's going to take a long time, you cancel it and kick it over to Mr Cool, which sends a request for the program to a server which emails the program to you. It works for web pages too, apparently – **http://www.cix.co.uk/~net-services/mrcool**. ▲

Expander for Windows is **SITEX10.EXE**. Double-click on that and it will download to your computer.

When you start out, you'll be downloading files other people have put online. If you want to upload your own files, you can use the FTP client built into Navigator to upload files. Open the directory on your computer that contains the file you want to upload. Get online, use Navigator to connect the FTP site, then open the directory where you plan to upload your file. Drag and drop the file from your directory into the Navigator window. Easy enough, though if you plan to upload a lot of files you're probably better off with a dedicated FTP program. When you're uploading something – say your personal web pages – to an online space maintained by your ISP, that space will be private: you will need a password and user name to gain access. Your ISP will supply you with details.

< 252 >

Troubleshooting

You can't actually get into the site of your choice
First, if you entered the exact location of the file, check that you got it right. If you did, it may just be that the site is busy. Like good web sites, the best FTP sites can get incredibly busy at peak times.

The file you want isn't where it's supposed to be
If you entered the exact address, it may be that the site has been reorganised and the file has been moved. Look for the index file and check there.

You're halfway through a lengthy download and you lose your connection
This used to happen an awful lot and it was hugely irritating. It still happens, but needn't be such a problem, especially if you're using one of the newer FTP programs which have a **Resume Download** feature. If you lose your connection and you've only downloaded part of the file, reconnect and double-click on the file again. A dialog box will come up and ask if you want to **Resume, Overwrite, Rename** or **Cancel**. Click the first and the program will pick up where it left off. Check the **Status** bar of your program when you first log in to a site to see whether it will let you resume aborted downloads. Some sites still don't. Incidentally, the latest versions of Navigator and Internet Explorer will also let you resume downloads. If you get cut off, just try to start the whole process again and both browsers should pick up where they left off. ▲

< 253 >

Working with downloaded files

So your **Download** directory is now bulging with all sorts of different files. Most likely, you've got a selection of **.exe**, **.zip** and **.txt** files. The latter present no problem, obviously. Click on them and an application on your computer should open them for you. Files with the **.exe** extension are also easy to handle. **.exe** indicates a self-extracting archive. Double-click on one of these and it should unpack itself automatically. Setup will kick in and on the way you'll be asked where you want to install the program. Pick your **Program Files** directory. Before you do this, <u>run a virus check</u>. <u>Always</u> virus check all **.exe** files you get from the net before you install them.

So far, so easy. **.zip** archives are a little more complicated. These are collections of files which have been compressed, using WinZip or something similar. You need to 'unzip' these archives before you can work with them. This is easy – especially since you have the latest version of WinZip. That's an **.exe** file, so it should be easy enough to install. The latest versions allow you to pick two different interfaces – Wizard or Classic.

Jargon file - Extension

As in File Extension. A group of letters which come after the file name and identify what type of file it is. ▲

< 254 >

Wizard makes unzipping files incredibly easy and it's good for beginners. Once you get used to it (and want to compress your own files), try the Classic interface.

Once WinZip is installed, just double-click on a file to unzip it. WinZip will start up. Then, if you're using the Wizard interface, just follow the directions and WinZip will decompress the archive and put its contents into a directory/folder called Unzipped. You can put it in a different folder if you wish. If you want to look at any text files in the zipped archive, click the **View Zip Documentation** button. Then click the **Next** button. WinZip is set by default to display the file icons after unzipping. So they will appear in a window and you can then double-click the **.exe** file (after virus checking it) to start installation. If you choose the Classic interface, you can do all this via the toolbar buttons. Just click the **Open** button and look for the archive you want to unzip.

Once your files are installed, you could clear out the Unzipped directory if that wasn't done automatically during installation. You could also delete the original archive from your Download directory. Alternatively, if

---

Tips – Virus Check

Your computer should come with a pre-installed virus checker. However, if it doesn't, you can download something from the net. One of the most popular virus checkers online is the McAfee VirusScan Security Suite. You can get an evaluation copy at **http://www.nai.com**. ▲

< 255 >

you want to keep copies of files from the net (just in case something goes wrong and you need to re-install), why not create a directory called **Archive** and put them there. You can use WinZip to compress files (perhaps before attaching them to email, or just to save space). Use the Classic interface and click the **New** button. A **New Archive** dialog box will appear. Write the name of your zip file in the **File name** text box, then click **OK**. The **Add** dialog box will appear. Use the drop down menu at the top to find the files you want to put in your archive. Hold down the **Control** key and click on each one you want to include. Then click the **Add** button.

File Types

You're most likely to come across **.exe** and **.zip** online, if only because PC users are in a majority on the net. Macintosh self-extracting archives come with a **.sea** extension. Archives compressed on the Mac using Stuffit come with the extension **.sit** – you'll see a fair amount of them. However, there are loads of other file types available online, either at web sites or FTP sites. Here's a few you may encounter, with details of the programs you need to view/open them.

.arc An older type of PC compressed archive. Stuffit Expander can handle this

.arj Another older PC compressed archive. Stuffit Expander also works here

.au, .aif Macintosh sound files. Double-click on these once downloaded and the Windows Media Player should play them

< 256 >

.avi Video for Windows file. Again, the Windows Media Player will play these once downloaded.

.bin MacBinary files. Macintoshes can cope with these automatically

.bmp Bitmap files. Windows has something (e.g. Paintbrush) which will display these

.cpt Mac Compact Pro archive. Stuffit Expander can decompress this

.doc A Word file. WordPad on Windows 95/98 will cope with this

.exe A PC executable file, to give it its official name. This will self-execute or extract itself when you double-click on it

.gif As in Graphic Interchange Format, an image file found on web pages. Your browser displays this automatically

.gz, .gzip A Unix compressed archive. Stuffit Expander and WinZip will deal with these

.hqx A Mac BinHex file. Stuffit Expander will convert it

.htm, .html As in Hypertext Markup Language. Your browser takes care of it

< 257 >

.jpg, jpeg Another type of compressed graphic found on web pages. Browsers display these automatically

.lha, .lzh Yet another type of compressed archive. You can add an external program to Winzip so it can cope with these. For more information, go to **http://www.winzip.com/xextern.htm** on the WinZip site

.mid, .rmi As in MIDI sound files. You need a external player/plug-in to handle these – for example, something like Crescendo

.mov, .qt QuickTime movie files. You can get a QuickTime player/plug-in to play these

.mpg, .mpeg Compressed video files. You can get a separate player/plug-in for these (e.g. Net Toob)

.mp2, .mp3 An MPEG sound file. You can get an external player for these (e.g. WinAmp)

.pdf As in Portable Document Format. You need Adobe's Acrobat viewer to open this

.pict Macintosh graphics file. Macs handle these automatically

.ra, ram Real Audio sound files. You'll need the RealPlayer plug-in for these

< 258 >

.sea Macintosh self-extracting archive. Just click

.sit Macintosh compressed archive. Use Stuffit Expander

.tar Another compressed archive you occasionally come across. WinZip will open it

.txt, .text ASCII text files

.uue, .uu UUencoded files. Winzip and Stuffit Expander can convert these

.wav Another type of Windows sound file. The Media Player will handle this

.z Another Unix compressed archive. Stuffit Expander will open it

.zip PC compressed archive. Winzip or Stuffit Expander will unzip this

---

Tips - Compression

You occasionally come across files with double-barrelled extensions – e.g. .tar.gz. This indicates that two levels of compression or encoding have been used. A good program like Stuffit Expander should automatically cope with both levels. ▲

< 259 >

Once you've got WinZip and Stuffit Expander, you can cope with a fair few of these. Browsers can also handle many of them. However, for some multimedia files you'll have seen that you need to augment your browser with various plug-ins or helper applications (e.g. RealPlayer). There's more on this on page 299. ▲

● ●

Finding files on the net

Searching for files, especially from FTP sites, can be a bit hit and miss. It's fine if you know the exact name of the file you want. Then you can use an old piece of net software known as Archie to locate an FTP site that contains your file. There's a useful program which combines Archie with an FTP program (i.e. it finds the file, then downloads it) called **fpArchie**, available from fpWare's homepage at **http://www.fpware.demon.nl**. However, it's probably easier to go to the web version of Archie at **http://src.doc.ic.ac.uk/archieplexform.html**. Here you enter the name of the file you want and Archie should produce a list of clickable links to FTP sites that have it. Very easy . . . if you know the exact name of the file you want. Often you don't, in which case Archie isn't much use. So sometimes, there's no better alternative than hunting around in a big FTP site just to see what's there.

A better bet might be to use the search engines or one of the big directory sites. If you're looking for software, try the 'software warehouse' web sites. Here are a few to be going on with. If you don't want to use

< 260 >

Tips - Doh!

You don't have to restrict yourself to downloading useful bits of software. Want to make your computer say 'Doh!' when you start it up? Go to Tim's Simpsons' Page at **http://www.timtoews.com. index2.html** and download soundfiles from the TV show. After something so manifestly pointless, make yourself feel better by visiting the Project Gutenberg site and downloading the electronic edition of a piece of classic lit – **http://promo.net/pg/**. ▲

---

your browser to do everything and want to see what other programs you could use for mail, news, FTP and chat, these are great places to look.

Download.com – **http://www.download.com**

Huge site maintained by ClNet. With a Quick Search and links to the top ten, newest and recommended downloads. While you're on the site, look out for a chart of the top fifty/hundred downloads. It can be interesting to see what everyone else is helping themselves to. Usually it's software. Recently it was bits of video from *South Park* and those *Dancing Baby* animations.

Shareware.com – **http://www.shareware.com**

Another huge ClNet site with lots of stuff for PCs and Macs. Again, easy to navigate and search.

< 261 >

Stroud's – http://cws.internet.com

The full name is Stroud's Consummate Winsock Applications, which is a bit of a mouthful and not strictly accurate any more but we'll let it pass because Stroud's is a terrific site. Links to lots of useful internet apps plus reviews and information.

Tucows – http://www.tucows.com

Another huge repository of net software for PCs and Macs and others. This link takes you to a general page. From here, click the links to find a UK mirror.

WinFiles.com – http://www.winfiles.com

This was Windows95.com. (Either Bill's lawyers have been in touch or they just decided to broaden their remit to cover other Microsoft flavours.) Another very useful site.

Tips – Download Times

A friend who downloads a lot of stuff has this method for cutting download times. First find the file you want. If it's on an American site and you're looking at a serious download time, take a note of the file name and then go to the FTP Search site at **http://ftpsearch.lycos.com**. You can then use it to search for a nearer site that contains the file you want and then download from there instead. ▲

< 262 >

When you go to a download site, you'll often be offered the choice of picking an alternative mirror site – i.e. a copy of the site maintained at another computer, perhaps on a different continent. The idea is that you can go somewhere less busy and save on download time. However, think before you pick a site. Don't immediately pick the nearest UK site. For example, trying to download some software from the Demon Internet site in the early evening would be asking for trouble. Instead, try to find a site in a part of the world that's asleep, and hence unlikely to be online. Alternatively, pick a site in a country that's unlikely to have a huge net population. US sites can be fine if you're downloading in the morning, UK time, when most Americans should be asleep.

Where to next?

Now you've got the hang of downloading files, you're in the perfect position to start beefing up your web browser with all sorts of multimedia plug-ins. For more on that, go to page 299. ▲

< 263 >

Online Chat

It may sound hard to believe now, but when the net was first hyped by the mainstream media it was considered exciting enough to be the centrepiece of nightclub events. People actually bought tickets for 'cyber nights' or 'interactive raves'. When things were just beginning to warm up at these events, everything would be brought to a halt and people would be directed to some bloke sat in front of a computer, who was 'accessing the future now'. (If you were really unlucky, this would be followed by a cyber fashion show.)

In a bid to make this rather dull spectacle more interesting, the bloke by the PC usually demonstrated online chat. The thinking must have been that at least chat was 'live', a (disjointed, disembodied, usually slightly daft) conversation, involving people from all around the world but scrolling out in 'real-time' text on your computer screen. Unfortunately chat and chat rooms are also pretty unpredictable. The glowing reports about the net that first appeared in the press suggested that it was packed with articulate and witty people. But somehow, when you needed them, these people were elsewhere.

At one net club night I attended, we all sat around and watched as the hapless demonstrator looked for a coherent conversation or someone willing to talk. He eventually started nattering with Jed from somewhere in Texas. He typed in his textual questions, which appeared on large screen projected above the desk. 'How's it going, Jed?' After a while the textual response blipped across the screen. 'Great. Hey this is really

< 264 >

cool :-).' Cue a long pause as Jed thought of what to say next. 'So, what's the weather like over there?'

Not surprisingly, this kind of thing did lead to a sense of anti-climax and perhaps helped spark the backlash that British journalists were dying to unleash. Events like this were sniggeringly dismissed as symptomatic of the net as a whole, which was written off as a nineties version of Citizens' Band radio. What the sarcastic press pack didn't realise (and perhaps you can't blame them) is that the net is not a spectator sport. Online chat is particularly dull to watch. But if you do it yourself, even if you're exchanging banalities, it can be surprisingly exciting seeing words appear on your computer screen that come from someone else on the other side of the world (well, it is at first).

Many net users agree that online chat is a bit too close to 'breaker, breaker, ten four good buddy' nonsense for comfort. Occasionally, chat achieves a brief respectability – usually when there's a war on and people

---

Read about it online - Chat

Some academics have taken a particular interest in chat. MIT professor Sherry Turkle had some interesting chapters on chat and chat worlds in her last book, *Life on the Screen*. You can find out more at her home page at **http://web.mit.edu/sturkle/www/**. There are some good links to interviews with Turkle and some of her essays at **http://www.uiowa.edu/~commstud/resources/digitalmedia/digitalpeople.html**. ▲

< 265 >

are using chat rooms to get news out from the frontline. But in general, lots of net users think it's a bit of waste of (cyber)space. Perhaps there is a slight class dimension to all this. The net is still primarily populated by upper/middle-class people whose business is information. For them, the net is an invaluable resource and they use it mainly for research (with perhaps a little online shopping/gaming/surfing for pleasure on the side). But what about people who aren't involved in 'knowledge work', people who get online in the evening for looking for entertainment and diversion?

Unless they're particularly obsessed, they aren't going to want to spend their time locating all the Quentin Tarantino interviews from the last three years. What ordinary people usually want to do when they get online is communicate with other people – in other words, chat. A while back a British TV programme about the net introduced a group of Welsh house-wives with no previous computer experience to the online world. They remained pretty unimpressed by much of what they saw but immediately warmed to online chat.

Online services like AOL recognised the 'will to chat' of ordinary people, and built their businesses up by catering to it. Their chat rooms were (and are) a hugely popular part of their general operation. Indeed, in the early days of the net, it became clear that chat was one of the few online things people were prepared to pay for. That sparked a mini boom a few years ago, with companies looking for ways to make more money from chat. As a result, chat spread to the web. However, since then it's become clear that chat isn't quite the route to easy money many had hoped.

It worked for the online services because they charged by the minute for the time people are connected, but most web chat sites rely on adver-

< 266 >

tising and it's becoming clear that when people chat, they stay in one place. They don't move around and hence don't see that many advertising banners. Consequently (and not without reason), many advertisers feel they're not getting value for money. Some also worry that chat rooms can be rather wild and might not create the right associations for their particular brand. As a result, even those companies who made a big success of taking chat to the web now see it as something of a dirty word. Intending now to create chat applications for the business world, the company iChat recently announced that it was going to change its name to something that didn't contain the dreaded 'c' word.

However, at the moment chat seems to be anything but a four-letter word for British politicians who are queuing up to show how modern they are by 'interacting' directly with the people in a chat room. Usually they get someone else to type for them and the questions are vetted beforehand. And it's possible that the politicians aren't there at all but have sent their spin doctors instead. (The perfect way to stay on-message?) So when it comes to interacting directly with the voters, chat rooms are slightly below radio phone-ins.

Despite the politicians' love affair with chat, it remains one of the wilder things you can get involved with online. For beginners, simply following and then joining in a conversation can be tricky. Everyone seems to be talking at once, often in weird variants of something that once resembled English. In a chat room where everyone is telling jokey riddles, because of delays caused by the connection, the opening questions can come at once, followed by a jumbled set of punchlines – which is funny, though not in the way intended. Like everything else online, chat is constantly being

< 267 >

upgraded. You can now chat in rooms that are presented onscreen as 2D or 3D environments. You can even send sounds to certain chat rooms (and as you might expect, a lot of fart noises travel down the wires).

Despite this kind of thing, chat rooms have been described like supermarkets and galleries, as 'the singles bars of the nineties'. It's true that a fair amount of chat online is about sex. In fact, to a lot of people it is a form of sex in itself. People meet online then head off to private rooms to type dirty to each other.

Some people get rather hot under the collar about one-handed typing, writing it off as perverse, empty, unreal and psychologically damaging. Other see no problem with consenting adults exchanging sexual/textual fantasies, so long as they keep a sense of proportion about it (though on one level, a sense of proportion is something clearly lacking in people describing themselves as 'Busty Babe' and 'Big Boy'). Men hassling women with indecent propositions is another thing entirely.

However, in contrast to the real world, when you're on the net you can set your software to remove all traces of a person who's hassling you. Men who hit on women should be aware that you can never be sure who you're chatting with online. Those who make a big deal of presenting themselves as women are often men goofing around. If nothing else, this can help them to realise the amount of hassle women have to put up with in online chat rooms. For that reason, many women keep their gender secret.

Sexual deception is one thing. In some online chat rooms, you might even find yourself in conversation with something that isn't human – in other words, a chatterbot, a program designed to greet new arrivals or even hold a sort of conversation. A small percentage of chat rooms are also home

< 268 >

Read about it online – Online Sex Chat

For some interesting thoughts on online sex chat, try the excerpt from Lisa Palac's *The Edge of the Bed* published by the webzine Salon – **http://www.salonmagazine.com/21st/books/1998/04/cov_27books.html**. Palac used to edit a magazine called *Future Sex* and is a little more open than most about the ups and downs of sex chat. ▲

to hackers who indulge in silly but usually harmless mischief. For some people, chat can become incredibly compelling and end up taking over their lives. Even ordinary users who keep their chatting under control can find themselves facing sizeable telephone bills at the end of the quarter.

For that reason, parents should check on their children's use of chat rooms. Chat can be as compelling for teens as the telephone. And yes, there is some evidence that paedophiles frequent chat spaces trying to engage children in conversation. So children's chat use should be supervised in some way. Parents should not let their kids chat without giving them some general rules and tips about what to look out for or avoid. After you've read this section, go to page 351 for specific advice on this.

As ever with the net, don't get too hung up over the potential problems. For most people, online chat is an entertaining way to pass the time, make friends and build a sense of community. Take all those stories about online relationships that turned into real-world marriages. They usually started in chat rooms. ▲

< 269 >

Places to chat online and the software you need

Online Services

Beginners might find the chat rooms at the online services the easiest places to start. You get all the software you need when you sign up. They are easy to use. There are thousands of different rooms, each devoted to different subjects. Chat in the online services is generally a pretty organised thing, with regular events in which users can get advice from experts and put questions to celebrities and, yes, politicians. Chat here is also subject to some control. If you're bothered by someone you can report it to a moderator who will take appropriate action. Parents who want to make sure their kids aren't exposed to dirty typing can take measures to block access to certain chat rooms. Of course, what some see as the advantages of the online services – that chat is easy to access and is controlled – may be a problem for others. Also, you pay extra for the online services' chat rooms, which may become annoying once you realise how easy it is to cope with the cheaper chat spaces on the net.

Internet Relay Chat, aka IRC

IRC was given to the world by the Finnish programmer, Jarkko Oikarinen, in 1988. It was pretty popular with net users right from the start, though it started to get more attention from the mainstream world

< 270 >

Read about it online - IRC

For an interview with Jarkko Oikarinen in which he talks about the ideas behind IRC and how he thinks it will develop in the future, go to **http://www.mirc.co.uk/help/jarkko2.txt**. ▲

during the Gulf War when it was used to send out live (uncensored) reports about the conflict. To chat using IRC, you have to connect to a chat server. Groups of chat servers around the world are hooked up into networks, known as nets. Much like an online service, a particular net will host a bewildering amount of chat spaces (known as channels), each in theory devoted to a particular subject. Though it's nowhere near as organised as the online services, IRC nets do host celebrity chats, special events and even games. In general, IRC is very free and easy – which may attract some and worry others. Certainly, compared to the online services, IRC is more confusing. However, it also offers a less American experience.

To use IRC you need the right software. PC owners should go for mIRC, available from **http://www.mirc.co.uk**; Mac users should try IRCLE, available from **http://www.xs4all.nl/~ircle**. If you downloaded the full version of Internet Explorer 4.x you should have Microsoft Chat, which you can use to access the IRC network, but I wouldn't advise it. You can also get an IRC plug-in for your browser – WWWIRC. You can download it from **http://www.fiu.edu/~zyang01/wwwirc/**. Again, I wouldn't advise using it if you can get your hands on something like mIRC. There's more on plug-ins on page 302. If you skipped the section on downloading, go back to page 236.

< 271 >

Web chat

Many web sites now feature chat rooms. They're popular with the big search sites (for example Yahoo and Excite) currently trying to turn themselves into 'portals' – i.e. user-friendly gateways to the net. The basic format is the same as IRC and the online services – a selection of spaces devoted to different topics. Again, they sometimes host special events; there will usually be details of these on the web site in question. The main attraction of web chat is that it's happening on the web, so you can use your browser without resorting to separate software. To access many web chat rooms, all you need at first is an up-to-date browser – i.e. one that can run Java or Javascript. When you enter the chat room, a Java applet is loaded by your browser which enables you to participate in real-time chat. If you decide web chat is for you, you may have to go on and get a proper chat plug-in. Most web chat rooms will have links for the kind of chat plug-in they support. The most popular is made by iChat – it's available for download from **http://www.acuity.com/ichat/download/index.html**.

Jargon file – Java, Javascript, Applet

Java is a programming language which, among other things, can be used to create interactive multimedia effects on the web. Javascript is a similar sort of language. An applet is a small program written in Java which can be placed on a web page. ▲

< 272 >

Chat Style and netiquette

Chat style is very similar to email style. If anything, the TLAs and smileys people use in their mail are more useful in real-time chat. Once you get used to them, the former can speed up your typing; it still won't be anything like normal spoken conversation, but it helps. The latter can help resolve any potential misunderstandings caused by bad typing or delays on the line. (If all this sounds like gibberish, you probably skipped the chapter on email. Go back to page 175 for some general style tips.)

As for chat netiquette (or chatiquette), again it is really an extension of email and newsgroup netiquette. So typing using capitals is the equivalent of shouting and should be avoided. Similarly, you should always think a bit before you type. Don't immediately kick off a flame war in response to something that seems like an obvious insult. It may not be intended that way and even if it is, sometimes it's best to ignore it anyway.

As with newsgroups, the best policy when you join a group is to lurk for a while, not say anything and find out what the group is talking about and what kind of language is acceptable. Each chat room or channel has its own codes of conduct, so in some bad language may be fine. One difference between chat rooms and newsgroups is that in the former everyone knows you are lurking; your arrival in a chat room/channel is always announced to all the other users. So if someone does say hello, it's bad form not to respond. In fact, it's generally considered rude to ignore people (unless you're being hassled).

The basic idea with chat is to keep the conversation going smoothly and to remember that it is a conversation. Don't change the subject of an

< 273 >

ongoing chat or start talking about something unconnected with the room's designated subject. Attention-seeking pranks which break up the collective flow are frowned upon. It's bad form to 'flood' a chat room or channel – i.e. dump a huge amount of text (or even your latest piece of ASCII art) into a conversation. If you have a lot to get off your chest, it's better to break it down into shorter chunks. Keeping things short is always the best policy with chat.

With each kind of online chat there are specific things you can do to protect yourself (and your computer) from potential hassle. Here are a few all-purpose tips which hold for all chat spaces. Never, ever give out personal information in a chat room or channel – i.e. your real name, address, credit card number or details of your net account and password. The person asking for such information may flash what seem like authoritative credentials, but don't believe them. Most chat programs let you create a personal profile. Think about the details you include if you choose to put one together. Putting details of what you do or your hobbies is fine. Don't put your address and telephone number or any other important personal details.

Read about it online – Chat Netiquette

For an exhaustive (and somewhat specialist) guide to chat/IRC netiquette, which advises you to 'Consider the lag factor', avoid 'attention-seeking gimmicks' and much else, go to **http://mirc.stealth.net/mircrulz/**. For more general tips on netiquette, try **http://www.albion.com/netiquette.index/html**. ▲

< 274 >

Think about the nicknames you pick for yourself. If you call yourself something like 'Hot Hunk', you are asking for a certain kind of attention (and signalling that you are a sad fool in the process). Women should go for chat room nicknames or screen names which don't indicate their gender. Otherwise, they will be hassled by the troglodytes who populate some chat rooms. Finally, don't always believe everything you read in a chat room. People are often not really what they say they are. ▲

● ●

Chat on the online services

As with everything they do, the online services try to make chat as easy as possible. I'll focus on AOL here, because they're the biggest service, but the others work in roughly the same way. After you've logged on to AOL,

---

Tips – Parental Control

Parents worried about their kids chatting on AOL should use the **Parental Control** button. Click this and you'll get information on how to block your kids from all chat rooms or the rooms created by AOL members in the American chat areas and how to stop hyperlinks sent in chat (in other words, links that, if clicked, will open a web page). ▲

< 275 >

click the **Chat** button on the main screen. You'll go to the main **Chat** screen and can then choose between UK and US chat. There are many more active chat rooms in the US section but the UK rooms are still worth a look. On this screen, there should be details of special UK Chat events and links to useful information. Click on **UK Chat** and a list of the various rooms will come up. Pick one and double-click on it (**AOL Chat** or **Shake the Shack** are usually fairly lively).

Once you enter a room, a new window will open. At the top you'll see various buttons – most fairly self-explanatory. The main part of the chat window is taken up with the ongoing conversation. You'll see a person's screen name and then their particular contribution. At the bottom of the window is a text box. Write your contribution here and press the **Send** button to have your say. To the top left of the chat window you'll see a list of the AOL screen names of the people who are in the room. Double-click on a name in the list, then click **Info** and you can see their personal profile. When you double-click on a person's name, you can also send them a private message. Just click the **Message** button, then write your message. You can carry on a conversation in this way.

However, it might be more advisable to create a private room. Go to the main **UK Chat** page and click the **Private Room** button. Enter a name for your room, then click **Go**. To enter a private room, use the same method. You can only enter an AOL private room if you know its exact name. It's a good idea to pick a fairly distinctive name for your room, just so that there isn't any confusion with other people's private rooms. Incidentally, a private room exists only as long as there's someone in it. When you leave, it disappears.

< 276 >

The mainstream media tend to assume that people go into a private chat room for one thing only. But often they're used for pretty dull conversations between family members, friends or work colleagues. Use a private room for any kind of online chat you don't want broadcast in a public forum. That said, you might want to think a bit before you accept an invitation to enter a private room. The AOL moderators (guides) won't be around to help you in there – though if there is a problem, just close the window. Do the same thing to leave a public chat room.

If you find there's not much going on in the UK, you might want to go to the US rooms. These are always buzzing and there are plenty of them. To access a list, click the **Rooms** button. (The **Center Stage** button will take you to the place where AOL hosts most of its celebrity chats.) You can also create your own chat space, known as a Members Room. Click the **Rooms** button, then look for the appropriate button.

Before you start chatting, it's a good idea to read AOL's Conditions of Service documents and other help files. They tell you what is and is not acceptable (though in many Stateside rooms people seem to ignore most

---

Tips – Saving Chat

You can save the conversations you have in AOL chat rooms. Select the **File** menu, then **Log manager**. In the top half of the dialog box that opens, enter a name for the log in the text box, then click the **Open Chat Log** button. Just click the **Close Chat Log** button when you're done with the chat you want to save. ▲

< 277 >

Tips – Private Messages

Here's one scam you're likely to encounter in AOL chat rooms (especially the American ones). As soon as you enter a new room, you may get a private message from someone who says they are a guide/moderator/member of AOL staff and that they need your password for a routine check. Ignore them. No one from AOL will ever ask for your password onscreen. Incidentally, when you enter some US chat rooms, you may suddenly get a few pieces of junk mail which feature embedded links to web pages. Ignore these links and delete the mail. ▲

of these rules), warn you about scams and potential hassles and have details on how to get help from the guides. One thing that will come in handy is the **Ignore** function. If someone in a chat room is being a pain, double-click on their name in the list of people in the room, then put a tick in the box next to **Ignore**. That way, their ramblings won't show up on your screen. However, if they leave the room and come back, you'll have to do this all over again. ▲

< 278 >

Internet Relay Chat

If the online services are too cosy for you, the place to go is IRC. There are so many different conversations happening on IRC at any one time that you're bound to find something to interest you. However, IRC is relatively complex. New users probably need to take more care than they would on somewhere like AOL. The first thing you need to do is get your IRC program – mIRC or IRCLE. Next, configure your software. To give you the basic idea, we'll run through what you do with mIRC. The other programs all work in a similar way.

When you first try to open mIRC, a **Setup** dialog box with come up, with the **IRC Servers** box displayed. First you need to specify an IRC server to connect to. As mentioned before, chat servers are hooked up in nets. Whatever chat server you connect to, you'll be able to access the channels that the particular net it is a part of is hosting. There are all sorts of different nets, each with their own distinctive flavour. Here's a few you could try. Check their web pages for more details on the channels they offer and their rules.

Undernet – **http://www.undernet.org/**
Dalnet – **http://www.dal.net/**
KidLink (an IRC net for kids) – **http://www.kidlink.org/IRC/**

For more information about other nets, try
http://www.irchhelp.org/irchhelp/networks/

< 279 >

When you're just starting out, you shouldn't get too hung up about which net you use. mIRC has a good list you can use. So, on the **IRC Servers** dialog box, use the drop-down menu to find a chat server reasonably close to home.

Next you need to enter **Full Name**, **Email Address**, **Nickname** (and an alternative choice) in the relevant boxes. You could enter your real name and address, but women in particular might want to put something fake in here. There are various computer commands which let IRC users look at the information you enter – they might discover you are actually a woman, for example. So if you're worried about this, enter a fake name in the **Full Name** box or just a witty one-liner. You could also enter a fake email address. However, it's probably worth only faking the first part of your address – the part before the @ sign, since your program will always tell those who know how to ask what your internet domain really is – so if your address is **janesmith@newisp.net**, you could put **elvis-presley@newisp.net**.

Nicknames are fairly straightforward. However, remember not to pick something too provocative if you can't stand the potential heat. In addition, some names won't be acceptable in some IRC channels. If you want to retain a degree of privacy on IRC, you could tick the box next to **Invisible Mode**. That means that people won't be able to find you online unless they know your exact nickname. You don't really need to do much more, though you should click the **Identd** tab and make sure that the **Enable Identd server** box is ticked. Many IRC servers quickly check your user ID when you log on. mIRC, like a lot of other programs, will take care of this automatically (if you tick this box). If you entered a fake email address before, don't worry. It won't matter.

< 280 >

Now you're ready to connect. Either click the **Connect** button (the one with the lightning on it) or select the **File** menu, then **Connect**. You'll then connect with the server you chose when you configured mIRC. When you connect, a screen should come up with some general information about the computer you're connecting to. Often there will also be a message of the day and some details about the person responsible for the server. The **Channels Folder** should then open automatically. If it doesn't, you can call it up via a toolbar button. This lists all the channels available on the server. To join one, just click the **Join** button. When you're just starting out, look for channels like **#newbies**, **#newusers**, **#beginners** or **#ircbeginners**. (Note that all IRC channels start with the # sign.)

mIRC and other new IRC programs feature plenty of user-friendly toolbar buttons. However, you can also use text commands to get things done. You type the command then press **Enter/Return**. If you really get into IRC, you'll probably prefer using commands (there are hundreds of them). Anything preceded by a **/** is interpreted by mIRC as a command. So if you wanted to join a channel, you would write **/join #newbies** in the main text box, then hit **Enter/Return** and you would go to that channel. Always remember the **/** sign. If you miss it out, mIRC assumes what you've typed is chat and broadcasts it to the channel. Result? Everyone now knows you are a new user who doesn't know how to work their software.

Once you've joined your channel, you should see a listing of the people currently on the channel on the right. The main chat window (which may show a welcome message at first) takes up most of the room. Below is the text box where you enter your contributions. It's polite to say hello to everyone. Type 'Hello' in the text box then hit **Enter/Return**. After that, it's

< 281 >

Read about it online - Chat Circuit

For more IRC speak and lots of, ahem, newz and viewz, see the IRC webzine Chat Circuit at **http://www.chatcircuit.com**. ▲

a good idea to lurk for a while and see what's happening. If it seems that this channel really isn't you, you can leave by typing **/part** and look for another one. Alternatively, just close the window. If you do want to get involved, just type your thoughts in the text box and hit **Enter/Return**. Remember that smileys and TLAs are big on IRC channels, as is a fairly distinctive way with spelling. (You often feel as if you're in a world filled with people who learned to read and write via the sleeve notes on Prince records; there's lot of 'I would die 4 U' and 'Chat Rulz' business).

If you want to chat privately with someone in an IRC channel, double-click on their nickname in the people list. A query window should open. Alternatively, right-click on a nickname in the list and a mouse menu will appear which will let you open a private query window with that person. If the person you want to talk to privately is not in your channel (and you know their nickname), type **/query**, then their nickname. If you want to find out if they're actually on the system, type **/whois**, then their nickname, which is also a good way of finding out a little bit about the person involved (or rather the information they entered when they configured their chat software). mIRC has a function called DCC Chat which lets you chat more securely with individual users (basically, it connects directly to their IRC program). To use this,

< 282 >

click the **DCC Chat** button on the toolbar or select the **DCC** menu, then **Chat**. You can then send a message to someone and, if they accept, you can start chatting and even exchange files.

As you explore IRC, you'll find out that there's all sorts of things you can do in a channel, from sending coloured text and messages when you leave to creating a new channel. Look in the mIRC help files for a good list of commands you can use. Here's a few to be going on with:

/list will get you a list of all channels currently running on the computer you're connected to

/list *subject* will list all channels devoted to the subject specified between the asterisks, as in **/list *football***

/list -min 5 max 20 will list all the groups with at least five people in them and no more than 20. Obviously you can set the variables yourself

/part message leaves a channel with a message which tells everyone else what you're up to as in **/part bye everyone, off to get some lunch**

/away tells everyone in a channel that you're temporarily away from your computer

/away message will tell everyone why you're away, so if you really want to share you can type **/away off to the loo**

< 283 >

/**nick** can be used to change your nickname

/**bye** ends an IRC session

You can use commands to set up your own channel on an IRC net. Think of a new name for it, then type /**join**, then the name you came up with, as in /**join #mychannel** (always remember the # sign). That's all it takes. Since it's your channel, you might as well make yourself the channel 'op' (as in 'operator', the person in charge). Type /**op**, then your nickname. Everyone who enters the channel will now know that you're in charge. Of course, power may not be your thing at all, so you can start a channel and make someone else the op using the **Mode** command. Type /**mode** then your channel name, then o, then the nickname, as in /**mode #mychannel o sid.**

You can invite other users to your channel by typing /**invite**, then their nickname and the name of your channel, as in /**invite dave #mychannel**. Of course, people might turn up off their own bat if you pick an interesting topic for discussion. To set the agenda, type /**topic**, then details of the subject you want to talk about. As channel op, you are in charge, which means that if someone is being disruptive, it's up to you to keep order. If necessary, you can kick troublemakers off the channel. Type /**kick**, then the channel name, then the name of the troublesome user. One of the general principles of IRC netiquette is that you should use power with responsibility. So don't set up a channel and then act like some sort of demented digital dictator.

IRC is mostly made up of ordinary people shooting the digital breeze. However, some channels are hacker hangouts. For some bored computer

< 284 >

teens, IRC is a wonderful playground. They can create bots or special sets of commands that will do all sorts of things on chat channels. Some hackers seem to like nothing better than trying to take over certain IRC channels. You aren't that likely to run into the more malevolent kind of IRC user if you don't go looking for them. However, there are precautions you can take. First and foremost, if someone asks you to type a particular computer command, **don't ever do it**, whatever they say. It will do something nasty to your computer and may even let someone else control it.

Don't tell the truth about your name and address. Remember you don't have to accept private messages. If someone hassles you via private messages, raise the problem in the public part of the channel or get help from the channel op. Alternatively, type **/motd** to get the Message of the Day which should feature contact details for the system administrator. You can set your software to ignore certain users. Type **/ignore** then the nickname of the user. (mIRC allows you to be much more specific when it comes to ignoring people and messages, so look in its help files.)

Tips – Timers

For some people, chat can be remarkably compelling. You can lose track of time quite easily. mIRC has a useful Online Timer function (look for the Clock button on the toolbar) which tots up the hours you've been nattering on about Manchester United's defensive problems or the wondrousness of George Clooney. ▲

< 285 >

Read about it online – IRC

It is a world all its own and you could easily write a book about what goes on there (and some people already have). For more information about IRC and what you can do, try the web. IRC Help is good place to start, particularly the IRC prelude – **http:///www.irchelp.org**. Alternatively, try the links to more information at the bottom of the MIRC homepage – **http://www.mirc.co.uk/**. ▲

When it comes to getting by on IRC you also have to make allowances for the system in general. Lag (delays on the line) can be a problem sometimes; the best way round this is to always connect to a server near you. Sometimes channels can split. Basically, you and the users on a particular server lose contact with the users in the same channel who were logging on to a different server. Channels stay up but half the users disappear. Splits aren't that much of a problem and usually right themselves fairly quickly. ▲

Chat on the web

For those who don't want the full-on chat experience of IRC but don't want to sign up with an online service, web chat offers a good halfway house. You don't need to get new software, but you can use IRC-like

< 286 >

Read about it online – Yack

A good place to find out about special chat events on the web is
Yack **http://www.yack.com/**, a kind of chat listings site. It features
details of various events plus links along with information about
whether you need a plug-in or not to take part . ▲

commands to do a little bit more than just type. Web chat has a little of
the free-and-easy feel of IRC chat but it also has the structure, the big-
name celebrity chats and special events you associate with the online
services. Web chat rooms are generally hosted by well-known companies
who have rules about appropriate conduct and mechanisms for reporting
those who get out of line. Perhaps the only difficult thing is finding the
right place to chat. There are chat spaces all over the web these days.

Yahoo's chat rooms are as good a place as any to begin. (Others work
in roughly the same way.) Go to the Yahoo site **http://www.yahoo.co.uk** and
click the **Chat** link. You should go to an introductory page which asks you
whether you want to register or try things out first as a guest. It's up to you.
As a guest, you can still chat. However you can't create different identities.
As a member, you'll be able to take part in the full range of activities.

If you choose to register, you have to fill out a form, pick a chat
name and usually a password. You then get a chance to create your chat
'identity' – in other words, write a user profile for the name(s) you have
chosen. Once again, you don't have to fill this in. If you decide to be a
guest, you just have to pick a guest name and then you can dive in. You

< 287 >

Read about it online - Talk City

Talk City – There are web sites where chat is the main business, not just a gimmicky add on. Try Talk City **http://www.talkcity.com/**, a kind of chat community site which features all sorts of themed chat rooms (accessible via a directory) and various celebrity chats and advice forums. You can even play games on Talk City – trivia quizzes and the like; some pit you against other users while others are automated affairs in which a bot plays Magnus Magnusson and you squirm in the hot seat . ▲

used to need a plug-in for most web chat rooms, including Yahoo. Now if you've got a Java-capable browser, you're fine. Incidentally, if you do need a plug-in for another web chat site, there's always a link somewhere on the site where you can get what you need.

When the chat window proper loads (which may take a while), it's packed with frames. To the right of the window, you see a list of people in the particular room you're in. Then there's scrolling list of 'emotions' or gestures – words like 'cackle', 'cringe', 'snicker' and 'snivel' – which you can use during the chat. To the left of these, taking up the bulk of the window, is the chat proper. Yahoo uses a colour-coding scheme to make it easier to follow. People are shown in red type, what they say is in blue and the emotions they send are pink.

Below this is the text box. Type your contribution in here, then press **Enter/Return** to get involved. To 'send an emotion', select one from the

< 288 >

scrolling menu, then double-click on it. It will appear on the screen in pink. You can create your own emotions as well. In the text box, type : then your 'emotion' then hit **Enter/Return**. For example, : **sighs sadly**. If you want to send an emotion to another user, click on the emotion from the list, click on the user, then click on the **Emotion** button in the pop-up box that appears. To talk privately with someone, click on their name, then fill out the pop up box which appears. Alternatively, if they're not in the same room as you, write **/tell**, then the **username**, then your message in the text box, then hit **Enter/Return**. Although the text will appear on the general chat screen, only you and the person you're talking to can see it.

Below the main chat frame, in the bottom right-hand corner, is a general navigation menu. The buttons are generally pretty easy to understand. Clicking on **Who's Online** calls up a vast list of everyone currently on Yahoo, along with the chat room they're chatting in and some information from their personal profiles. If you see a friend's name and you want to meet up, write **/goto**, then their username, then hit **Enter/Return** and you'll go to the room they're in.

Click on **Create A Room** and a menu comes up which lets you choose a name for your chat room, specify whether it is public or private, describe it and pick a 'rating' which allows you to choose whether you want bad language in your room to be automatically filtered. If you create a public user room, it appears on the general rooms list. A private room won't. The only way people can enter it is if you tell them you're there via a private message. They can then use the **goto** command (as in **/goto**, then your **username**, then **Enter/Return**). Once you and your chums are all

< 289 >

inside, you can lock the room and keep others out by typing the command **/room secure on**.

In a way, the biggest problem with web chat is finding a place where coherent chat is going on. They don't seem to draw crowds of regulars or build up a real sense of community. Web chat rooms seem to be populated by people who are there on a whim. As a result they can be chaotic. Since they are so easy to access, you get a few people dropping in to shout rude words or otherwise wind people up. As usual, you can choose to ignore people who are a pain by typing **/ignore**, then the **username** then **Enter/Return**.

There are a few other commands that might come in handy when it comes to general security. If you click on a person's name, you'll notice that you can click on the **Follow** button and, yes, follow that person as they move from room to room. This does have its uses. If a friend chooses to follow you, when you create a private room they will go to it at the same time as you – there's no need for a private message. On the other hand, the very idea of a **Follow** button is enough to get tabloid hacks sharpening up those 'CyberStalker' headlines.

Tips – Help Files

This may sound obvious, but with web chat sites, always start by reading the help files/introductory guides. They're all slightly different and if you don't read the guides you won't know whether functions like following are possible in a particular chat space and whether there's anything you can do about them if they annoy you. ▲

< 290 >

Luckily, you can stop people following you. Type **/stop follow** then the username, then hit **Enter/Return**. Alternatively if you type **/autofollow ask** then hit **Enter/Return** at the start of a chat session, you'll be notified if someone starts to follow you. Typing **/allow** then the **username**, then **Enter/Return** will allow them to continue. Typing **/disallow**, then the **username** will stop them. **/autofollow no** will automatically block all attempts to follow you. Of course, the **/goto** command is a kind of following too, and you can block that in the same way using **/autogoto** and the options above.

Instant Messages

One of the most popular chat-like tools on the net at the moment are instant message programs (also sometimes known as buddy lists). These are a bit like intelligent online pagers. You can send messages which are halfway between email and chat. You can carry on conversations using instant message programs or use them to set up proper chat sessions. First you have to register with the company running the software and network, get a password and a screen name or number. You then pass this to friends who use it to send you instant messages.

You can create a 'buddy list' of friends who also use the same software, so that when they come online you're notified, via a small window on your desktop (obviously you have to be online too) and then you can page them to say hello. If you (and your friends or work colleagues) spend a lot of time online, this can be incredibly useful. Obviously, one of the pleasures of being online is that you can't be bothered by other people, so most instant messages have various privacy features which let you block messages (and in effect hang up a virtual Do Not Disturb sign).

< 291 >

AOL users have long been able to track friends and send them quick messages (via a function called the buddy list). In the last year or so, instant messaging has spread on to the net in general. The program that's made the biggest splash is ICQ (as in 'I seek you'). In fact ICQ made such a big splash that AOL bought the company behind it – Mirabilis. You can download a beta/evaluation copy from **http://www.mirabilis.com/**. When it comes to the big names, Yahoo has launched a pager which is available for free **http://pager.yahoo.com/** and AOL has also taken its buddy lists on to the net, with AOL Instant Messenger, which lets you 'page' AOL users and anyone else who has registered the software. This is obviously a lot of people and AIM is now bundled with Netscape Communicator, which means that its potential user base is massive. And obviously with messaging systems (which are incompatible) the number of users you can reach is one of the key things to look for.

Given that you can get AOL Instant Messenger for free, you might as well try it, but ICQ is really the one to go for. AOL Instant Messenger does the basics and will let you send friends web site URLs. It allows you to block certain users and includes a **Warn** feature which lets you send a warning to abusive users (and the AOL authorities). However, with ICQ you can also send files via instant messages. You can easily use ICQ to set up chat sessions. If you send an instant message to someone and they're offline, ICQ will hold on to the page and send it when they come online. It also has good privacy controls – your authorisation is required before people can add you to their buddy list and you can block messages from certain users. Mirabilis, the company behind ICQ, add new features fairly regularly. So it's worth going to their web site to find out what's new.

< 292 >

Graphic Chat

A couple of years ago, graphic chat (online conversations in which the speakers were represented onscreen as characters or avatars in 2D or 3D space) was supposed to be the future of online chat. It might still be, but at the moment, most users don't have the fast connections or fast machines you really need to make this kind of thing work. In addition, visuals often take something away from the chat proper (which remains a textual thing and appears in speech bubbles above the characters' heads). People inevitably start talking about each other's avatars. Adding a visual dimension, setting the chat in space station, the bar from *Star Wars* or a *South Park* type environment, often winds up making the whole experience less interesting. Text is such a 'low-bandwidth' thing, it leaves space for imagination, projection and fantasy. Visuals lock you into a particular (often rather corny) space.

If you feel like checking it out, you can try 2D chat spaces, which look like variations on comic books. The best known of these is probably WorldsAway which used to be confined to Compuserve but has now moved on to the net (for info, go to **http://www.worldsaway.com/**). The easiest 2D chat to access is **Microsoft Chat** which you will get if you download the full version of Internet Explorer. Once you start the program, you can design your own character, connect to Microsoft server, then chat as you would in a normal IRC chat room. Alternatively, 2D visual chat is available on the web courtesy of The Palace **http://www.thepalace.com**. Go to the web site and you'll get a chance to check out the various 'Palaces' that have been set up around the world. (Some are business-oriented, some are just for fun; all are cartoony spaces in which you are represented by

< 293 >

cartoon faces, flowers, animals and the like.) You can download a Palace plug-in but if you have a Java-capable browser, you don't need one and can just drop in to a room to check things out. For the full 3D chat experience, try WorldsChat. Here you can create your own avatar and wander around a giant space station, chatting as you go. However, you will need to buy special software – go to **http:// www.worlds.net** for more information. For more about online 3D worlds, go to page 400.

MUDs

Some users may see chat as one of the more trivial of online activities. But for an example of how seriously some people take chat (and what strange places it can take them to), check out a MUD. Multiple User Dungeons (or Dimensions or Dialogues) are chat spaces in which users have collectively talked up a whole world, with its own rules and customs. Relying simply on text, users create an alternative geography (and alternative identities) where they can play out ideas, theories and fantasies.

At a more basic level, MUDs are programs on a remote computer. Users log on and explore them, via their own computerised character. You can wander round the textual spaces other users have created, chat with other users, play games, even create your own rooms and buildings. Typically, when you log on, some text will appear on a screen telling you that you're in, for example, an entrance lobby and that in front of you are three doors, a table and a book. You move around by typing textual commands. So you can choose to go through one of the doors. If you do, some text will come up telling you what's behind it. You can continue like this for hours, and some users do. For those who

< 294 >

Jargon file – Identity Hacking

As in the creation of alternative identities online. Much as you hack code, you can also apparently hack your own personality and try out different versions of yourself . ▲

get into them, MUDs seem to be among the most compelling of online activities.

MUDs used to be very popular online. They're not such a big thing these days, though some (for example, the cyber-boho world known as LambdaMOO) remain very busy. They started as a kind of online extension of Dungeons and Dragons role-playing games. As you moved around them, you competed with other users, tried to gain more power, move up the MUD hierarchy and eventually become a wizard or some such. You can now play these sorts of games in MUDs themed around novels (for example, those by Tolkien and Terry Pratchett) and films (*Star Wars*).

Some users didn't really get into this and began to develop MUDs which were more social, in which people kicked around ideas rather than each other. Strictly speaking, these often weren't really exactly what you called MUDs. These alternative MUDs were often called TinyMUDs or MUSHes, MOOs, MUSEs or MUCKs (you really don't need to know what all these stand for). In one of the alternative MUDs people pretended to be small, cute, furry animals and spent their time having 'cyber sex' with each other. In others, people explored identity hacking and alternative lifestyles.

< 295 >

These alternative MUDs were almost the online equivalent of the communes of the sixties and early seventies. Unlike chat in general, they were taken very seriously by the digerati, who devoted plenty of academic papers to them. For one example, try Julian Dibbell's *A Rape in Cyberspace*, a fascinating account of a 'sexual assault' that took place in LambdaMOO; it's available at **http://www.levity.com/julian/bungle.html**.

MUDs are an example of the pre-Web net. To use them, you really need an old piece of software called Telnet. This lets you connect to a remote computer via the net and then use the programs on that computer. You can use Telnet for lots of things (searching library databases, for example) but it's mainly used now by MUDers. You may have been given a Telnet program as part of your ISP's introductory software package, or

Jargon file – Digerati

Aka the self-styled cyber-élite – a group of software programmers, business people, theorists, gurus, old hippies, rich people and self-publicists who are bravely helping us all out by living the future now – on expenses, naturally. The premier digerati web hangout is Edge **http://www.edge.org** where you can find out who's in with the in-crowd and see what they're currently thinking about. Leaving aside the snide comments, the site does feature some interesting discussions about science and technology. However, if you want an antidote, try ditherati – a regular selection of dumb things the digerati have said – **http://www.ditherati.com/**. ▲

< 296 >

Read about it online – Telnet

For a useful guide to other computers and resources you can
access using Telnet, try the HYTELNET site at
http://www.cam.ac.uk/Hytelnet/index.html. ▲

you may already have a version if you're running a Windows 95/98 PC.

However, it's probably still easier to pick up Telnet from the net. PC
users could try CRT (available from **http://www.vandyke.com**). Mac users
could try NCSA Telnet (available from **ftp://ftp.amug.org**). Telnet programs
all work in roughly the same way. You have to enter the domain
name/address of the computer you want to log on to, along with the port
number. When you connect, you'll usually see an introductory screen
which should give you some useful details on the commands you need to
move around the system, For more help, type **help** then hit **Enter/Control**.

One of the best places to go for information about MUDs is the web.
You could start with a very useful general FAQ at **http://www.lysator.liu.se/
mud/faq/faq1.html** (this site is worth exploring – there are some good links
to programs designed to make using MUDs more easy.) There's a good list
of MUDs at the MUD Resource Collection at **http://www.godlike.com/
muds**. Yahoo has a huge list of the various different sorts of MUDs
online – go to **http://www/yahoo.co.uk/Recreation/Games/Internet_Games/
MUDs_MUSHes_MOOs_etc_/**. Usenet newsgroups are also a good place to
go for general information about MUDs. Try **rec.games.mud** or
rec.games.mud.announce.

< 297 >

When it comes to getting into MUDs, the best thing is to take your time. It does take a while to find your way around and master the text commands a particular program requires. Always read the help files. Starting out in a social MUD might be a good idea. Users here aren't going to be trying to wipe you out and accumulate more wizard points (or whatever), so you'll get the time to get used to the whole concept. Finally, one piece of advice about MUDs that is fairly crucial. They're clearly not for everyone. But those who do get into them can end up stuck. It's not unknown for users to spend hours on end in MUDs and to experience real grief if their online persona gets killed. If you do get hooked, fine. But try to keep the whole thing in perspective.

Where to Next?

By now the net is pretty much your oyster. Next, you could beef up your web browsing – on page 299 there's information on the web and multimedia and offline browsing. However, if you've had more than enough of the web, you could cut to page 351 for some tips on security and survival online. ▲

< 298 >

TAKING THE WEB TO THE NEXT LEVEL

4

• •

I hope you now feel as if you know your way around the net. You've done the work, slogged your way through the basics. You know your FTP from your HTTP. But of course there is more to learn (there always is with the net). This section looks at web multimedia and the software you need to check it out. It also covers offline browsing (which may be able to save you some time and perhaps some money), and finishes with an introduction to net shopping. By now, we're assuming you're more comfortable with the net and net software (and know how to find a Help file), so there isn't so much detail about how to work individual programs. ▲

• •

Multimedia on the web

A few years ago a friend came round to my house to check out the net. She'd caught some of the hype and wanted to see what all the fuss was about. I set everything up and left her to it. After a while, she came downstairs looking disappointed. What was it with all the text, she asked.

< 299 >

Where was the MTV-style multimedia sound and fury you were supposed to get? The answer was that, despite the impression given by the hype, it wasn't on the net. However, it is now . . . sort of. The net, or rather the web, has gone multimedia in the last two years. You can now listen to sound and watch video in real time. You can play games or watch animations bounce around web pages.

Whether this is an uncomplicated Good Thing is open to question. Is your browsing experience radically improved by web pages which play Beethoven's 'Ode to Joy' on what sounds like Rolf Harris's old stylophone? Do pages with twirling logos, jumping type and rolling tickers of 'breaking news' really engage and inform you more than simple legible text? It's true that much web multimedia still feels like something of an indulgence, a programmer's high-tech toy. However, as with lots of things online, it's getting better all the time. It won't be long before multimedia stops being a gimmick and becomes an essential part of the average browsing experience (some would argue that it's there already). As for now, the best thing is not to expect too much and just have some fun.

Getting Started

To get the best out of web multimedia, you will need a reasonably up-to-date computer. The old PC you bought five years ago won't cut it. The minimum you need is a soundcard, a good graphics/video card with at least 2 Mb of memory (more will make video look better), a reasonably speedy Pentium processor and a fast modem – 28.8 Kbps is the slowest you can get away with. A fairly big hard disk is also useful. You'll need some extra software, most of which you can download for free from the

< 300 >

Tips – Plug-ins

Your ISP may supply you with a browser that is already kitted out with a few essential plug-ins. If you're running Navigator you can quickly check to see what you've got. Select the **Help** menu, then **About Plug-ins**. ▲

web – which means it's easy to fill up your hard drive without realising. However, browsers are now multimedia devices with built-in programs which can handle video and sound. When you click a link to most sound files, your browser will usually play them, sometimes in a separate window. The same goes for video files, once downloaded. Don't worry about whether your browser can or cannot handle a particular file. If it has problems, it will tell you that you need more software.

You will be told you need either a plug-in or an ActiveX control. You can also get a separate viewer or helper application to handle some sound/video/image files but we'll get to those later. A plug-in is a kind of booster program which enables your browser to handle a specific sort of web multimedia. You don't need to know how to use a plug-in; you just click a link and it goes to work, playing the multimedia content within your browser window. The plug-in idea was first developed by Netscape. Of course, you can get plug-ins for Internet Explorer, but, just to be helpful, Microsoft has also introduced its own way of handling multi-media within the browser – ActiveX. As a result, if you're using Internet Explorer, sometimes when you go to get a plug-in you'll wind up with an ActiveX control instead. ActiveX controls are a bit like plug-ins in that

< 301 >

they are integrated with your browser and enable it to play multimedia within its main window. Navigator can play ActiveX controls so long as you install the NCompass ScriptActive plug-in. You can get it from **http://www.ncompasslabs.com/**. If all this sounds confusing – well, it is, but it really isn't an issue when you're browsing.

Getting Plug-ins and ActiveX controls

If you're using Navigator and you click a link to a multimedia file it can't handle, a dialog box will appear, directing you to the Netscape plug-in page. Often web sites which use multimedia provide links to the appropriate plug-in. Once you've got what you need, close your browser (and any other applications you're running) and start the installation process. Internet Explorer comes with a variety of ActiveX controls. If you come across a page that uses one you haven't got, your browser will start to download it. It may flash up a **Security Warning** screen to check that it's OK. Some ActiveX controls go to work once you've downloaded them. Others will need to be installed. You can get new ActiveX controls from Microsoft – go to **http://www.microsoft.com/activex/** or try the ActiveX site put up by C/Net: **http://www.activex.com/**. If you want to get your plug-ins before you browse, you could start at the software sites mentioned in the chapter on FTP.

Download.com – **http://www.download.com**
Shareware.com – **http://www.shareware.com**
Stroud's – **http://cws.internet.com**
Tucows – **http://www.tucows.com**
WinFiles – **http://www.winfiles.com**

< 302 >

Download.com runs a special sub-site for browsers, called Browsers.com at **http://www.browsers.com/** which has a vast list of all available plug-ins. It's worth investigating this list later, but for now, start with the Browsers.com chart of the most popular plug-ins (rated in terms of the number of downloads).

One plug-in you're bound to use is RealPlayer, so we'll get that one first. RealPlayer started out as RealAudio, which handled streaming audio – the files play as you download them, you don't need to wait until they're completely downloaded. RealPlayer now handles streaming video and animation as well. Quality isn't always up there with files that you download, then play, but it's getting better all the time. Start your browser and go to Real Networks' UK web site at **http://uk.real.com/**. There should be a current version of RealPlayer available for free download. Enter various details – your computer's operating system and processor, your connection speed, your name and email address – and then click the **Download Free RealPlayer** button. If

Tips – Plug-ins

Take care if you're downloading plug-ins from sites you haven't heard of before. Recently stories circulated online about a porn site which required users to download a special viewer. This turned out to be a bit of software designed to hijack users' telephone lines and run up huge bills. So it pays to look around the site and think a bit before you download. ▲

< 303 >

you read the chapter on **FTP and Downloading,** the rest is straightforward. If not, go back to page 236. Generally plug-ins are self-extracting compressed files with the extension **.exe** or **.sea**: just double-click them and the installation process will start up. Sometimes you may come across a plug-in that has been compressed using WinZip or Stuffit – for details on this, go back to page 254.

Once the download is complete, close your browser and any other applications, find the RealPlayer file (it will be called **rp32_50.exe** or some such) and double-click it. You'll then be walked through installation. That's it. So what can you use RealPlayer for? The UK Real Networks have some good links to sites that use their technology (for example, there's a link to live broadcasts from the Ministry of Sound nightclub). The US Real Networks site also showcases sites making the best use of its plug-in – **http://www.real.com/ content/index.html** or **http://www.real.com/ showcase.index/html**.

Now you know how to download plug-ins, you might as well spend some time beefing up your browser. The other plug-in you definitely need is Shockwave. Developed by Macromedia, this is free and is the standard tool for interactive multimedia and animated gimmicks on web. Shockwave will play multimedia created using three of Macromedia's development programs – Flash, Director and Authorware. Download the plug-in/ActiveX control from **http://www.macromedia.com/shockwave/**. For links to sites using Shockwave/Flash, try the Shockzone **http://www.macromedia. com/shockzone** or Shockrave **http://www.shockrave.com/** for, amongst other things, links to web cartoons (everything from *South Park* to 'Dilbert' and 'Peanuts') created using Shockwave. Shockwave animations and games

< 304 >

Tips – Online Radio

Most big radio stations use RealPlayer tech to put their output on the web. That's fine if you're worried about missing a broadcast while you're abroad, but if you're in the UK it's a costly alternative to the transistor radio. Why not try some of the web radio stations proper? For example, **http://www.pirate-radio.co.uk/** which features some excellent sessions by underground dance DJs after six in the evening GMT. ▲

---

often take a while to download. Once they have, you don't have to be online to view/play them. Save money and log off for a while.

The latest versions of Internet Explorer should come with something called ActiveMovie, which plays pretty much every sort of video you find online. However, it won't hurt to try something new. You can download the full version of Apple's QuickTime, which includes plug-ins amongst other things and handles sound and 3D visuals as well as video. Go to **http://www.apple.com/quicktime/**. Read the QuickTime documentation. Once you've installed QuickTime proper, you'll need to locate the plug-ins and then put them in the **Plug-in** folder of your browser. Alternatively, try the VivoActive plug-in which handles streaming audio and video and is also free – download it from **http://egg.vivo.com/products/products.html**. Another useful video (and audio) plug-in is Net Toob. Get an evaluation copy at **http://www.nettoob.com/**. When it comes to audio plug-ins/ActiveX controls, try Live Update's Crescendo, which plays sound files created

< 305 >

using the MIDI format **http://www.liveupdate.com/**. Another audio plug-in worth a quick look is the MODPlug which plays sound files made using the MOD format. Fans claim it is superior to everything else online – everyone says that about their particular toy **http://www.castlex.com**. Finally, Navigator users should definitely try Beatnik, an interactive sound/music plug-in created by Headspace, a company started by Brit techno-popster Thomas Dolby **http://www.headspace.com/**.

Plug-ins aren't just about interactive multimedia. They can do more boringly useful things too. Try the Adobe Acrobat Reader plug-in which lets you read documents created using Adobe's Acrobat graphics program **http://www.adobe.com/**. Alternatively, there's NetZip, which lets you unzip compressed files via your browser **http://www.netzip.com/**. There are yet more plug-ins you can get which will let you use your browser to navigate 3D environments and make long-distance telephone calls. Since these are more for the tech fetishist, you'll find these in the Power User section on page 393.

Tips – Unused Plug-ins

As you try out various plug-ins, you're bound to download some you don't use much. Don't let them clutter up your disc: get rid of them. And if you want to keep your hard disc in good order, get a decent utilities/uninstall program to take care of this. ▲

< 306 >

Helper Applications

You can use a helper application (or helper app) to handle some multimedia files you find on the web. Usually a helper app deals with one sort of file (though not always). Unlike a plug-in, it's a separate program which isn't integrated into the browser. If you download a sound file from the net, you can then log off, close your browser, and use the helper app to play it. However, you can also configure your browser so that if you come across the file type your app handles, the browser will start it up and it will then play the file in a separate window. Helper apps mostly come in handy if you want to edit multimedia/graphics files that you download from the web once you're offline. For example, you could try L View Pro 2.0 which you can use to view, edit and create images **http://www.lview2.com/**. Alternatively, try WinAmp (or MacAmp), an excellent audio player which handles most MPEG audio files, specifically files with the .mp3 extension **http://www.winamp.com/**.

If you do want a helper app to automatically handle a particular kind of file while you're browsing, you need to associate it with that file type. To do this with Navigator, select the **Edit** menu, then **Preferences**, then **Applications**, then just fill out the relevant boxes. Use the **New Type** button to add a new file type. Aside from the file extension, you'll be asked for the MIME type – something like **audio/x-mpeg** or **video/ quicktime**. Don't worry too much about this: it's just another way of identifying and organising files on line. If you don't know the MIME type for a file, check in the documentation for the helper app you're using. If you're using Internet Explorer, open Windows Explorer, select the **View** menu, then **Options**, then the **File Types** tab. This process can be a bit

< 307 >

fiddly but you can get a neat free utilities program which does it all for you. WAssociate is available at **http://home.worldonline.nl/~wmail/ Associate/index.html**.

Java

Java is a programming language developed by Sun Computers which, amongst other things, can be used to deliver interactive web content. Programmers use Java to create applets, small programs which are placed directly on web pages. They can also add interactivity to their pages with something called JavaScript, a scripting language. You need a reasonably up-to-date browser for JavaScript and Java applets. Often you probably won't be aware when your browser is running a Java applet. But sometimes you have to wait for an applet to download before you can do anything. Java is mostly used to create little animations on web pages, scrolling news 'tickers' and interactive games/routines – everything from calculators to real-time chat. Most web chat rooms now use Java applets rather than plug-ins. If you want to see what applets can do, try the mildly diverting demos at **http://www.gamelan.com/** or **http://www.java.co.uk** or go to Sun's own Java page at **http://java.sun.com** for more applets and updates on Java in general.

Jargon file – Scripting Language

A set of programming shortcuts which make it a little easier for programmers to create interactive routines. ▲

< 308 >

Read about it online – Java

For a more balanced look at Sun's much-talked-about programming language, try the special report put together by Wired News, a reasonably critical look at the 'virtual religion' that is Java and the conflicting claims made about its future effects on the computing industry – go to **http://www.wired.com/news/news/java/**. ▲

Java will undoubtedly continue to develop and become ever more crucial to the all-singing all-dancing web. As it does, worries about its security implications will probably grow too. When you access a Java-boosted web page, you download a small program on to your computer, a program that could in theory contain a virus. So what can you do? Play and pray seems to be about the size of it. Sun insists its security measures are top-notch, but people are always saying that and then being caught out by hackers. Unscrupulous types can also use Javascript to snatch your email address while you browse their site. You can then find yourself on

Tips – Applets

Even if you're not worried about security, it can be a good idea to disable Java. Applets can be unstable and crash your browser. They can slow down your time on the web too. And a fair few of them are so trivial or irritating that you're often better off without them. ▲

< 309 >

the receiving end of a lot of spam. If you're worried, get your browser to block Java applets and Javascript. In Navigator, select the **Edit** menu, then **Preferences**, then click on **Advanced** and look for the Java section. In Internet Explorer, select the **View** menu, then **Internet Options**, then click the **Security** tab. Click the box next to the line **Custom (for expert users)**, then click the **Settings** button. In the **Security Settings** dialog box, look for the **Java Permissions** section. ▲

• •

Offline browsing

For hardcore webheads, a good offline browser is the software holy grail. They dream of programs that will go online while they sleep, download the web pages they want and have them all ready for fast clicking the next morning. It's not hard to see why people drool slightly when this subject comes up. It combines saving money with eliminating long waits for pages to download. At the moment, however, the perfect offline browser is a fantasy. Current programs obviously can't target the links on web pages that you might actually want to check. Instead, they have to download all the links, which takes time. As a result, while you sleep, you spend your money packing your hard disk with huge chunks of data you'll never look at. That said, offline browsers are getting better and they can be useful for certain tasks. But the better ones are fairly complex programs that are often part intelligent agent, part search tool, part geek indulgence. However, you can start browsing offline without having to

< 310 >

get extra software. First, as mentioned earlier (on page 125), your browser's history file makes basic offline browsing very easy (particularly in Internet Explorer 4.X). If all you do is read web pages and click the odd link, you should use it. The **History** file is just an interface for the documents stored in your browser's cache. There are other ways of accessing these files. You can get separate programs which make your cache (often a confusing jumble, especially in Navigator) legible. Try Unmozify **http://www.evolve. co.uk/** or Cache Explorer **http://www.mwso.com/**. Both put a nice and easy Windows Explorer-style interface on your cache.

You can also use Internet Explorer 4.X as an offline browser, courtesy of its subscriptions feature. When you make a particular site a Favourite, you're also given the option of subscribing to it. You can then get Internet Explorer to check the site for updates and automatically download new content you can read offline. If you do subscribe, click the **Customise** button and you can then enter information about your subscription. To convert existing Favourites (or Internet Shortcuts) into subscriptions, select the **Favourites** menu, find the site you want and right-click on it. Choose **Subscribe** from the menu. A **Subscribe** dialog box will appear. Again, if you choose to have Internet Explorer download page updates, click the **Customise** button.

The **Subscription Wizard** then starts up. You'll be asked whether you want to download the page or the pages it links to. If you choose the latter, you'll need to specify how many links deep. The default is one link. If you set it any higher, your browser may end up downloading an awful lot of data. When it comes to updating your subscription, you can choose to do it manually or schedule an automatic download. If you go for the

< 311 >

Tips – Task Scheduling

If you experience problems automating subscriptions, it may be that you need Task Scheduler. This is included in the full Internet Explorer download. However, if you only got the browser, you won't have it. Use the **Product Update** link (on the **Help** menu) to get it – it only takes around five minutes to download . ▲

latter (and you're connecting via a modem) tick **Scheduled** and **Dial as needed if connected through a modem**. To set the schedule, click the **New** button. You can then choose to update daily, weekly or monthly. Think about the time you set for your automatic download. If you're subscribing to an American site, pick a time like 6 a.m., when US traffic will be tailing off but European/British traffic won't have started. If the site requires a user name or password, enter them when prompted. Once the **Subscription Wizard** finishes, you need to go back to the main Internet Explorer screen to automate your modem connection. Select the **View** menu, then **Internet Options**, then the **Connection** tab. Tick **Connect to the Internet using a modem**, then click the **Settings** button. Pick the name of the connection you want to use, fill out the various boxes and tick **Connect automatically to update subscriptions**. Make sure **Disconnect if idle for X minutes** is ticked. Two or three minutes here is sensible. That way, Internet Explorer will terminate the connection once your pages have been downloaded. There's yet more information you could enter. Select the **Favourites** menu, then **Manage Subscriptions**. Right-click one

< 312 >

of your subscriptions, then select **Properties** from the mouse menu. Click the **Subscription** tab to access general information about the site and an **Unsubscribe** button. Click the **Receiving** tab and, if you've chosen to download pages for offline viewing, the **Advanced** button. The next dialog box lets you choose not to download images, sound and video, ActiveX controls and Java applets. You can also limit the size of the overall download by ticking **Never download more than X Kb per update** and setting a figure of your choice. Incidentally, if you set this too low, you won't download anything you can actually use. Once your subscription is downloaded, set Internet Explorer to work offline, type in the URL and access it as normal.

Is all this something of a performance? Yes. Is it worth it? It's difficult to say. Using Internet Explorer subscriptions for offline browsing is still fairly crude. You may be connecting at night, but your browser will be online for longer, collecting material you may never look at. If you tend to look at the web in the morning (and mostly access American sites), an offline browser is pretty pointless. On the other hand, if you can only use the web in the evening, when American sites become busy, it might prove

Tips - Sleep Mode

If you are going to attempt to automatically download web content at night, you obviously have to leave your computer on. However, you don't need to leave your monitor on. Some computers also have a Sleep mode which saves some power. Check in your manual. ▲

< 313 >

handy. What current offline browsers offer is the chance to spend money (on longer, indiscriminate downloads) to save time waiting by your machine. As such, they're more for people in the web business who want to download a whole site so that they can check it out or perhaps demo it easily at presentations. Ordinary users might be better sticking with the **History** file. Alternatively, set up your subscriptions but forget automating them and update them manually – when you get up, for example – then read them in the evening. ▲

● ●

Shopping on the net

Net analysts love to talk about the billions of bucks net shopping will apparently generate by the year 2000. Neo-luddites dismiss it and go on about how computers won't ever replace the deep sensual pleasures of shopping in the real world. The truth, as ever, lies somewhere in between the two. Net shopping is becoming more popular but plenty of people still have a bit of a problem trusting online retailers enough to make a purchase. Of course shopping on the net won't replace real shops. On the other hand, it is possible to overstate the sensual pleasures of the weekly supermarket shop.

If you actually try it out, you will realise that online shopping isn't the same thing as real-world shopping. It gives retailers the opportunity to sell in a very different way. Some mistakenly attempt to simulate a real-world environment (from supermarket shelves to shopping malls). The

< 314 >

smart online retailers know that graphics aren't the best use of computer power. Go to Amazon **http://www.amazon.com/**, the leading online bookstore, and you get all the top ten recommendations you might expect. But shoppers are invited to post reviews of books they've bought. And Amazon cross-references its records, so that as you check out a possible buy you'll see a list of titles also purchased by people who bought the book you're contemplating. And when you go back after making a purchase, you see a list of books bought since by people who also bought the same title as you. You can also get email updates about new titles on subjects you're interested in. The main problem with all this is that it is so effective it becomes very hard not to buy something after a while. Net shopping also allows for different sorts of retail models to develop. For example, at some American online car retail sites (for example, Auto-by-tel – **http://www.autobytel.com**), you say what you're looking for then various car companies compete with each other to come up with the best quote. Car Source **http://www.carsource.co.uk** is attempting something similar over here.

The advantages of online shopping are fairly obvious. It's convenient – if your net access is up to speed. It gives you access to a wide range of goods. You can buy American products that often never make it over here or have sold out – for example, that hard-to-get Christmas toy. At the moment, even with telephone and shipping charges, net shopping can be pretty cheap. Many online retailers use discounts to persuade people to give them a try. Not all products are suited to net shopping. You obviously wouldn't buy designer clothes online. But books and CDs are another thing entirely. The latter are among the growth areas for net

< 315 >

shopping, along with computer hardware and software, travel, videos, financial services and, yes, pornography. Porn doesn't completely dominate net shopping, despite what you may have heard. And other types of product are becoming available all the time. Once they solve the logistical problems involved, the big supermarkets will become major online players. Even if you don't actually buy, the net is great for researching purchases and prices. In addition, classified ads are also coming online. On the net, it's much easier to find an ad for something you want. Then you go ahead and telephone the seller in the usual way. In the UK, many of the major classified ad outlets are online, from the general: *Loot* **http://www.loot.co.uk** and *Exchange and Mart* **http://www.exchangeand mart.co.uk**, to the specialist: *Autotrader* **http://www.autotrader.co.uk**.

Read about it online - The Future of Shopping

Some critics have pointed out that the discounts that come with net shopping are another example of tax breaks for the rich. Of course, whether you worry about exacerbating social inequality as you play with the half-price laptop you got online is down to you. But clearly, if it takes off on a large scale, net shopping will have massive social effects. For thoughtful speculation on what these might be and some interesting ideas on how the net might let ordinary people buy and sell, try the Guaranteed Electronic Markets site put up by TV presenter/cyber-pundit Wingham Rowan **http://www.gems.org.uk**. ▲

< 316 >

Making an Online Purchase

This tends to work in the same way at most online shops. You browse for the product you want then add it to a 'net shopping cart'. Once you're ready to pay, you go to the checkout and enter your details – name, address, credit card number. You also choose a shipping method. The total cost will be totted up and you're given an opportunity to confirm the purchase or change your mind. Then it's just a question of waiting for your goods to arrive. Some online retailers mail you to confirm the purchase and will also send an update about your order's progress.

Obviously, security is a worry when shopping on the net. However, as mentioned before, this has more to do with the novelty of the online world and less to do with real risks. Giving your credit card number to someone over the telephone is potentially risky, but most of us do it without thinking. To protect yourself online, first make sure that personal information and credit card details are sent to a secure server. Both Navigator and Internet Explorer are set up for secure transactions (essentially this means that important information is encrypted). If you're connected to a secure server, the padlock and key at the bottom left of your browser screen should be intact/locked. If they are not, you're not on a secure server.

You can also check by looking at the address in the browser text box. If you're on a secure server, the URL should start with **https://**. You can check a site's security status by looking at its security certificate. In Internet Explorer, select the **File** menu, then **Properties**, then click the **Certificates** button; in Navigator, select the **View** menu, then **Page Info**. If you're really worried, you shouldn't buy at sites that don't offer secure connections. But many people who shop at non-secure sites say they've

< 317 >

Tips - Online Ratailers

One thing to look out for is how quickly online retailers process your credit card purchase. Ideally, you want them to do it as soon as possible, the way it happens in most real-world shops. Some online retailers save up their credit card purchases and process them all in one go. This is not ideal. The longer your details are sitting around on someone's computer (or desk), the more vulnerable they are to misuse. ▲

never experienced problems. In the end, it's your call.

If you are worried about sending details over the net, good online retailers always give you the option of telephoning them in. Don't send personal/credit details by email. And don't give out any more information than you would with a standard credit-card purchase via the telephone. Incidentally, if you use a credit card, you are protected in various ways against fraud. Note that many online retailers also offer protection (money-back guarantees and the like), if you can prove that you were the victim of online fraud. There are a few general precautions you can take when shopping online. First, check out the retailer. Make sure they have a real-world address and telephone number. Don't buy from an organisation with just an email address. Check refund and return policies before you buy anything. Ask for confirmation of your order. At the very least, save and print the order screen when you make your purchase. Use your common sense. Be suspicious of incredible offers or discounts.

< 318 >

Tips – Shopping and Privacy

Obviously shopping on the net raises certain privacy issues. An online retailer like Amazon can remember who you are and what you've previously purchased because it creates a little identifying file on your browser – called a cookie. There are benefits to this. Net shops can tell you about special offers in an area you've shown an interest in. But there are problems too. What will they do with your data? Will they sell it to junk emailers? Can you stop them? For more about net shopping and privacy, go to page 322. ▲

Net Shopping in the UK and the US

Obviously Britain lags behind America when it comes to shopping on the net. Many more Americans have made an online purchase. There are many more US-based sites for them to visit. Of course, American net shops are just as accessible to UK surfers. There are lots of reasons to try them out, aside from the greater variety of what's on offer. Many products – books, CDs and computer software and hardware – are a lot cheaper in the States. And often online they're discounted as well. Even when you pay the shipping costs, they are still cheaper than buying at home. Incidentally, although books are exempt, you are likely to be charged duty on other items that you buy from America. Again, even with this added on, you may still save money. Online shopping is a big part of the so-called portal web sites. Many offer shopping areas and directories which are worth a look. Try Yahoo **http://shopguide.yahoo.com** or Excite's

< 319 >

Read about it online - Buying From American Sites

Obviously if you do choose to buy from an American site and experience problems, it will be difficult to sort them out. There are US organisations that monitor commerce on and offline. Try the Better Business Bureau at **http://www.bbb.org/**. ▲

Shopping Channel **http://www.excite.com/channel/shopping**. For general information on what's out there, try Netbuyer **http://netbuyer.zdnet.com/**. Otherwise, try Yahoo's general directory for links to online shops.

The US may be leading the way, but there are still plenty of online shops in the UK offering everything from books and CDs to football shirts and flowers. Here's a quick list of some of the contenders in the most popular online sales categories.

BOOKS

The Internet Bookshop – **http://www.bookshop.co.uk**
Amazon UK – **http://www.amazon.co.uk**
Waterstones – **http://www.waterstones.co.uk**

CDS AND VIDEOS

The Interactive Music/Video Shop – **http://www.musicshop.co.uk**
CDZone – **http://www.cdzone.co.uk**
Entertainment Express – **http://www.entexpress.com**

< 320 >

COMPUTER SOFTWARE AND GAMES
Software Warehouse – **http://www.software-warehouse.co.uk**
CD Direct – **http://www.cddirect.co.uk**

COMPUTER HARDWARE
Dell – **http://www.dell.co.uk**
Gateway 2000 – **http://uk.gw2k.com**
Byte Direct – **http://www.byte-direct.co.uk**
Network Solutions – **http://www.network-solutions.co.uk**

TRAVEL
A2B Travel – **http://www.a2btravel.com**
Bargain Holidays – **http://www.bargainholidays.com**

For tickets to all sorts of entertainment events, try Aloud **http://www.aloud.com**. Both Tesco **http://www.tesco.co.uk** and Sainsbury's **http://www.sainsburys.co.uk** are now running online shopping trials – it's worth having a look at which shops are involved. New Lads can now go online to sort out their designer Y-front needs at Male Direct – **http://www.kiniki.com** and their replica football shirts courtesy of Allsports **http://www.allsportsretail.co.uk**. Apparently Chelsea and Arsenal are also open for business online. There are links on Shop Guide, a useful UK net shopping directory, at **http://www.shopguide.co.uk**. If you don't know what you want and just want to browse, try some UK net malls – Shoppers Universe **http://shoppersuniverse.com/**, UK Shopping City **http://www.**

< 321 >

ukshops.co.uk, Yell's Shopping area **http://www.shopyell.co.uk** and Barclays' Barclaysquare **http://www.barclaysquare.co.uk**.

Electronic Cash, Online Auctions and Shopping Bots

Early enthusiasts for net shopping claimed that soon we would be doing it with special electronic currencies that would protect our privacy and enable all sorts of micropayments which would eventually build up into a thriving info-economy. E-cash and micropayments have yet to take the world by storm, for various reasons. First, it's a difficult thing to pull off technically, before you tackle the real problem of building trust in it. Second, we already have a kind of secure electronic currency we trust – our credit cards. Third, people can't be bothered with such small purchases. As one net theorist put it, do you want to be nickel-and-dimed to death? Nevertheless you can try out a form of e-cash (and make a few micropurchases), courtesy of Barclays' Barclaycoin **http://www.**

Read about it online – Online Banking

Though many of the big high-street names are now offering online banking, their services aren't quite up to scratch yet. Call your bank to find out what they offer. The insurance business seems to be ahead of the banks when it comes to taking advantage of the net. Take Screentrade **http://www.screentrade.com**, which lets you compare quotes and buy home and car policies online. ▲

< 322 >

barclaycoin.co.uk which you can use at their Barclaysquare online mall. You can also catch up on current developments in the field at the CyberCash site – **http://www.cybercash.com/**.

One net shopping innovation that does seem to be catching on is the online auction. These are slightly different to the offline variety. Bids are sent in via the net and products go the highest bidder before a set time. Often people try to wait until the last minute and things can get a bit hectic close to the deadline. Alternatively, in some online auctions, known as 'Dutch' auctions, the seller gradually reduces prices until someone bites. Many online auctions specialise in computer hardware and software, but you can buy all sorts of products, from toys to jewellery. The leading British online auction house is Quixell **http://www.quixell.co.uk**, which deals in computer hardware and software. American operations worth a look include Onsale **http://www.onsale.com** and First Auction **http://www.firstauction.com**. Alternatively, try Bidfind **http://www.vsn. net/af/**, which lets you search many of the online auctions to find out if a particular product is on offer and what the current price is.

Bidfind is what's known as a 'shopping bot' – an automated program which searches sites for shopping information, specifically price. Something like Bidfind helps you find what's out there on sale. Other shopping bots do price comparisons so you can find the lowest price for a particular item. Again, techno-gurus see a bright future for shopping bots. They think that in the future they will go online, interact with the bots run by shops, buy items and arrange shipping all by themselves, leaving us free to get on with our lives. That's a long way off yet. However, price comparison is available now and is worth looking into.

< 323 >

Read about it online – SET

Visa and Mastercard are working on something called SET, aka Secure Electronic Transaction, a new way to pay for things online which will bring increased security. Both shops and customers will be able to confirm each other's identities and all transaction information will be encrypted. For more information, try the Visa and Mastercard sites – **http://www.visa.com** and **http://www.mastercard.com**. ▲

Try Acses **http://www.acses.com**, which searches online bookshops for the lowest price on a title. Alternatively, try Bottom Dollar **http://www.bottomdollar.com**, Roboshopper **http://www.roboshopper.com** and Shopping Explorer **http://www.shoppingexplorer.com**. Both Yahoo and Excite feature shopping bots in their shopping areas and there are plenty more to try out – look for a list on the excellent Bot Spot **http://www.botspot.com**. Many of these aren't perfect yet. But they could change the nature of net shopping. At the moment, online retailers are spending money on marketing, brand building, security and cultivating trust. A shopping bot bypasses all that costly online branding. It lets smaller operations without the money for marketing compete in terms of price. So will the bigger online retailers continue to let shopping bots access their sites? If they don't, they lose business. If they do, they still might not get the sales. The end result might be that the net turns into the place for bargain shopping. We'll see.

< 324 >

Next Step

It may bring lots of benefits, but online shopping does raise concerns over privacy online. If you want to find out more, go to the next section. Alternatively, if all the talk of shopping bots has whetted your appetite for more gizmos, go to the Power User section on page 393 ▲

< 325 >

The Essential Clicks

Net guides and manuals usually find space for long directories of interesting places to go. These can be pretty useful, but they're not without problems. By the time you sit down to read the book, more than a few of the links can be out of date. Sure, general guides tell you what's out there. But they can never really be a match for online directories. And I'm not sure how much people really use them. Perhaps they pick out a few categories and try the links. But pretty soon, if there's something they're interested in, if they've got any sense they'll get online and search for sites themselves.

We've decided to take a different approach. The following isn't supposed to be a comprehensive listing. It features one hundred sites and there are millions online. The idea behind this book has been to give you the skills you need to find the information you want on the net. We've now got to a stage where everything that happens in the real world is represented in some way online. If you're interested in something – gardening, sailing, fashion – it's there on the net. Just go and look. That said, there are some things online, a net culture, that you wouldn't know about unless somebody told you. And there are some sites that are so useful or entertaining, you can't afford to miss them. So we thought we'd put these into a list. The resulting Essential Clicks are strongly tilted towards net culture. There are a few dumb sites here that we particularly

< 326 >

like but which may leave you cold. However, there are also plenty of sites you'll find yourself returning to on a regular basis. Think of this as a kind of Favourites/Bookmarks starter pack. As ever with the net, feel free to edit and add your own.

SEARCH

Yahoo – **http://www.yahoo.com**
Now packed with all sorts of add-on services (from chat and free mail to shopping) but still the leading general net directory.

HotBot – **http://www.hotbot.com**
Fast, easy to use and reliable. Beginning to establish itself as the search engine to beat.

AltaVista – **http://altavista.com**
An excellent search engine but falling just a little bit behind HotBot now.

Deja News – **http://www.dejanews.com**
Simply brilliant Usenet archive site. Come here if you're looking for answers or if you just want to make sense of the newsgroups.

Liszt – **http://www.liszt.com**
Looking for a mailing list? Want to search the mailing lists for answers? This is the site you need.

< 327 >

The WebCrawler Search Ticker –
http://webcrawler.com/SearchTicker.html
One of a growing number of sites which let you find out what other people are searching for (and whether they can spell) – voyeurism reconfigured for the net.

MetaCrawler – **http://www.metacrawler.com/**
Want to make your searches more comprehensive? Use several search engines at once courtesy of this useful site.

RESEARCH

Scoot – **http://www.scoot.co.uk**
Brilliant research tool that lets you track businesses, people, products and films. Results are served up quickly and in a very legible form. Essential.

Research-It – **http://www.itools.com/research-it/research-it.html**
A research and reference tool that lets you search all sorts of dictionaries, use currency converters, delve into map databases and much else, all on the one page.

Learn2com – **http://www.learn2.com**
Don't know how to carve a turkey, make a compost heap or tie your bow tie? Come here for useful tutorials (2Torials as they put it) on just about everything.

< 328 >

SOFTWARE

Download.com – **http://www.download.com**
Huge software warehouse site maintained by the computer information network CNet. Along with links to software, this has reviews, recommendations, news and charts showing what's currently being downloaded.

Stroud's Consummate Winsock Applications – **http://cws.internet.com**
Yet another software warehouse. If Download.com feels too overwhelming, try the more focused selections at Stroud's.

CULTURE

Jodi – **http://www.jodi.org**
What do you want from art on the net? Not copies of famous art works that take for ever to download and look sort of flat when they do. You want art made to be seen only on the net. You want the mad code games and screen-crashing wind-ups of Jodi.

Irational – **http://www.irational.org**
For some British net art, try this site maintained by techno-artist/provocateur Heath Bunting with links to his various online art escapades, from the Internet Beggar to online graffiti.

< 329 >

Po Bronson – **http://members.aol.com/pobronson/**

Most print world writers leave the net to their publishers' press department. Po Bronson (author of high-finance satire *Bombadiers* and Silicon Valley comedy *The First $20 Million is Always the Hardest*) just got on with things himself. A low-tech site which delivers what fans want: extra bits and pieces relating to his books (including deleted chapters and the like), interviews, journalism and much else.

McKenzie Wark –
http://www.mcs.mq.edu.au/Staff/mwark/home/homepage.html

OK, so cultural theory sounds dry and it usually is. But Australian academic Wark makes it work, as it were. A theorist not afraid of arguing the toss in the papers and online. Here's a selection of his thoughts on everything from Aussie culture to net politics.

Levity – **http://www.levity.com**

Excellent selection of links to post-sixties boho literature, which means everything from the official avant-garde of Burroughs and Acker to psychedelic rambling from the likes of Terence McKenna. Luckily, there's space in between for cyberpunk authors like William Gibson and technocult critics like Mark Dery and Erik Davis.

AltX – **http://www.altx.com**

An online publishing network, no less, hosted by Mark Amerika, who contributes fiction and online hypertext literature and provides a space for others to add links and kinks to their fictional experiments.

< 330 >

ENTERTAINMENT

Ain't It Cool News – **http://www.aint-it-cool-news.com**
You don't want the same old reviews when you go online. You want reviews from punters who catch the advance screenings of big Hollywood films – reviews the studios often don't want you to read.

The Force.Net – **http://www.theforce.net**
Geeks love 'Star Wars' which means that the web is packed with coutless Force-obsessed sites. This one takes the biscuit. Filled with all sorts of SW gossip, including endless details on the scripts and visuals for the upcoming prequels.

Internet Movie Database – **http://uk.imdb.com**
One of the great net resources – put together and consulted by the film fans of the world. Obsessively detailed databases about any film you might care to wonder about.

The Onion – **http://www.theonion.com**
One of the most reliably funny comedy sites. Takes a favourite net joke genre – the spoof press release – to another level with its selection of news stories that sound as if they ought to be true (e.g. Nike to stop producing trainers in order to concentrate on advertising). Much ripped off but rarely bettered.

Mr Showbiz – **http://www.mrshowbiz.com**
Celebrity gossip. All the usual tabloid fare.

< 331 >

Shockrave – **http://www.shockrave.com**

Site designed to showcase Macromedia's Shockwave plug-in, but not just another piece of corporate PR. Try your hand at various games and music-mixing routines and check out the web cartoons – everything from Peanuts and Dilbert to current cult fave *South Park*.

Spumco – **http://www.spumco.com**

Home pages for the company run by John Kricfalusi, the creator of cult cartoon duo Ren and Stimpy. Bumped from that show because of his refusal to compromise, Kricfalusi has put his new work straight on to the net. Check in here for regular episodes of his new cartoon, featuring Jimmy the Idiot Boy and George Liquor, American.

interFACE Pirate Radio – **http://www.pirate-radio.co.uk/**

A web-based private radio station which spins a mix of dance genres every evening after six.

The Sync – **http://www.thesync.com**

A great experiment in reworking TV for the net. Rather than just pump out standard TV shows online, this site showcases indie film and various net-only videos and shows – everything from the Cyber Love interactive talkshow and The Jenni Show (featuring Jennifer Ringley, the woman behind, or rather in front of, the JenniCam) to Meeks Uncensored, a regular show on technopolitics featuring cyber hack Brock Meeks.

< 332 >

Sonic Net – **http://www.sonicnet.com**
Very flashy American pop/rock site which focuses mainly on indie/electronica and the like with news, streaming audio, radio and much else. Might crash your browser.

The Astounding B Monster – **http://www.bmonster.com**
Marty Baumann's reliably excellent fanzine devoted to B movies. Each issue covers a particular theme – from 'Rocket Jocks' to 'Monsters from the Deep'. Detailed, witty and well designed.

Glebe's Thrift Funnel – **http://www.koekie.org.uk/funnel**
When they're left to get on with it and not bugged by killjoy lawyers, fans inevitably produce the best web sites. Of course, it helps if the object of their obsession is as interesting as Chris Morris. Check in here for more than you really need to know about the anti-Paxman's brand of media pranks and comic terrorism.

GAMES

You Don't Know Jack – **http://www.bezerk.com**
Something of a web landmark. The online version of the hyperactive trivia quiz. You need extra bits of software but it's still worthwhile.

Gamespot – **http://www.gamespot.co.uk**
British version of an excellent computer/video games site, with news, reviews, demo downloads, tips and much else.

< 333 >

Digital Nostalgia – **http://www.negia.net/~msakey/**
Retro-gaming (hunting down versions of those arcade games of yore so you can play them on your PC) and emulators (programs which dumb down your PC so it resembles your old games machine of ten years ago) are big online. This is a good general page, with all sorts of games you can download and links to other retrogaming/emulator pages. Alternatively, try The Official Multiple Arcade Machine Emulator page – **http://www. mame.retrogames.com**.

Professional Gamers League – **http://www.pgl.com**
The future of spectator sport online or the ultimate gamers' fantasy site, a place they come to dream about turning pro and earning big bucks playing Quake. Details on the players, fixtures and current state of play in the league, along with webcasts of contests.

Yahoo Games – **http://play.yahoo.com**
There are now plenty of sites using Java apps to let you play trad games (poker, backgammon, chess and the like) with punters from around the world. Typically, Yahoo's effort makes it all very easy and accessible.

NEWS AND WEATHER

BBC News Online – **http://news.bbc.co.uk**
One part of the Beeb's online operation. An excellent news site.

< 334 >

Press Association – **http://www.pa.press.net**

Go to the place where the hacks go to get their stories. Another impressive news site.

Guardian – **http://www.guardianunlimited.co.uk**

Get your daily news fix here, along with regular columns, special net features and links to other *Guardian* sites – the football and cricket pages are particularly worthwhile.

Met Office – **http://www.meto.govt.uk/**

Get your forecasts from the people who are supposed to know, along with features on how they do it and lots of links.

COMPUTERS AND TECHNOLOGY

C/Net – **http://www.cnet.com**

A monster site which can tell you just about everything you need to know about computers. News.com is the place to catch breaking technology news, but elsewhere you'll find information on getting started online, software reviews and much else. Indispensable.

Wired News – **http://www.wired.com**

An excellent technology news site, updated daily, featuring sections on culture, technology, business and politics. Less bogged down by press-release details and with more analysis than the competition.

< 335 >

Tasty Bits from the Technology Front – **http://www.tbtf.com**
Highly digestible alternative to big tech/net news sites – a quirky selection of technology news culled from a variety of online sources.

Need To Know – **http://www.ntk.net**
A sarky British digest of the week's technology/net news, plus updates on geek culture, brilliant tips on web pages to check out, a rundown on the week's media for geeks and a fair few laughs. Sign up to get this in your mailing box every Friday. Otherwise, drop in at the web site every week.

WEBZINES

Salon – **http://www.salonmagazine.com**
The most dependable of the attempts to bring a *New Yorker*-style, intelligent, general-interest mag to the net. Updated daily, this has great news and media coverage, good travel writing and much else. 21st, the section on technology and culture, is unmissable.

Urban 75 – **http://www.urban75.com**
British webzine covering all strands of alternative culture, from direct action and road protesting to outdoor raves. Features the infamous Slap a Spice game, in which you can interactively take it out on Scary, Sporty and the rest. If that doesn't feel so good, give Tony Blair and Michael Howard a good clicking instead.

< 336 >

The Drudge Report – **http://www.drudgereport.com**
This daily dose of Washington gossip and planted 'scoops' has had more impact on mainstream culture than most web sites (it broke the Zippergate story, sort of). And parasitic, right-wing info-junkie Drudge himself is some sort of symbol of the age.

The Drudge Retort – **http://www.drudge.com**
An answer site to Matt Drudge's rants. Niftily using an address close to its target, this site parodies the Drudge Report's daily shots of gossip and has a brilliant list of links to left-leaning sites online.

The Obscure Store – **http://www.obscurestore.com**
Jim Romanesko's 'daily news zine' puts together links to all sorts of interesting stories from the US media and showcases some of his own writing. There are also useful links to US media sites and an online shop packed with excellent zines as well. A truly wonderful site.

The Obvious – **http://www.theobvious.com**
Michael Sippey's zine specialises in thoughtful speculation on digital tech, and points you to stories that matter on other sites. His map of interesting sites is also a good way into a network of young web-based creatives.

Rewired – **http://www.rewired.com**
David Hudson's stimulating weekly zine is the place for left-leaning, techno-cultural criticism, reports on European net culture and occasional pieces on Berlin life.

< 337 >

Feed – **http://www.feedmag.com**

Yet another excellent American webzine, covering pop culture and techno-culture. This one retains a commitment to words and links rather than flashy animations. Aside from features, there are attempts to annotate documents to reveal their meaning and ongoing panel discussions.

Suck – **http://www.suck.com**

Almost an institution now and, like all comic institutions, deemed to be not quite as funny as it used to be. Suck fires a daily blast of vitriolic analysis and wordy spleen at the big, soft target that is the net. Still funny, especially when Heather Havrilevsky is writing. Excellent cartoons from Terry Colon.

Disgruntled – **http://www.disgruntled.com**

A zine for all those who want to sound off about work. Lots of features which cover everything from dodgy bosses to workers' rights. Check out the special sections where working stiffs moan about their jobs – and maybe send in your own contributions.

SPORT

Soccernet – **http://www.soccernet.com**

If you're not going to use the *Guardian* sites for your footie fix, you could do a lot worse than this effort (co-created by the *Daily Mail*). Reports, stats and opinion from all round the world.

< 338 >

Cric Info – **http://www.uk.cricket.org**

This is a great site. News, scores and opinion from all round the world.

SportsWeb – **http://www.sportsweb.com**

Reuters' entry into the sports mega-site business is compellingly comprehensive. A global focus is tied to reports on all sorts of sports, along with the stats, scores and gossip fans crave.

TRAVEL

A2B Travel – **http://www.a2btravel.com**

A sizeable, UK-slanted travel resource from the media company Emap. You'll find everything here, from general information on booking hotels to the latest cheap flights.

Bargain Holidays – **http://www.bargainholidays.com**

Part two of EMap's plan to put travel agents out of business. As you might expect, a good place to snap up those last-minute cheap holidays.

Railtrack – **http://www.railtrack.co.uk**

Access the train information you need in a fraction of the time it takes to call the telephone timetable.

Lonely Planet – **http://www.lonelyplanet.com**

The web presence of the agreeably post-hippy backpacker guides. This

< 339 >

has excerpts from the books, travellers' tales, forums for people planning trips and excellent travel-related links.

Multi Media Mapping – **http://www.multimap.com**
Enter the name of the British town you're going to, or the street and get a map of the area you can print out.

AA – Where to Stay, Where to Eat –
http://www.theaa.co.uk/hotels/index.html
Useful site which lets you search the AA's reviews database for details on UK hotels and restaurants in the region you're travelling to.

SHOPPING

Aloud – **http://www.aloud.com**
Yet another Emap site. Find out about pop/rock/comedy gigs and festivals here and book your tickets too.

Amazon – **http://www.amazon.com**
Now facing serious competition, but still the best online bookshop. Great recommendations, easy searching, clever suggestions for other purchases, excellent service. If nothing else, come here to research, then buy the books from a UK site: Amazon recently acquired the UK site BookPages – **http://www.bookpages.co.uk**, and have just relaunched it as **http://www.amazon.co.uk**.

< 340 >

Shop Guide – **http://www.shopguide.co.uk**
Useful UK online shopping directory, with links to net shops, ratings and other advice.

Bidfind – **http://www.vsn.net/af/**
Online auctions can be a great place to pick up bargains, especially if you're after a computer. This search tool looks through all the auctions for the goods you want and comes back with current prices.

Bull Electrical – **http://www.bull-electrical.com**
Online heaven for those who like to build their own radios/computers. Get your components here along with some very odd end-of-the-line techno-toys. Fancy some solar panels or a tank laser? Check in here.

What's On Stage – **http://www.whatson.com/**
Another Emap site: this one's for theatre and classical concerts and though it has a London focus, covers the rest of the country too. Find out what's on and book your tickets.

WEIRD

Urban Legends Archive – **http://www.urbanlegends.com**
The web archive of the newsgroup devoted to logging and debunking urban legends. The place for all those stories about strange things in your burgers, ghostly hitchhikers and the extra apparently shown hanging himself in *The Wizard of Oz*.

< 341 >

The Smoking Gun – **http://www.thesmokinggun.com**
The web is packed with conspiracy sites which claim to have the truth. This offers something both odder and more 'real'. You can view actual documents relating to celebrity crimes and cover-ups: read the crime scene report filed when the man suspected of killing Tupac Shakur was bumped off, or have a gander at the police reports on Janet Jackson's stalker.

The Kooks Musuem – **http://www.teleport.com/~dkossy/**
This started out as a book, but now Donna Kossy's kookological studies have found their natural home on the web. Stories about inspired lunatics and visionary nuts neatly sorted into useful categories, from conspiracy theorists to people who have solved the world's problems but can't get the rest of us to listen.

Disinformation – **http://www.disinfo.com/**
The search service of choice for people looking for the 'hidden information' that 'falls through the cracks of the corporate-owned media conglomerates'. Categories include Propaganda, Revolutionaries, Censorship, Counterculture, Counterintelligence and Newspeak.

NET CULTURE

Cybergeography Research – **http://www.cybergeography.org**
The place to go if you want to know what a map of the net might look like.

< 342 >

JenniCam – **http://www.jennicam.org**

A camera placed in Jenny's bedroom and hooked up to the net so that everyone can see what she gets up to, twenty-four hours a day. Yes, she sometimes takes her clothes off. Net voyeurism or online happening/performance art?

Carl Steadman – **http://www.freedonia.com**

The homepage maintained by the net celeb who co-founded the webzine Suck. This has links to his multiple online projects, wind-ups, parodies and an ongoing diary.

Ghost Sites of the Web – **http://www.disobey.com/ghostsites/**

Steve Baldwin's excellent listings site tracks ghost web sites, sites that are online but show no signs of life, haven't been updated in months or years and are hence like time capsules from an earlier era. Web history on the hoof.

The Useless Pages – **http://www.go2net.com/internet/useless/**

The trash aesthetic has been alive and well online for ages, as proved by the continuing popularity of this collection of links to incredibly stupid or pointless web pages. Rather knowing now, so not as good as it used to be, but still very funny.

The Fray – **http://www.fray.com**

As in the real world, personal confessional is thriving online, in various forms. Your own homepage is the perfect place to vent your feelings. Take

< 343 >

this much-praised site, which has great design and personal pieces by creator Derek Powazek and his friends on everything from work to drugs.

The Bot Spot – http://www.botspot.com

We are not alone online: there are a lot of other people there too. But there are also lots of small automated programs beavering away doing searches for us. This site delves into the world of bots, covering search bots, shopping bots, chatterbots and much else.

Lee's Superfine Banana Label Collection – http://www.overmann.org/index.htm

Until you get on the web, you just don't realise how everything is collected by someone somewhere. This site is devoted to a collection of banana labels from round the world and features galleries of personal favourites and dancing banana animations, plus links to other banana-label collectors around the world.

The Ate My Balls Mega Page – http://www.mrev.net/mrzebra/ate-my-balls/index.htm

Yet more online idiocy. The net is great for passing on gags. It's also packed with blokish students with too little to do. Hence the Ate My Balls thing. First a page appeared which shows Mr T (from *The A Team*) grinning and saying 'Damn, these balls is good' or some such. Then other pages appear proclaiming that Homer Simpson/David Hasselhof/Han Solo 'ate my balls'. Now the net is groaning under the weight of balls-related traffic. To see how far a net fad can go, try this page.

< 344 >

Nua – **http://www.nua.ie/surveys**

Trivial but amusing collection of links to all manner of surveys and reports about the net. The place to tap into the latest collection of useless statistics about the rising number of grandmothers online and the like.

Edge – **http://www.edge.org**

Site hosted by power agent John Brockman, who scores techno-gurus and celeb scientists their big book deals. In return, they turn up here to ponder all sorts of interesting questions.

Police Scanner – **http://www.policescanner.com**

Use the net to listen in on the police and emergency services and hear what a fine job they do.

WOMEN

GeekGirl – **http://www.geekgirl.com.au**

Coming straight out of Australia, this is the original geek-girl zine, though there are now lots of imitators. Very flashy graphics tied to good writing and links.

iVillage – **http://www.ivillage.com**

Everyone's talking about creating portal sites – one-stop homepages with everything you need. Next step is specialist portals. iVillage is already there and fast cornering the thirtysomething female demographic online. A mix of different women's resources (from parenting info and financial

< 345 >

tips to links to software to help you work from home), plus message boards, chat rooms and an unpatronising tone. For the competition, try **http://www.women.com**.

Gurl – **http://www.gurl.com**

Another webzine possibly thinking of becoming a portal to the web, though aimed at a much younger audience than iVillage. The place for all your perky post-feminist features and links.

KIDS

Yahooligans – **http://www.yahooligans.com**

Typically dependable set of links to kid-centred sites, along with advice and all the usual community-building extras.

Bonus – **http://www.bonus.com**

Hugely enjoyable site packed with kids' games, some educational, some just for fun. Very bright and very American. You need to register and you also need a reasonable computer.

GCSE Answers – **http://www.gcse.com**

Parents may be a little worried about sites where kids can do their homework by buying ready-made school essays and papers. This is an altogether more responsible operation, offering revision tips and tutorials for English and Maths GCSEs.

< 346 >

POLITICS/NET POLITICS

Electronic Frontier Foundation – **http://www.eff.org**
Political pressure group of choice for the digerati and still a good site to go
to bone up on net history and follow current debates and news concerning
online issues, from censorship and privacy to intellectual property.

McSpotlight – **http://www.mcspotlight.org**
Direct action online – sort of. Set up during the McLibel trial, this is still
arguing the case against McDonald's and multinationals in general.

Global Internet Liberty Coalition – **http://www.gilc.org**
If the American/soft libertarian focus of the EFF isn't you, try this net
activist resource. More global in its scope, this gives you updates of the
state of play re. online free speech and privacy around the world, along
with excellent archives.

Cyber Rights and Cyber Liberties –
http://www.leeds.ac.uk/law/pgs/yaman/yaman.htm
Yaman Akdeniz's excellent site points you towards everything you need
to know about privacy and censorship on the net in the UK.

Junkbusters – **http://www.junkbusters.com**
Exhaustive, slightly exhausting but still brilliantly useful site aimed at
helping you rid your life of all forms of unwanted junk communication,
from spam to junk snail mail and those late-evening telephone sales calls.

< 347 >

Consumer Project on Technology – **http://www.cptech.org**
Imagine a highbrow *Watchdog* for the digital age and you get the gist of
this site put up by James Love and Ralph Nader – information on anti-
trust actions against Microsoft, biotechnology, pharmaceutical companies
and intellectual property, amongst other things.

RELATIONSHIPS

Swoon – **http://www.swoon.com**
Romance and relationships site put together by Condé Nast. This features
bits from various print magazines but the best bit is the Swoon Personals
– good for a browse even if you're aren't really looking.

Match.com – **http://www.match.com**
Billed as the premier online dating service, this charges (though this is a
plus point with users, since it apparently deters nutters). Sign on, browse
profiles of other members, look for people near you, get matched up by
the search engine of love.

Remind U-Mail – **http://calendar.stwing.upenn.edu/**
Something to save your relationship perhaps. Set up a calendar here and
get email reminders so you don't forget important anniversaries and
birthdays.

< 348 >

SCIENCE

NASA – **http://www.nasa.gov**

A vast site covering NASA's multiple projects, past, present and future. The place to come for those satellite photos and to catch up on current missions.

New Scientist – **http://www.newscientist.com**

The ever-wonderful British science mag has been online for ages, providing features, news and links to science stuff around the web.

HEALTH

Planet Health – **http://www.planet-health.com**

Useful site for hypochondriacs, featuring health news, a Health Explorer search engine/directory that lets you find sites about your particular pain and 'a personal health risk assessment', which identifies your problem and points you to web sites that can help.

The Keirsey Temperament Sorter – **http://www.keirsey.com**

Check your head, courtesy of this online personality test (these are very big online for some reason). Click your way through the seventy or so questions and then get slotted into one of around sixteen different types.

< 349 >

LOOKING AFTER YOURSELF ON THE NET

• •

Despite the claims of moral guardians, the net is not an alien hostile space. It's not a dangerous place. But you do need to take care. Like the real world, there are people online who do not have your best interests at heart. And, unlike the real world, the net is such a novel space that sometimes you might not realise you're getting into trouble. So here are a few . . . no, not survival tips, just bits of advice on how to make your time online as painless as it is enjoyable. ▲

• •

Pornography, free speech and protecting your kids online

It's a shame that a book like this inevitably has to devote more space to the 'threats' the net poses to children than to the benefits it offers.

< 351 >

Read about it online – Children's Sites

If you do have kids and you want a quick way of finding what's around online for them, try Yahooligans – basically a directory of children's sites put together by Yahoo – **http://www.yahooligans.com**. Alternatively, try Kid's Space – **http://www.kids-space.org** – a nice collaborative site where children can post artwork and exchange ideas, or Bonus – **http://www.bonus.com** – a vast compendium of interactive games. ▲

However, hysterical reporting has set the agenda and, in a way, become self-fulfilling prophecy. If they hear often enough that the net is awash with pornography, what do you think children are going to think about when they do get online? The net is not a risk-free environment. Parents should not let children use it without advice, guidance, boundaries and some form of supervision any more than they would let them play out in the street without the same. The best thing parents can do when it comes to their children and the net is learn about it, be realistic, balanced and sensible. Then they might have a chance of communicating the right attitude to their children.

Now, pornography. Yes, there is indeed a lot of it on the net. It doesn't generally jump out at you when you log on, despite what alarmists say. That said, junk email advertising porn sites is a problem – not the sort of thing you really want turning up unannounced in your mailbox, especially if you share it with the kids. On some search sites it's possible that

< 352 >

running a search on something like 'little women' might either turn up sites that are a long way from Louisa May Alcott or cause the various programs running the site to think that you're looking for something pornographic and hence load a series of ads for X rated sites. (Of course, the thing to do here is make your search more focused - for more information, go back to page 147). Some irresponsible webmasters do try to con people into coming to their porn sites - by using misleading meta tags which trick the search engines. (Their aim here is usually to make money from advertising other porn sites. The more people who turn up on their sites - whether or not they wanted to go there - the more money they can get for their advertising). Obviously, if a set of links to porn sites turn up on the results screen of your search site of choice, you will ignore them, refine your search and get on with your work. However, your twelve year old son might find it difficult to resist clicking the odd link. Parents should also be aware that some porn sites have web addresses which are very close to the addresses of popular sites. A favourite trick is to use a familiar domain name but change the top level domain. For example, the web address of the Whitehouse is **http://www.whitehouse.gov**. However, there is also a very popular porn site at **http://www.whitehouse.com**. Typos of well known web addresses (Netscape, Yahoo etc) are also sometimes taken up by porn sites.

So, it is possible for unwanted pornographic material to find its way onto your computer screen. But usually you have to look for it. If you're a consenting adult who likes that sort of thing, there's plenty online for you. If you're an adult who doesn't like that sort of thing, don't go looking for it. Of course, adults aren't the problem here. The problem is

< 353 >

hormonal teens and curious children accessing this material. However, many sites are pay-per-view commercial operations. You have to enter credit-card details and sign up with a service to verify that you are an adult to get in. That said, all sites offer free samples as a come-on. And there are plenty of completely free porn sites online. The more responsible use some sort of adult check service. But plenty don't. Pornographic images are also freely available in some Usenet newsgroups – usually the alt.binaries groups. These tend to be ads for web sites, complete with embedded links. However, some people just swap images for fun.

There are indeed newsgroups covering the more bizarre sexual practices. There are some groups devoted to paedophilia and child porn. It's likely that your internet service provider is already blocking access to these, though they are accessible via remote news servers outside the UK. There are other things for parents to worry about apart from sexual material. There are racist web sites put up by Nazi-sympathisers and White Power types, sites denying that the Holocaust took place, sites that feature information on making bombs and spud guns, sites that feature autopsy and accident scene photographs. There's also plenty of uncontroversial, non-visual material that just isn't suitable for children – discussion about recovering from sexual abuse, for example. The web and newsgroups aren't the only things parents should be aware of. Recently, stories have also emerged about paedophiles emailing schools and attempting to strike up relationships with children. Though they're mainly a text thing, chat rooms are often filled with talk about sex. It's also clear that some paedophiles do hang out in chat rooms frequented by children. Online, visual cues that might alert you to potential problems

< 354 >

are absent. So it's harder to spot dodgy characters. That said, according to those who work with them, many paedophiles are capable of great superficial charm in the real world. They know how to get people to drop their defences.

So there's material and people online you want to keep away from your children. The first thing to do is to get this into perspective. The net is not packed with pornography, paedophiles and perverts. It's mostly used by ordinary people like you. So don't believe the moral panic-mongers. They're not that concerned about your kids. They're more interested in selling their book or TV series. Second, the presence of pornography and dodgy characters online is no reason to keep your kids offline. Most children use the net happily without ever coming into harm's way. You kids will enjoy the net and learn from it. Don't deprive them out of ill-informed fear.

I once heard a net user point out that certain city streets are used at night by prostitutes but that doesn't stop families using the road system in general. I know what he was getting at, and I'm generally sympathetic, but the analogy doesn't hold. Red-light districts in cyberspace run 24 hours a day. Plus, your children aren't likely to wander into a real

---

Tips – IRC for Kids

Chat can be a risky area for kids. However, there are areas of the IRC network that are specifically for kids which might be worth a look. Try KidLink (an IRC net for kids) – **http://www.kidlink.org/IRC/**. ▲

< 355 >

red-light district in the middle of the night. But it's easy for them to find their way to porn sites on the net. The barriers we find in the real world – physical, legal, social – aren't yet there in cyberspace. In the real world there's a top shelf. Sure, there's bomb-making information around, but it's often under the counter at independent bookshops or hidden away in the less accessible parts of a library. Eventually a set of similar barriers will develop in cyberspace.

For example, a top-level domain for pornography has been suggested – X-rated sites would end in .porn for example – and it would then be easier to block children from that area of the net. It might work, though it wouldn't be without problems. But many pornographers would be happy to go along with it. Despite what alarmists say, the majority don't want children on their sites. They're not out to corrupt anyone. They just want to make money. Hence they generally want to avoid anything that might lead the police to stop them making money. Some people think governments should set up legal barriers online to protect children. There are areas where everyone seems to be in agreement (banning child porn, for example). But the law concerning things like hard-core porn and hate speech is different, country to country. And so far, the attempts of individual countries at drafting legislation have been so vague that, if put into practice, they would cover much more than pornographic material, would treat adults as children and ruin much that's good about the net (the fact that it connects everything and that it makes it so easy for information to move freely).

Some free-speech activists argue that, aside from being undesirable, censorship on the net is also impossible. Hang out online for a while and

< 356 >

Read about it online – Censorship on the Net

Net users campaigned successfully against the Communications Decency Act – an ill-conceived attempt to censor obscene material on the net – and they continue to keep a close watch on worldwide attempts at online censorship. For details on campaigns past and present, try the Electronic Frontier Foundation site **http://www.eff.org**, the Global Internet Liberty Coalition **http://www.gilc.org**. For a British site, try Liberty's Campaign against the Censorship of the Internet in Britain – **http://www.liberty.org.uk/cacib/**. ▲

---

you'll come across the claim that 'the net interprets censorship as damage and routes around it'. There is something glib about the way free-speech fundamentalists repeat this as if it closed the argument, as if the technology was going to decide things for us. But without taking draconian measures, national governments have found it difficult to block access to a site in another country that contains political or pornographic material they don't like. There always seems to be a way for smart people to get to the forbidden information. And the job of would-be censors is made harder by activists who delight in putting up mirror sites of banned web pages. Hence the rather bizarre spectacle of right-on activists hosting pages put up by scumbag Holocaust revisionists.

In the UK, the police have argued that plenty of existing laws do apply to the net and they have put pressure on UK ISPs to block access to newsgroups that carry illegal or obscene material or face prosecution

< 357 >

themselves. Critics argue that the police are setting themselves up as censors and are disregarding a complex set of legal issues. Put simply, the police claim the ISPs are 'publishers' of this material and are legally responsible. ISPs argue that they are merely carriers of this stuff and hence are not responsible. You don't prosecute the telephone companies if people use their lines to conspire to commit crimes, they suggest. The whole thing's a bit more complex than this, but you get the gist. In practice, though this isn't completely resolved, many UK ISPs have blocked access to newsgroups used by paedophiles.

The UK net industry argues that it can regulate itself and has set up the Internet Watch Foundation **http://www.iwf.org.uk**, which collects reports about child porn online – amongst other things – and alerts ISPs. The net industry in general is anti-legislation. It would prefer a system of ratings used in combination with blocking software. The idea here is that sites are rated according to their content. Then parents can install and configure special software that blocks access to certain categories of sites. This was deemed to be the perfect solution by many techno-gurus, since it seemed to put control in the hands of individual users but didn't affect the general space of the net. Unfortunately, it's not that simple. Critics say the ratings system currently being implemented – PICS, aka Platform for Internet Content Selection – actually brings an unacceptably high level of regulation to the net as a whole. Again, this is fairly complex, but the problem is that PICS allows for control beyond the level of individual. ISPs and even countries can use it to block access to certain sites. And once a site is rated and filtered, it will disappear completely. You won't know it exists. Worried by PICS, some net users have now come round to

< 358 >

Read about it online - Ratings

The leading ratings organisation online is the Retail Software Advisory Council **http://www.rsac.org** which started out rating video games but moved on to the net with its RSACi ratings. For the arguments against ratings, read the interview in the Internet Legal Practice newsletter with the American law professor Lawrence Lessig (who was briefly involved in the Microsoft anti-trust case) – **http://www.collegehill.com/ilp-news/lessig.html**. Alternatively, try the EFF and GILC sites mentioned previously. ▲

the opinion that carefully framed legislation might in the end be the best way to protect children online and preserve the freedoms made possible by the net. Unfortunately, the net has become caught up in the larger, ongoing moral panic about children. So it's highly unlikely that people will take the time to develop sensible ideas about how to make legislation work. But you can do your bit, simply by taking a sensible and realistic attitude to the net and your children. ▲

< 359 >

Setting guidelines and boundaries for children online

If you have a family computer, think about where you put it. Don't allow your child to keep it in his or her bedroom. Set it up in a communal space where they will at least feel you're keeping an eye on them. Don't let them password-protect areas of the computer. Use the computer yourself and keep an eye on any new bits of software or new files that appear on it. You may want to give older children their own computer (and net connection) but recognise the implications of that decision. Recognise that you will (a) have to talk to them more about what they do online (not something teenagers will relish) and (b) have to trust them more. You can make the choice not to let your kids use the net on their own. Certainly with younger children this is the best bet. With children over ten, it's not going to work.

So set some basic guidelines. Set time limits on their net use and the places they can and cannot go. Tell them they can and should talk to you if they find material that makes them uncomfortable, if they get nasty email messages and the like. Tell them to never give out personal information (everything from name, address, telephone number and the location of their school to personal photographs) without your permission. Incidentally, they may be at risk here not from dodgy individuals but from dodgy companies who often try to con kids – with the offer of prizes

< 360 >

– into handing over information about their parents. It's always worth checking the privacy policy on sites your kids use a lot. Finally, impress on your kids that they must never meet online friends without checking with you first. If you do agree to meet someone, go with your children and make sure the meeting is in a public place.

If you don't trust your children to resist temptation, you can set up a few technological barriers. First, the online services and many ISPs sell themselves as family operations and will provide ways for you to block access to 'unacceptable' material. If you want uncensored access to the net for yourself, sign up with a more liberal ISP and install blocking software. Several programs are on offer. The best known are probably Cyber Sitter **http://www.solidoak.com/cysitter.com**, Cyber Patrol **http://www. cyberpatrol. com**, Net Nanny **http://www.netnanny.com** and Surf Watch **http://www. surfwatch.com**, but plenty more are coming on the market. These do the same sorts of things but all work in slightly different ways, so visit the web pages for more information. Filterware blocks access to certain sorts of sites and let you set times during which the net can (or cannot) be used. They all use some sort of list of unsuitable sites, which they compile in

Read about it online – Larry Magid

He has established himself as an authority on child and teen safety online. Check his sites **http://www.safekids.com** and **http://www.safeteens.com** for advice, tips and some good links to kids/teens sites. ▲

< 361 >

various ways. Some let you unblock certain sites if you think they're fine for your kids. Some let you choose more sites to be blocked. Most record attempts to access restricted web sites. Some let you restrict access to certain areas of your computer as well.

These programs are fine if you want to let younger children use the net unsupervised. If you've got teenage children, it's more complicated. For one thing, computer-literate teens might find a way round blocking software. In general, filterware needs maintenance. The list of banned sites is constantly changing. New sites appear. Old ones disappear. So you need to download a new list of censored sites fairly frequently. More importantly, many of these programs come with a built-in political agenda. As part of their right-wing family-values approach, they block access to non-pornographic sites promoting gay/feminist politics. Unfortunately, it's often unclear what some programs are blocking. Not surprisingly, some of the companies who make these programs won't reveal what's on their banned list. They work hard on compiling it and see it as their crucial piece of intellectual property. You could always try one of the newer, more flexible programs which give you more information and control over the material they block – for example, Surfin' Annette – available from Spycatcher **http://www.spycatcher.com**.

You don't necessarily need to install software to begin blocking sites. Internet Explorer allows a form of web filtering. Select the **View** menu, then **Internet Options,** then click the **Content** tab. Click the **Enable** button in the **Content Advisor** section. You then have to set a password. Once you've done that, you go to a **Content Advisor** dialog box which lets you use a little slider control to set acceptable levels as far as Language,

< 362 >

Read about it online – Filterware

There's no problem with people using filterware, so long as they're aware of what it actually blocks. But some free-speech fundamentalists hate the very idea of filterware. For more info, try the Censorware Project – **http://www.spectacle.org/cwp/intro.html**. Net reporters Brock Meeks and Declan McCullagh were the first journalists to reveal what some filterware programs were actually blocking. For their 1996 report, go to **http://peacefire.org/archives/cwd.12.20.96.txt**. One of the most determined filterware critics is Bennett Haselton, founder of Peace Fire, the Youth Alliance Against Internet Censorship. His site – **http://www.peacefire.org** – has extensive reports on the problems of each individual piece of software along with revealing reports of his rather rancorous dealings with Solid Oak, the makers of Cyber Sitter. ▲

Nudity, Sex and Violence are concerned. This uses the RSACi ratings (pretty much the standard online now), is fairly crude and only blocks web access. Netscape are apparently planning to add content filtering to the next version of Communicator.

Blocking access isn't the only option. You can also snoop on your children's use of the net. Filterware programs allow a measure of this. But there are now specially dedicated surveillance programs that will tell you everything your child gets up to online and will even mail you at work if they click on something naughty. Basically these are home versions of the

< 363 >

programs that are now used in many offices. The leading product in this area is something called Prudence **http://www.bluewolfnet.com/pru.htm**. How you feel about using surveillance technology on your kids is up to you. If you install it, you can either tell them you're using it or keep it secret. The latter seems a particularly unhealthy option. Parents might find out more than they bargained for about their children (and what they think of their mum and dad). Are you ready for outing by software, for example? On the other hand, if you do tell your kids you're using surveillance software, you can see how it might be incorporated into adolescent rites of passage. When they seem old enough to look after themselves, you can make a big deal of turning the thing off. Netscape is apparently planning to introduce parental surveillance features into the next version of Communicator (which may be out by the time you read this book).

Of course, your browser is already a surveillance tool. It keeps a record of where you've been (in the **History** file), stores pages you've visited in the cache, retains addresses entered in its text box and has a file filled with cookies – special identifying files placed by some sites on your hard disk (more about these later). So if you do want to keep a less invasive check on what Junior has been up to, look in these. If you use Internet Explorer, your cookies will be in a **Cookies** folder in the general Windows directory. In Navigator, the cookies will be in **cookies.txt** in the **Users** folder. Of course, smart kids will know about all this. But a completely clear **History** file and an empty cache after a couple of hours' surfing is suspicious. Note that Collabra and Outlook Express also save details of newsgroups that have been subscribed to, then unsubscribed. Just spend some time looking around in the files and folders. If you're

< 364 >

really obsessive, a good utilities program will also enable you to recover deleted files. So you can tell if your child has downloaded images, transferred them to a floppy disc, then deleted them. Of course, if you're that obsessive, especially without grounds for suspicion, it may be you, and not your kids, who needs help.

Finally, when people talk about protecting kids online, it always seems to be in the context of dangerous material or people. In fact, plain vanilla chat can up being harmful. Some children find it incredibly compelling. Even if all they're doing is nattering about Leonardo DiCaprio or the new Arsenal away strip, it can be a problem if done to excess. So keep a tactful

Tips – Clearing Your Machine

If you choose to check out porn on the net using the same software as your kids, that is, of course, your business. However, your browser can easily make it your kids' business. The URLs will be in the **History** file and the pages in the cache unless you clear them out. Some sites may put cookies in your browser which identify whoever happens to be using the browser as a porn consumer. Some sites will then target what they see as appropriate advertising at whoever is using your browser. So, if you want to protect your kids (and keep your late-night surfing to yourself), you'll need to clear History, the cache and your cookies. If you use Navigator, Cover Your Tracks – available from **http://www.geocities.com/SiliconValley/Vista/5610/cyt.html** – will do this for you. ▲

< 365 >

eye on them and make sure that chat (and the net in general) doesn't stop them from enjoying other things. You could always try one of those pieces of software that tots up the time spent online (also useful when it comes to keeping your own net use under control). Try Net Meter http://www.cracker.u-net.com/. ▲

• •

Privacy on the net

The fact that the net allows ordinary people to communicate anonymously has been much discussed. The online porn business clearly benefits because its customers feel they are acting (if that's the word) in private, that there's no one watching them download those dirty pictures the way there might be if they reached up to the top shelf in their local newsagents. In chat rooms and MUDs people continue to play fast and loose with the truth about themselves, because they feel that other users only know the personal details they choose to reveal. However, it's become clear that there are people taking note when you download porn. And some chat-room users know how to sniff around your software and retrieve the email address you may have entered during configuration (an email address that might reveal your real name). The net may allow a superficial kind of anonymity. But at a more fundamental level, much of what you do online is accessible to all sorts of people who know how to look. The web, in particular, now looks almost purpose-built to collect and process personal data about ordinary users. As privacy activists have

< 366 >

Read about it online – EPIC

For information on privacy online, try the Electronic Privacy Information Centre at **http://epic.org**. For more general information on privacy, try Privacy International **http://www.privacy.org/pi/**. For British information about net politics, including privacy online, try Yaman Akdeniz's excellent Cyber Rights and Cyber Liberties site – **http://www.leeds.ac.uk/law/pgs/yaman/yaman.htm**. ▲

pointed out, the net is redefining the nature of privacy, is allowing governments and corporations greater and greater access to the lives of ordinary people. So first, be aware of the lack of real privacy online. Don't assume that anything you do or say online is private. Take precautions and get involved in the ongoing debate about privacy online.

Privacy Online at Work

This should really be the shortest section in this book. Put simply, there is no online privacy at work. Assume that your boss is using software to track your use of the net. Assume that he or she owns whatever you say online. The law has tended to back this up so far. Don't use the net at work for personal communications. Don't use email for anything that might get you into trouble. It will be impossible to delete it easily, since it will be stored in all sorts of places. And simply deleting sensitive email is never enough. People will be able to retrieve it, if they feel the need. To really get rid of email you need a file wiping utility. Also, don't use the

< 367 >

web for non-work related activities. It's likely the boss will know exactly what you're up to. Download porn on company time and you may end up fired. You can keep personal communications at work private by using web mail but your boss will still know if you spend a lot of time at a web mail site. The only thing you can really do at work is find out what the privacy policy is and whether surveillance software is being used.

Internet Service Providers and Privacy

When you're thinking of signing up with an ISP, check their privacy policy. Make sure they're not going to sell your personal details to junk mailers, on or offline. Check whether they include any personal/sensitive information in their member directories. Remember that it's possible for them to track what you do online, if they want to. Be careful with the password to your net account. Obviously, if someone gets your password, they will be able to read your mail and use your account to cause mischief in your name. Don't ever give it out to anyone online, even if they identify themselves as working for your ISP. Your ISP will never ask for your password online. Never email your net account password to anyone. Change it frequently and choose a random combination of letters and numbers.

Email and Privacy

The first thing to realise about standard email is that it is not private. On its way to and from your computer it will sit around unprotected on various computers. Even after you download it, read it and delete it, it will still be accessible to someone with a good utilities program. Again,

< 368 >

the only way to completely remove it is with a file wiping program. The only way to ensure email privacy is to use encryption. An encryption program scrambles your messages so that they look like random gobbledegook. The most popular form of encryption online is public key cryptography. The idea here is that a net user has two 'keys', one public, one private. The public one is distributed to friends and colleagues. Often people tack it on the end of their emails. The private key is kept secret and secure. If you want to encrypt a message to someone, you use their public key. When they get your message, they need their private key to decrypt it. Without access to the private key, communications encrypted in this way are very difficult – if not impossible – to unscramble. Encryption software also allows you to create digital signatures so that you know for certain who sent a particular piece of email.

Sounds simple, doesn't it? Unfortunately, it isn't. Though the business world is more than a little keen, the government and the police remain unhappy about the spread of so-called strong encryption software. They argue that it will be used by terrorists, drug dealers and other criminals to frustrate law enforcement. So they've tried to introduce encryption programs which, in various ways, allow the police access to encrypted communications. The net community is campaigning vigorously against this and some have resorted to direct action. In 1991, a programmer called Phil Zimmerman finished a public key encryption program called Pretty Good Privacy. He sent it to friends who then made it freely available on the net. Zimmerman was then taken to court by the US government on a charge of illegally exporting munitions. The case collapsed a couple of years ago and Zimmerman

< 369 >

has since gone into the encryption business proper, selling commercial versions of PGP. It remains the most popular encryption program online, thanks to its rebel history.

However, the US government still prohibits the export of strong encryption technology. If you want to use PGP, you need to get it from a European site. At the moment, the UK government appears to be similarly keen to restrict the use of strong encryption (despite at times also saying that they didn't want to stop ordinary people using software like PGP). Current noises indicate that the government wants encryption software to leave all sorts of useful back doors for the security services. However, since the government seems rather confused on this subject, it's possible that things might change. There are plenty of web pages where you can catch up on the latest – try the Cyber Rights and Cyber Liberties page mentioned previously. Alternatively, try the page maintained by UK crypto activist Ross Anderson **http://www.cl.cam.ac.uk/~rja14/** or S. Simpson's page **http://www.hertreg.ac.uk/ss/** which has some excellent links and some interesting software to download too. Incidentally, both

Read about it online – PGP

Phil Zimmerman's PGP Inc is now part of Network Associates. Go to **http://www.nai.com** for more details and look for links to info on his past, PGP and the trial. Alternatively, try the EFF site and look for the archive **http://www.eff.org**. To download a version of PGP, go to the International PGP homepage **http://zone.pspt.fi/pgp/**. ▲

< 370 >

browser mail programs allow you to encrypt and sign your mail. They're not as good as PGP, but still worth a look. If you use Outlook Express, you first need to get a digital identity from Verisign, Microsoft's chosen commercial certifying authority. Select the **Tools** menu, then **Options**, then click the **Security** tab, then click the **Get Digital ID** button. After that you can choose to digitally sign your email and encrypt it by ticking the boxes in the **Secure Mail** section. In Navigator, click the **Security** toolbar button. Click the **Messenger** tab and you're given the option of encrypting or signing your mail. You need a personal security certificate. To get one, click the **Yours** tab. You're given a choice of certificate authorities. To select one, click the **Signers** tab.

Of course, email privacy isn't just about stopping nosey people from reading what you say. Sometimes you want people to read what you say. You just don't want them to know it was you that said it. For example, you might want to post personal messages to a public mailing list about depression or alcoholism. You might want to send anonymous email blowing the whistle on malpractice where you work. You can, if you use an anonymous remailer. You send your mail to one of these, it strips away identifying

Read about it online – Anonymity

For more information about anonymity online, with links to software, academic research and other resources, try the site put up by the American Association for the Advancement of Science at **http://www.aaas.org/spp/anon**. ▲

< 371 >

details then sends it on. Some remailers also permit replies to anonymous messages. Remailers remain controversial with police and journalists, who in the past claimed they were primarily used to send abusive mail and circulate child porn. The most famous anonymous remailer – anon.penet.fi – closed after coming under fire from hysterical hacks and the Church of Scientology. There are still a few anonymous remailers up and running. There's a list at **http://www.cs.berkeley.edu/~raph/remailer-list.html**. Alternatively, try the Nymserver, which you have to pay for – **http://www. nymserver.com**. Incidentally, you can also achieve a superficial anonymity by entering a false name and address when you configure your email software. It means people won't be able to reply to your mail, though. You can use a non-gender specific nickname rather than your real name in your email address. You can also set up multiple web mail accounts and use them for specific things – keeping your ISP mail account for select recipients.

Newsgroups, Mailing Lists and Privacy

In theory, you should attach your email address to newsgroup postings. That way, people can respond privately if they wish. In practice, if you reveal your email address in newsgroups it may be collected by the programs used by direct marketing monsters and you may soon find yourself deluged with spam. So when you configure your newsreader, you may want to enter a bogus name and email address. You could also use an anonymous remailer when participating in newsgroups. There's another reason why false names or anonymous remailers are also useful with newsgroups and mailing lists. Many sites now archive newsgroups and mailing lists (for example, Deja News) and some suggest that these

< 372 >

Tips – Avoiding Spam

This advice comes from Internet Magazine. When you put a return email address on your newsgroup postings, try something that will confuse the automated programs used by spammers but will be easily decoded by human readers. One popular choice used to be yourname@nospam.yourisp.net – though the spam kings are wise to that one now. Try **yourname@yourisp.net.strip.this.bit. out.to.reply** or something similar. ▲

---

databases are being used for something beyond simple research. It's claimed that some employers run searches on potential employees to see what they've said in the newsgroups/mailing lists. Contributing anonymously might avoid any potential problems. Some search sites allow you to add details to your postings which prevent them from being archived and searched. Check in their help files.

The Web and Privacy

By now it may have dawned on you that your browser collects all sorts of information about what you do on the web. The information stored in the cache and the **History** files is only the half of it. The real problems as far as the web and privacy is concerned are cookies. These are little identifying text files which some sites place on your computer when you visit them. When you go back to a particular site, it will be able to read the cookie to tell what you did there before. It will also be able to add more

< 373 >

Tips - Cookies

One of the neatest ways to deal with cookies is to use Luckman Interactive's free Anonymous Cookie program. This disables all the cookies on your browser while you surf, so no one can sneak a look. But when you get to a site that has put a cookie on your file and you want to take advantage of it, you can immediately re-enable them, then turn them off again when you leave. Download it from **http://www.luckman.com/**. ▲

information. There are obviously benefits to this. Many sites use cookies to log your personal preferences. Shopping sites use cookies so that they can remember what you bought before and direct you to other things you might like. Whilst this sounds fine, you might feel less comfortable about companies surreptitiously snooping around your cookies, building a database on you and then sharing it with others who use the information to target advertising at you. And some cookies may be used to store all sorts of personal details – your address, even your credit-card details. As mentioned before, you can check on which sites have put cookies on your computer. In Navigator, look in the **User** folder. If you use Internet Explorer, look for the **Cookies** folder in the general Windows directory. You can instruct your browser to refuse cookies. In Internet Explorer, select the **View** menu, then **Internet Options**, then click the **Advanced** tab, then scroll down to the section on **Cookies**. In Navigator, select the **Edit** menu, then **Preferences**, then **Advanced**. In the **Cookies** section you can

< 374 >

choose to block all cookies or **Accept only cookies that get sent back to the originating server,** which in theory ought to offer more privacy, if you trust the originating server. For more information about cookies, try Cookie Central **http://www.cookiecentral.com**.

Cookies aren't the only threat to privacy on the web. Some sites use JavaScript to copy your email address while you're browsing. One way to stop this is not to enter your email address into the relevant sections of your browser. Of course, that means you won't be able to use it for email. Alternatively, change the settings on your browser to block Java and JavaScript. In Navigator, select the **Edit** menu, then **Preferences,** then **Advanced** and look for the Java section. In Internet Explorer, select the **View** menu, then **Internet Options,** then click the **Advanced** tab, then scroll down to the **Java** section. You can achieve complete anonymity on the web via an anonymiser, which sets up a protective barrier between you and the sites you surf. Try Anonymiser.com, a commercial service which also offers anonymous email **http://www.anonymiser.com**. For free web anonymity, try Bell Labs' Lucent Personal Web Assistant **http://lpwa.com**. The neat thing about these tools is that when you have to enter personal details to access a particular site, they will come up with false information but remember it next time you visit. In other words, you can enjoy the benefits of customising/personalising certain pages without giving away anything really personal.

Giving away personal data without realising is one thing. What about information you choose to hand over, when you register with a site or buy something? The first thing you should do here is consider who's asking for the information. Do they have a real-world address? Do they have a

< 375 >

Tips - Anti Junk Mail

You can run a quick check to see if your browser is giving away your identity – i.e. your email address – to sites you visit. Go to the Junkbusters site **http://www.junkbusters.com**, a terrific general anti-junk mail resource. Specifically go to **http://www.junkbusters. com/cgi-bin/privacy** and look for the privacy test link. ▲

---

privacy/security policy? Do they tell you what they're going to do with your information? It's become clear recently that, after insisting it be allowed to regulate itself in this area, the net industry is doing a very bad job of protecting consumer privacy. Information collected when users register at sites or buy something is being sold on and swapped without their knowledge or consent. In an attempt to show willing, some web sites are beginning to sign up with an organisation called TRUSTe, which is attempting to set certain standards regarding privacy and commercial web sites. If a site has signed up, you should see a little TRUSTe logo somewhere. For more information, go to **http://www.truste.org**. Aware that they are losing the PR battle over online privacy, various big corporations (Disney, Apple, Microsoft, Dell and others) have set up something called the Online Privacy Alliance, which will apparently attempt to set down standards to protect net users – for more information go to **http://www.privacyalliance.org**. ▲

< 376 >

Harassment on the net

Some techno-gurus used to talk about how the net would help people escape old prejudices and work together productively. It's now clear that, like everything else, this technology can be abused and some people deliberately use it to make mischief and cause problems. This can encompass everything from sabotaging mailing lists and newsgroups with wind-ups and spoof messages to making someone's life a misery with abusive and unwanted email. The press love to refer to the latter as cyberstalking, which may seem somewhat overstated to some. However, email is such an intimate form that a continual unwanted presence in your mail box does feel like some sort of invasion of your personal space. And if someone is technologically literate, it's clear that the net can help them obtain information that would enable real-world stalking.

This obviously isn't a problem that only afflicts women but clearly women in particular need to take precautions. Problems often start in chat rooms. So, as mentioned in the section on chat, configure your software so it doesn't reveal anything important or real about you. Pick a

Read about it online – Harassment

For advice about tackling online harassment, lists of safe chat rooms and MUDs and much else, try the excellent Women Halting Online Abuse at **http://whoa.femail.com**. ▲

< 377 >

non-gender-specific nickname. If someone gets on your nerves, use the **Ignore** function on your chat software to make them disappear. If problems persist, report them to the people running the chat room. If someone gets hold of your email address and sends you abusive mail, use mail filters to block it. But not before saving some of it and sending it to your tormentor's ISP to complain (try mailing **postmaster@ispname. com**). If their mail gives a false name and address, look at the header for more information about them and their messages. Get help from your ISP. Ultimately, if you're worried, save the mail and get the police involved.

Email and Harassment

Abusive or obscene messages are something that could come by ordinary mail. However, the net makes new forms of mail abuse possible. A technologically literate net user who wants to give you a hard time can mail bomb you – in other words, flood your mailbox with thousands of messages, thus rendering your mail account useless. There's not a lot you can do about this apart from wait until the dust clears. You can attempt to see if the bulk mail reveals details of where it came from. If it does, contact the ISP responsible. But if someone is smart enough to send you thousands of messages, they're usually smart enough to cover their tracks. Sometimes, people attempt to crash your mail by signing you up to lots of high-volume mailing lists. Here the only thing you can do is to sit down and unsubscribe from all the lists. If you have multiple web mail accounts, you will be able to continue emailing people while your mailbox proper is cleared. However, it is a hassle. But you're unlikely to receive a mail bomb, unless you're nasty enough to send out junk email

< 378 >

and foolish enough to include your real return address. Mail bombs are sometimes used against spammers (and supportive ISPs) by activists – punishment in kind.

Spam

People who have never been online get incredibly het up about pornography on the net. People who are online don't worry that much about it. The thing they get really uptight about is spam – unwanted junk email sent to hundreds of thousands of users at once. It's fair to say that, for the net community, spam and spammers have now replaced the government and clueless journalists as number-one hate objects. Now, don't get me wrong. Spam is a major pain. But it's interesting to speculate on why the net hardcore despise spam with such intensity. Perhaps it's because it's a daily refutation of their misplaced idealism about the net. Every day there's more in their mailboxes. And whatever it actually says, the basic message is always the same: the net is not automatically a force for good. Perhaps it's also that much spam – with its idiotic get-rich-quick schemes – feels like a cruel parody of some netheads' early fantasies about making their first million on the net.

Leaving aside pseudo-intellectual speculation, it's pretty obvious why net users don't like spam. It costs time and money. Deleting the stuff every morning can be a lengthy process. And in contrast to real world junk mail, the recipient actually pays for the privilege of getting spam. There's also no disincentive to spammers to stop spamming. In contrast to the real world, there's not much difference, cost-wise, between sending one piece of mail and several hundred thousand copies. Spam has also

< 379 >

Read about it online - Spam

The web is packed with sites about spam, how to deal
with it and what to do about spammers. For legal angles and
links, try the Coalition Against Unsolicited Commercial Email
http:// www.cauce.org/. For news, history, links and practical
information, try Junkbusters **http://www.junkbusters.com**.
For another wonderfully useful site, go to **http://www.mcs.com/~jcr/
junkemaildeal.html** . ▲

destroyed certain online communities – some newsgroups for example.
There are further problems if you actually take the time to read the stuff.
Some spam is offensive. Most of it consists of fraudulent get-rich-quick
offers, fake charity appeals, pyramid schemes and other cons, all designed
to trick the gullible into handing over money.

So the first piece of advice for net newcomers concerning spam is: don't
read it. If you do, don't believe it. Sick kiddies collecting email addresses/
business cards/money for charity? A can't-fail chance to get in early on the
next hot stock? A killer scheme in which if you send money and addresses
of friends now you will, in just a few weeks, receive thousands of pounds?
All rubbish. The second tip is: get angry by all means, but don't let it take
over your life. Spam has become a fact of life online. You can do certain
things to minimise the problems it causes. But you can't make it go away
completely. So do what you can and get on with your online life.

< 380 >

Many junk emailers assemble their mailing lists with email addresses they get from newsgroups and web pages. So you could simply never contribute to the newsgroups and avoid putting up a web page. Of course, if you did this, there'd be little point in being online. A better alternative might be to use false email addresses when posting to Usenet. In addition, don't post your email address publicly on the web. Don't use your browser for mail (that way, people can't sneakily snatch your address while you're browsing). If you do give personal details to web sites, check their policy on this. Incidentally, in recent months, several major sites with good reputations online (from Amazon to Wired) have been accused of spamming. Setting up several email accounts (and keeping one for dealings in the newsgroups) might be one way to keep one mailbox spam free.

You can also use filters and blockers either to automatically send anything that looks like spam into the trash folder or to stop your mail program from downloading the stuff in the first place. None of these will block everything but they're still worth trying. There's some good advice on how to set up spam filters in Eudora at **http://wso.williams.edu/~eudora/ eudora-3-0-spam-filter.html**. Even if you use Outlook Express or Messenger, it's worth checking this out, since it will help you attempt something similar with your software. You can get extra bits of software to deal with spam. Try Spam Exterminator **http://www.unisyn.com/ spamex/**, the SpammerSlammer **http://www.spammerslammer.com**), Spamicide **http://www.compulink.co.uk/~net-services/spam** and Email Chomper **http://www.sarum.com/echomp.html**. The best of these programs (e.g. Spam Exterminator) let you identify spam before you download it.

< 381 >

They also provide safeguards so you can avoid deleting mail you actually want. Another program worth looking at is POP3 Scan Mailbox **http://www.netcomuk.co.uk/~kempston/smb/index.html**, which is a useful general mail utitility which can also scan for spam on your ISP's mail server. Your ISP should also be taking anti-spam action. Some of the best spam blockers work at the server level. So if you are having problems, call your ISP and find out what they're doing. If they're not doing much, you might want to change to someone else. However, many are trying their best to deal with spam and (in the States) some are even taking legal action against persistent spammers.

If spam does get through, don't try sending an email bomb back. More than likely, the spammer won't have given a real return email address, so there won't be any point. But it's not a good idea anyway. If the spammer has been using a legitimate ISP, you will only succeed in annoying them and they will thus be less likely to help you. Instead, write to the spammer and ask to be removed from their mailing list. This sometimes works. Some direct mailers buy emailing lists in good faith. They think people want to get their messages. If you politely protest, they will take you off their list. Alternatively, send mail saying that you're happy to receive spam but charge £10 per piece of mail. Apparently, if the spamming persists this will help you sue the spammer, if you take things to court. That's unlikely, but sending the mail won't hurt. Of course, most spammers don't supply a working email address. In that case, try protesting to the spammer's ISP (for example, send email to **postmaster@ispname.com**.

If all the addresses on the spam are faked, look at the header to see if you can figure out where it came from. The Junkbusters site has infor-

< 382 >

Tips – Spam Lists

Treat with a degree of suspicion any sites that say they will remove you from mailing lists. In the past some of these have actually been set up by spammers looking for more email addresses. ▲

---

mation on how to understand headers. Get That Spammer **http:// kryten.eng.monash.edu.au/gspam.html** has more information on tracking down spammers. You can get software which helps you decode headers, track down spammers and draft legal threats to send them – try Spam Hater, **http://www.compulink.co.uk/~net-services/spam/**. The newsgroups are a good source of information about spam. Try **news.admin.net-abuse.email**. Alternatively check at **news.admin.net-abuse.sightings** to see if the spam you're getting has been encountered by others. If not, report it to the group. For information about spam in newsgroups, try **news.admin.net-abuse.usenet**. ▲

• •

Trust and security

A couple of years ago, Pierre Salinger, JFK's spin doctor, went public with 'proof' that the TWA Flight 800 plane crash had in fact been caused by a US Navy missile. In fact, the crucial piece of evidence was a document Salinger had found online, a document which looked official but which

< 383 >

had already been widely discredited. Result – he looked pretty dumb and the online media and net culture in general had a field day. They shouldn't be so smug. Every now and then, everyone online gets taken in by something that seems on the level but turns out to be bogus. Recently, a speech circulated on the net which was widely thought to be by American writer Kurt Vonnegut. It wasn't. It turned out to be a newspaper column by a journalist. She hadn't intended to fool anyone. Someone had put her column online. It got passed on. The authorial credits got lost. Imagination filled in a few gaps that weren't there in the first place.

It's pretty easy to fool people if all they've got is words (and their willingness to believe). This kind of thing is generally harmless, though Pierre Salinger might not agree. If you don't want to make the same mistake, don't automatically believe everything (or everyone) you read online. There's plenty of useful and reliable information online. There's also tons of rubbish. And there's lots of information that is tricked up to look official and reliable, but isn't. Some people are similarly tricked up. In the early days, a certain amount of playing with identities was seen as part of the net experience. It can still be fun, but as the net has become more commercial, there's a little more at stake. Put simply, there are conmen and women online looking to part you from your money. They might do this with spam – with chain letters and 'unmissable opportunities' to make money fast. They might do it with official-sounding email which seems to have come from your ISP and requests you send in your personal information and credit card details again. As a rule, remember that ISPs never ask you to send important information in emails. If you get mail like this, at the very least ring your ISP up to check it out.

< 384 >

Faking mail which seems to have come from someone else, aka mail spoofing, is very easy to do and much used by net pranksters. So if you get mail from **tony.blair@newlabour.org**, don't start planning the outfit you'll wear to Number 10. Instead think hard about which of your friends might play that kind of trick. If you get mail from a friend that seems completely out of character, don't immediately assume they sent it. Similarly, on mailing lists and newsgroups, if postings turn up from someone that don't seem to fit their previous image, it's likely they're spoofs. If you want email that you and your friends can definitely trust, you can start using the encryption software mentioned above which lets you create digital signatures which prove you sent a particular piece of mail. In general, be sceptical when you're on the web. Remember it doesn't cost that much to make a web site look good or official. So think about who put the site up and why they're telling you what they're telling you. Always look for a real-world address/contact number before you hand over information to a site. Be sceptical about 'guaranteed money-making stock offers' and the like. For more information on net cons, go to Internet Fraud Watch **http://www.fraud.org/internet/intinfo.htm** or try Internet Scambusters at **http://www.scambusters.com**. ▲

● ●

Viruses and Hackers

A common and hugely pointless net scam is the fake virus warning – a message warning of an email virus which will infect and crash your

< 385 >

computer if you download and read it. These messages *are* viruses of a sort: mental viruses which infect your brain cells and cause you to waste valuable time worrying about whether they're true. Ignore them. Don't pass them on. However, do take precautions about viruses. You're mainly at risk from software you download from the net. Get a good anti-virus program and always virus-check programs before you install them. (There are three big anti-virus programs: Doctor Solomon's Home Guard – **http://www.drsolomon.com/**; Norton AntiVirus – **http://www.symantec.com**; and McAfee's VirusScan – **http://www.nai.com**). Similarly, be wary of documents created using Word which are attached to email. These may contain macro viruses and should be checked before you open them.

People worry an awful lot about viruses online, more than is strictly necessary. You could say the same thing about hackers. Some people seem convinced that once you get online, these info-age folk devils will seek you out and make your life a misery. The truth is, most hackers spend their time either trying to make other hackers' lives a misery (and hence prove how hardcore they are) or trying to break into government/military computers (and hence prove how hardcore they are). Generally, they won't bug you if you don't bother them. That said, there are a few digital-era grifters out there, trying to use their net skills to turn a buck or score some free telephone calls at your expense. So take care, especially on IRC. If you're in a chat room and someone tells you to type a particular command, don't do it. It may let them take over your computer. Be careful about the software you download from sites that seem less than reputable. Note that both big browsers warn you about software you download and information you send. Both let you 'turn up' the security features. However, if you want to

< 386 >

do something more, you can always install so-called anti-vandal software – something like Guard Dog **http://ww.cybermedia.com** or eSafe Protect **http://www.esafe.co.uk**. These programs will watch over you while you are online, track cookies and tell you if someone tries anything dodgy (for example, accessing private files on your computer). ▲

● ●

Copyright and libel on the net

Digital technology makes it easy to make copies of things. The net makes it easy to share those copies with other people. As a result, according to some net theorists, old intellectual property laws shouldn't really apply online and we need to work out a new way of compensating people for the content they create. Unsurprisingly, many old-school lawyers (and their mainstream clients) don't see things in quite the same way. They're perfectly happy to hang on to the old laws and see if they can make them stick in cyberspace. Hence a regular net news story in which artists on their own or creative industries as a whole take action against web sites they claim are illegally using copyrighted material. Everyone from Oasis to Rag Doll (the people behind the Teletubbies) have attempted to crack down on fan sites which, they claim, are abusing their material.

There are obvious problems with this. The web is what it is today thanks to fan sites. They're often great resources and brilliant adverts for

< 387 >

the objects of their devotion. So hardline crackdowns seem somewhat perverse. On the other hand, what if a fan site is making lots of money using someone else's material? There are other problems which seem more clear cut. The net takes home taping to another level. People can record tracks from their favourite CDs, upload them to the net and swap them with other users. This is illegal, obviously, though not without benefit to the artists being copied, according to some. If you download a track by a band you've never heard before and you like it, you might just go out and buy the CD since downloading a whole album is still a time-consuming process. However, technology is getting better all the time and soon it won't take so long, which is why the music industry is making a fuss about net bootlegging. They're only following the lead of the computer software industry which has long been attempting to do something about the spread of pirated programs online.

Bootlegging is a fairly familiar crime. The net makes possible all sorts of novel abuses of copyright and infringements of trademarks. Take domain squatting, in which smart net users buy up the right to use familiar corporate names online (as in **mcdonalds.com**) in the hope of getting money from selling them back to the real world businesses involved. In general, where it's clear that this has been done with some sort of intent to make money, the courts tend to find in favour of those who own the trademark in the real world. But things aren't always simple. Recently in America a toy company attempted to get heavy with a child whose nickname was the same as one of their products. They claimed, to general derision, that his personal web site **http://www.pokey.org** infringed their intellectual property rights.

< 388 >

Some businesses have gone to court to argue that links made by one site to stories on their site were an attempt to benefit illegally from their intellectual property. More recently, *Playboy* attempted to take action against a former Playmate whose site used the word 'Playboy' as one of its meta-tags – the things web designers use to indicate what's on the site to roaming search engines. They claimed the meta-tag constituted copyright infringement and was an attempt to steal their traffic. The Playmate argued that since she talked about her experiences with the magazine, it was legitimate. Celebrities are also beginning to take action against web sites that circulate pictures of them in the nude – many of which are deliberately faked.

It will be interesting watching all these problems get sorted out over the next few years. In the meantime, what you really need to know is how you can avoid getting a letter from a lawyer about something you've done online. First, think about the copyright status of material you use online. If you put pictures on your web page that you've scanned in from magazines, it's likely that, legally, they belong to someone else, so try to get permission or give credits and indicate who owns the copyright. If you re-post material to a newsgroup – an interesting newspaper story, say – make sure you say where it came from and put in the appropriate credits. Check with people before you re-post something they sent to one newsgroup to another group or mailing list. It will probably be fine, but since they will own the copyright, you should check anyway.

Incidentally, you own the copyright on any original material that you put online. So you might want to put a little copyright sign on it. That way, if someone decides to put it in a print collection of the wit and

< 389 >

Read about it online – Intellectual Property

Some activists argue that, under cover of responding to the challenge posed by the net (and digital technology), various corporations are trying to extend the intellectual property laws in a way that would drastically curtail free public discussion. For more information, look at the Intellectual Property section on the Consumer Project on Technology **http://www.cptech.org**. For some utopian but interesting thoughts on intellectual property, try John Perry Barlow's essay on 'The Economy of the Mind on the Global Net' – **http://www.eff.org/pub/Intellectual_property/idea_economy.article**. ▲

wisdom of the net, you have a chance of getting some sort of credit (and possibly even payment). The thing to remember about material you put online is that if it's any good, it will be passed around. Be flattered. Don't immediately call a lawyer. (A few of the features I've written have turned up without my permission on various web sites. So long as my name is still on the copy, it's fine by me. It means more people get to read my work.) Finally, with regard to your own creations, written or otherwise, remember that the libel laws do seem to apply on the net. People have been successful in suing for libel over things that were said online. The unresolved area is whether ISPs have some legal responsibility for libels circulated by their users. Luckily, the courts seem so far to have decided that they don't. The person who is responsible is the person who posted the original message. In other words, you. So think before you sound off

< 390 >

on the web, in a newsgroup, in mailing lists or in chat rooms. People are reading and taking notes. Make sure you cover yourself.

Next Step

There is only one place to go next. You know pretty much all you need to know when it comes to getting round the net. What you can do now is try out a few cutting-edge programs and gimmicks, buy some more software to tweak your browser still further, learn how to do it yourself online and look into the history of the net. So onward – to the power users section. ▲

< 391 >

6
POWER USERS

● ●

If you've got this far, you at least deserve honesty. So let me be completely straight with you. 'Power User' is something of a double-edged term. There are plenty of people who glory in the label, who think it indicates that they are on a different level to the average net/computer user. Then there are those (usually the sad, resentful types who work in computer-support departments) who think that 'Power Users' are the kind of clueless techno-macho types who go on about how powerful their computer is, how fast the processor is, how much disk space it has, but then only use it for tapping out letters. There is something naff about that 'power' prefix. But were it not for that 'Power User' label, this section would be called something like 'Advanced Internet', which is kind of dull.

By now, you know about nearly all of the useful, basic things you can do with the net. What's left are the expensive purchases (faster connections) you need to make if the net becomes more business than pleasure. That and a whole series of toys, gizmos and gimmicks you could try out. They might not improve the quality of your time online to quite the extent

< 393 >

they claim. But they can be fun to play with. And incidentally, if you find you can't resist the latest plug-in, if you find yourself up in the small hours trying to get your new browser booster to work, you'll know that you've definitely made that evolutionary cross-over from Homo Erectus to Homo Connectus. Welcome to the club. ▲

● ●

Power connections

Everyone on the net figures that their connection could be faster. Power Users are the ones who pay a lot of extra money for that much-craved download speed. There are several options beyond the standard telephone line when it comes to connecting to the net. Those in the net business could get a leased line (a high-speed, high-cost connnection that's open all the time). A cheaper option that's also appropriate for home users with a bit of money is an ISDN line (the letters stand for Integrated Services Digital Network). BT is currently giving ISDN the hard sell, with an offer to hook you up for less than £100. ISDN is a digital telephone line which offers faster connection times than current modems – up to 128 Kbps, with some jigging about. ISDN also lets you do two things at once; you can be connected to the net and talking on the telephone at the same time, all via the same line. However, you will need to get various bits of hardware and software to connect, and rental and call charges are a lot higher than normal telephone lines.

< 394 >

Read about it online – ISDN

For more information about BT's ISDN service, try their web pages at **http://www.homehighway.bt.com**. As you might expect, there are plenty of web sites that aim to help you get to grips with ISDN – most put up by high-tech firms that hope you might actually pay for some real help. For some useful general info, try the ISDN Zone at **http://www.isdnzone.com/dyndefault.htm**. Alternatively, there's a British ISDN page at **http://www.timm.demon.co.uk/index2.html** (watch out for the truly diabolical background music) . Finally, the people at Dope.com (Digital Online Production Enterprises) have put up the story of their ISDN connection, which takes you step by step through the whole process, at **http://www.dope.com/isdn.htm**. ▲

There are other connection options which offer much higher bandwidth than ISDN. For example, you could try a wireless/satellite connection. With this you receive data at very fast speeds (10 Mbps, according to some claims), but send it back at more standard rates. For an idea of what's out there, try DirecPC – **http://www.direcpc.com/** or their UK supplier at **http://www.easat.co.uk**. Some techno-gurus say that satellite net connections will be the way cheap high bandwidth connections come to the masses. Others have their money on cable modems.

The leader in this field is the American company @home. Apparently it has started cable modem trials in the UK and earlier this year signed some sort of agreement with a British company – ComTel – with a view to

< 395 >

providing cable modem access to the net over here at some point in the future. For more information, try @home's web site **http://www.home.net**. It may be that your electricity company will sort you out with a fast net line. In 1997, the regional electricity company Norweb annnounced that, in conjunction with the American company Nortel, it had developed something called Digital Powerline which lets you connect to the net via normal powerlines and transmit up to 1 Mb of data per second (around ten times faster than an ISDN line). You can find out more at **http://www.nortel.com/powerline/**. Reports surfaced last summer suggesting that tests weren't going that well, so it may take a while for it to reach the mainstream market. Home users who feel the need for speed now should probably cough up for an ISDN line.

Even though Power Users crave speed, when they get it, they're not always happy. They're always convinced they're not making adequate use of their connection, that bandwidth is not being used. Now they have software they can use to tweak their net connections and monitor download speeds. For example, there's Net Medic **http://www.vitalsigns.com**, which monitors your connection and checks to see if everything is fine. If there's a problem at your end, it tries to help you fix it. If it's at the ISP's end, it gives you the data you need to make a complaint. Alternatively, try TweakDUN. a utility which tackles low connection speeds by initiating something called the Windows Max MTU fix (for more information about what this is exactly, and on TweakDUN, go to **http://www.infinisource.com/maxmtu.htm**). You can also try DU Meter which reports on data transfer rates as you download pages from the web, showing the results in a nice graphic form **http://www.hagel.threadnet.com/dumeter/**. ▲

< 396 >

Power mail

Email used to be just a text thing, but now that most mail programs are HTML capable, it has gone multimedia. You can make your birthday message to a friend resemble the most Java-jumping web page – if you have the time and the inclination. Of course, downloading it may take a big chunk out of his or her happy day. Even the most hardcore of net users would probably be happy with an old-world card delivered by the postman. But what do you care? Remember the Power Users' creed – if it can be done, do it. Don't waste time wondering why. The simplest way to create graphic email is to use one of the pre-set templates that come with programs like Outlook Express. If you know how to write HTML (or if you have a program like Word 97, which lets you create a fancily formatted document and then save it as HTML), then you know one of the more straightforward ways of adding some more personal graphic flash to your mail. Of course, it's unclear how much that adds to your message, though including hypertext links in mail – so that friends can just click on them to launch their browser and visit the page in question – is useful and saves a bit of time and effort too. There's more on writing HTML coming up.

You can also get programs to help spiff up your mail. LiveMail uses Java to let you add sound, visuals and even animations to your messages **http://www.pslivemail.com**, as does E-Mail Magic **http://www.arcamax. com**. With the former, you're given around 200 basic formats you can customise and change to suit your purpose. Good for special occasions maybe, but not the sort of thing you want to send to the boss. You can also attach sound and video files to your email. CineMail

< 397 >

http://www.baraka-intracom.com is intended to make it easier to send email with attached video files of yourself saying 'Hi'. Of course, video files are very big, so this will take a while to download. As a result, it's best inflicted on family members. One form of email multimedia which does seem to be finding favour is what I suppose we might, somewhat confusingly, call voice email. Here you record yourself singing 'Happy Birthday' to your grandchildren, or whatever, then attach the soundfile to some email. One program that is proving popular is Voice E-Mail **http://www.bonzi.com**, a browser plug-in which makes creating and receiving voice email very easy. The thing with all these multimedia mail packages is that, whilst they will give your messages more impact, they may cause a few problems. Check that the recipients of your sound/video files have the software/viewers to handle them. Check that the message isn't too long and doesn't lead to a monster download. Also remember that once you start sending people mail loaded up with Java applications, security begins to be a problem.

The other thing about Power Users and mail is that they want it all the time. When Power Users travel, they want to keep getting that daily or even hourly email fix. Actually, this really isn't hard now. If you have a POP3 account (and pretty much everyone does now) and you're connecting via a friend or an overseas office, it's just a question of adding your name and password and the address of your ISP's net server to the mail software on the computer you're using, then connecting and getting your mail in the usual way. Alternatively, set up a Web mail account which will be accessible to you wherever and however you connect in your travels. You could also see if you can get your messages forwarded on to that web mail address whilst you're travelling. Finally, if you are

< 398 >

going to travel a lot, pick your ISP carefully. Some are international players. Sign up in one country and you can get net access in another. The online services are sometimes a good choice for travellers, in that they have points of presence all round the world. ▲

● ●

Power browsing

There's always something unfinished about web browsers. They always feel like work-in-progress, never the finished item. You know that someone somewhere is always working on the upgrade. However, you generally have to wait until Microsoft, Netscape or whoever puts out a new version of their browser. Plug-ins changed all that and thus were fatal for Power Users. The problem is that they let users take control of this update/boosting process. Thanks to plug-ins, Power Users can now spend all their time looking for the killer bit of software which will speed up their web use, make their searching more relevant and efficient and generally smarten up their browsing. Take some of the claims made for plug-ins and browser companion software with a pinch of salt. They may speed up your web access, but the difference is hard to quantify sometimes. Load up with accelerator programs and you risk becoming the digital equivalent of those boy racers who rush, bully and generally cut people up, only to end up stuck in a jam, a mere two cars ahead of more easy-going drivers. In addition, these programs generally cost money. It's possible to spend quite a lot and not see a vast improvement. However, the choice is yours. ▲

< 399 >

VRML

If the plug-ins mentioned in the previous section on web multimedia just weren't enough, try CosmoPlayer **http://cosmosoftware.com** which lets you explore computer-generated 3D worlds via your browser (Internet Explorer users could also use the VRML ActiveX control). The letters stand for Virtual Reality Modelling Language – a text-based programming language developed in 1994 that is used to create online 3D worlds. You may remember that Virtual Reality – a sort of three-dimensional, computer-generated world users were able to enter and interact with, courtesy of

Read about it online – VRML

If you want to see some of the more interesting VRML worlds currently online, you could do worse than wander round the galleries section of the Cosmo Software site **http://cosmosoftware.com/galleries**. Fairly typical of what's on offer is CNN's virtual 3D trip round the International Space Station. Load up with the right plug-in and you'll get a computer-generated preview of the latest giant leap for mankind at **http://www.cnn.com/SPECIALS/multimedia/vrml/iss/**. Self-styled technopagan Mark Pesce was one of the co-creators of VRML. His vast web site contains some interesting thoughts on online virtual worlds (and lots of wackier stuff as well). Look out for a link to a history of VRML's development, entitled 'The Great Leap Downward' and written for the online mag Feed **http://www.hyperreal.org/~mpesce/**. ▲

< 400 >

goggles and gloves, was the big techno-buzz before the net took over. It's still much hyped by adherents but it has to be said that VRML worlds don't quite match up to the ecstatic visions of the VR hypesters. They're still fun to mess around with, but you do need a powerful computer, with plenty of processing speed and a fast net connection. Otherwise, pointing and clicking through a world that is supposed to be in three seamless dimensions resembles one of those comic flick books with half the pages removed. You also have to wait a while for the worlds to download before you can do anything. When you do enter one, you'll generally see a little menu of commands which you click to walk or fly around. Often VRML is used to create worlds that are product demos ('Walk through your new kitchen!') or 'you are there' educational spectacles which take you through the last space flight to Mars. It's fair to say that VRML has yet to find the killer app that convinces ordinary people to do more than play with it once. ▲

Internet telephony and videoconferencing

Internet telephony sounds as if it should have no problem taking off with ordinary people. In theory, it gives you the chance to use the net to make long-distance international calls, for which you are charged at local rate. As a result, when net telephony first appeared there were suggestions that the big telephone companies might try to block its development, but more

< 401 >

Read about it online – Internet Telephony

For a good introduction and how to use the various software packages, try the Computer Telephony Depot at **http://www.ctdepot.com**. ▲

recently they seem to have accepted its inevitability and are now trying to get involved in the process of setting standards. When net telephony programs first appeared, they were little more than geek indulgences. Call quality was bad and both people had to use the same software before they could communicate. Most of those who did try it at first were nerds trying to put one over on the hated telephone companies.

More recently, net telephony has improved somewhat. Aside from talking to someone, you can send files back and forth and much else. More importantly, you can use net telephony software to call normal telephones, which increases their usefulness at a stroke. To try it out, you need a computer with a decent full-duplex soundcard (full-duplex means that you and the person you're calling will both be able to talk at the same time,

Tips – PowWow

For a multi-purpose free communications client, try PowWow **http://www.tribal.com**, which handles basic chat as well as telephone calls and sends pictures and files, amongst many other things. ▲

< 402 >

rather than waiting, walkie-talkie style, for one person to finish and say 'Over'), a microphone and speakers. When it comes to software, the market pioneer and still one of the leading players is Vocaltec's Internet Phone **http://www.vocaltec.com**. The current version is especially worthwhile because it allows net-to-telephone calls. A good alternative to Internet Phone is Web Phone **http://www.netspeak.com**.

The full download of Internet Explorer includes NetMeeting, Microsoft's voice/video communications software. You can use it to make telephone calls, but it's really a prototype business tool, designed to allow videoconferencing. Some techno-gurus see this as the next logical step

---

Read about it online – NetMeeting

Thanks to Microsoft's giveaway marketing strategy, NetMeeting has become very popular. For links to the various cultures it has spawned around the world, try NetMeeting Place at **http://www.netmeet.net**. A word of warning: although it's sold as a business thing, video-conferencing is used by plenty of people for video sex chat and much else. If you give the wrong signals, especially if you're a woman, you may find your videoconferencee dropping his pants and showing you what he's got. As ever, women should be aware of the potential for hassle and choose screen names accordingly. *Salon Magazine* ran an interesting story on NetMeeting's sexual circuits recently **http://www.salonmagazine.com/21st/feature/1998/07/cov_21 feature.html**. ▲

< 403 >

from Internet telephony. Certainly, if you've ever dreamed of having a videophone, then this, for the moment, is the closest you'll get. The sound is crackly and the visuals very stiff and jerky, but they do turn up on your screen at the same time. For videoconferencing, you will need a high-powered computer and a fast connection, with soundcard, microphone, speakers and camera, so it's not really for everyone yet. Since NetMeeting is free, you may as well get it and mess around with it. However, there are plenty of other video-conferencing programs you could try. Developed at Cornell University, CU-SeeMe was the first one to appear and it's still going strong. The commercial version is available at **http://www.wpine.com**. Alternatively, try iVisit, yet another video-conferencing package, at **http://www.ivisit.com**. ▲

● ●

Push

Push was hyped like crazy two years ago as the next big thing. The idea is that instead of going online and choosing to 'pull down' certain documents, net users sign up to channels and information is 'pushed' at them at regular intervals. Net purists/theorists didn't like push much when it was first hyped because it seemed to impose models and metaphors from television on to the net. Net sceptics delighted in pointing out that the new thing had been around for a while in the form of mailing lists (aka retro-push).

< 404 >

Read about it online - Push

One of the great champions of Push was Wired magazine. Where they lead, left-leaning intellectuals inevitably follow, brandishing critiques and taking pot shots. One of the best attacks on Push (and Wired's hyping of it) came from Dutch theorist Geert Lovink. Read it in the archives of Rewired at **http://www.rewired.com/97/0303.html**. ▲

Push hasn't really caught on with ordinary net users, mainly because it doesn't work that well. All the TV-style channel imagery may suggest it's something designed to appeal to mainstream home users, but push is yet another net thing best left to business. For it to work properly, you have to be connected all the time and you need to be in the market for regular info-updates. By the by, it's unclear whether even the info-blips and drips pushed at business users constitute what the jargonauts call 'mission critical information' or whether they just turn into so much newzak cluttering up your computer screen.

All this is one way of saying that push is really still a toy for Power Users. If you want to find out more, go to the sites maintained by two of the companies behind it – Pointcast **http://www.pointcast.com** and Marimba **http://www.marimba.com**. Alternatively, both Microsoft (with its channels) and Netscape (with Netcaster) included push programs in version 4 of their browsers. You can start up Netscape's Netcaster via the Communicator menu. If you didn't get the complete version of Communicator, download it via **Software Updates** on the Communicator

< 405 >

menu. When it loads, you'll see a Netcaster window on the right of the screen. (Click the little tab to hide the window.) The bulk of the Netcaster window is taken up with **Channel Finder,** a list of various channels, provided by the likes of Wired and ABC News, aimed at business and home users. Below are various self-explanatory toolbars. You then have to subscribe to various channels and choose when to get updates. Netscape seem to have acknowledged that push isn't quite ready for the mass market - it didn't include Netcaster in the update on Communicator (4.5) which appeared just as this book was going to press. Certainly, Netcaster does need a fair amount of memory to run properly. Otherwise it can be hugely frustrating.

Despite some rumours, Microsoft insists it is still committed to push and its channels. To try them out, click the **Channels** button on the Internet Explorer toolbar and a list of Microsoft's channels (provided by the likes of *Vogue*, the *BBC*, the *FT* and *New Scientist*) will open in a browser bar. Click on one to subscribe. You'll then be walked through the subscription process and will have to specify how often you want updates. You can add your own sites to the channel list. Visit the site in question, choose to make it a **Favourite,** click the **Create** button and put it in the **Channels** folder. If you try the BBC channel, you may notice that you're given the chance to add something called the **Companion** – a little window featuring news headlines, weather info and the like – to your desktop. If you're running Windows 95, before you can do this you need to install Active Desktop. ▲

< 406 >

The Active Desktop

When Internet Explorer 4.X first came out (in autumn 1997), it picked up a lot of flak, mainly because of Active Desktop. At the time, it was intended as a preview of the way Windows 98 would integrate the net into your computer desktop and let you move 'seamlessly' between the two. People tend not to like it when you change their computers without really warning them – hence the general outrage. Windows 98 has now made 'web integration' more stable. If that's what you want, it's your best bet. However, any power users still running Windows 95 can get a preview from Active Desktop. However, you do need a fair amount of RAM for it to run properly (admittedly that probably isn't going to be an issue for power users).

Once installed, Active Desktop puts a browser-like interface on many of the files and apps on your computer. You can set it so that you access files the way you would on a web page. Rather than clicking to select something and double-clicking to open it, you move the cursor over a file to select it and click once to open it.

If you don't like this, you can change it or customise it by right-clicking on an empty space on the desktop and working with the mouse menu that appears. Active Desktop also adds a few things to the **Start** menu and the taskbar at the bottom of the desktop – all fairly self-explanatory. You'll also notice a menu of Microsoft Channels. If you (a) don't use channels much and (b) don't want any more corporate logos on your desktop than is absolutely necessary, you can get rid of this. Right-

< 407 >

click on an empty part of your desktop, select **Customise my desktop** then click the **Web** tab and remove the tick next to **Internet Explorer Channel Bar**. The latter is a desktop component. You can add others, like the BBC companion. Just click the link and follow directions on the BBC channel. Then you'll have a little window on your desktop which, if you're connected, will flash news headlines at you while you're using your word processor. It's fun, sort of, but potentially costly. ▲

• •

Accelerators, Search Agents and Offline Browsers

Hanging around is one of the thing that bugs Power Users the most. They tot up all those seconds and minutes spent twiddling thumbs whilst a particular page downloads and conclude angrily that they're losing three hours a week to the World Wide Wait. Hence the market for programs known as accelerators. These claim to speed up your browsing drastically, usually by retrieving links to pages before you've clicked on them. That way, when you do decide to click a link, it's already there on your computer and loads really quickly. Most now use something called 'intelligent caching', which means that the program checks on the pages in your cache and gets updates so that if you decide to access them you'll get them a lot quicker too. Take all the meaningless claims about twentyfold

< 408 >

Read about it online – Intelligent Agents

Not everyone on the net thinks that intelligent agents will necessarily be a good thing, even if they ever work properly. Cyber-celebrity Jaron Lanier (he was involved in the first wave of VR hype) has written some interesting rants against the whole agent idea. Try Agents of Alienation on his homepage at **http://www.well.com/user/jaron/agentalien.html**. For the alternative view, try Intelligent Software by Patti Maes at **http://pattie.www.media.mit.edu/people/pattie/SciAm-95.html**. ▲

---

increases in browsing speed with a pinch of salt. For accelerators to work, you have to be someone who reads a lot while online, rather than scanning quickly to find links you need, clicking them and then reading when you're offline. But some of these programs are very good and contain useful search features too. The best at the moment is probably Surf Express **http://www.connectix.com**, though PeakJet **http://www.peak.com** and Net Sonic **http://www.web3000.com** are both good too.

Intelligent agents are another online fantasy. Ultimate techno-guru Nicholas Negroponte started the ball rolling in his book *Being Digital*, when he went on about agents that would learn about your informational likes and dislikes and hence would get the stuff you wanted from the net unprompted. The kind of imagery he used was rather strange – he talked about having a kind of digital butler to take care of your informational needs – and suggested that this was an odd upgrade of that old fifties

< 409 >

futurist fantasy about robo-butlers serving us cocktails on the space-station veranda. That hasn't happened yet. And it's fair to say that agents, as Negroponte describes them, are still a way off. There are products on the market – try Autonomy's Agent Suite **http://www.agentware.com** – which will do searches for you while you're off doing something else and will also (another great techo-fantasy) assemble an individual newspaper according to your preferences.

How does Autonomy's software know your preferences? You have to train it. The more you use your agent, the more it learns about you and the information you like and the better it gets at finding that information. There's some serious technology in the Agent Suite, though that means it's perhaps not necessarily the best bet for the home user just trying things out. Instead home users could try the various programs which claim to be agents, but aren't really. There are any number of programs around which say they will speed up your searches and make them more efficient by searching several engines all at once. Try Copernic **http://www. copernic.com** and Zurf Rider **http://www.zurf.com**. More interestingly, Alexa attempts to add 'smartness' to your browsing by tracking the sites

Read about it online – Alexa

For one of the more enthusiastic responses to Alexa, plus some interesting links, try Steven Johnson's The Alexa Effect at Feed – **http://www.feedmag.com/html/feedline/98.06johnson/98.06 johnson_master.html**. ▲

< 410 >

you visit and suggesting some you might also like: these sites are selected by analysing a database of other Alexa users and the places they chose to go **http://www.alexa.com**. The very latest versions of Netscape's Navigator include Alexa's technology.

Alexa has been received enthusiastically by some people on the net who have dusted off all those 'power to the people' arguments that were in fashion a while back. The suggestion is that, by pooling the collective wisdom of different users to build a database of recommendations, Alexa is helping people avoid the big corporate search engines and mass-market directories, that because it is a guide that travels with you, it is more suited to the net than the new big portal web sites that attempt to keep you in one place (reading advertising). You can see why people like Alexa, though the recommendation feature has a way to go yet. However, it is definitely worth playing with. Most interestingly, Alexa will let you view pages that have been taken down from the web. It's hooked up to a massive net archive. If the page you're after turns out to be missing, presumed dead, Alexa quickly searches its archive to see if it has it stored away. For more on the archive part of this project, go to **http://www.archive.org**.

We did briefly cover offline browsing a few chapters back. It probably won't come as a surprise to learn that there are lots of offline browsers that you could try out. I'm not sure if any of them quite deliver on the promises they make, but they are worth a look. Some download whole versions of sites, which are then displayed in a Windows Explorer-style window – something which lets you see a web site as a directory structure and allows you to go to the documents much more quickly. Others simply download the pages you want plus random assorted links. The pick of the bunch at

< 411 >

the moment are Anawave Web Snake **http://www.anaserve.com** and NetAttache Pro **http://www.tympani.com**. Web Whacker **http://www. bluesquirrel.com** and Secret Agent **http://www.ariel.co.uk** are also worth a look. Finally, here's a few programs that are either fun or useful and don't quite fit into any particular category. Internet Explorer users should probably download PowerToys, a collection of tweaks and gizmos which, amongst other things, lets you change the search engines called up by the **Search** button and zoom in and out of images **http://www.microsoft.com/ ie/ie40/powertoys**. If you want a sort of Swiss army knife of a program, download Naviscope **http://www.naviscope.com** which will speed up searches, track your downloads to see how efficient they are, block cookies and a whole pile of other things. Speaking of which, online grumps who can't stand the ads, animated gifs or cookies could try Intermute – **http://www.intermute.com** – which removes ads, stops animated gifs and blocks cookies. Last of all, why not have some fun with Picture in Picture, aka PiP **http://www.katiesoft.com/pipzone.htm**, which lets you view four web sites at a time – basically it splits your browser window into four sections. Think of it as serious multi-tasking made that bit easier. ▲

< 412 >

History

There's more to net history than the list of web sites you visited in the last week. Perhaps it's should be mandatory for all would-be power users to learn about the online world and how it developed. However, this guide doesn't contain a chapter about history; not because we don't think it's important, but because we think it's too important (and interesting) to be crammed into a couple of pages. To a certain extent, the basic details of net history have entered mainstream consciousness. You may have come across the basic historical details – how the net was developed during the Cold War as part of a drive to create a message system with no central point, a system that as a result wouldn't be so vulnerable to attack. Created by a hierarchical military industrial complex obsessed with top down control, the net paradoxically advanced a different way of doing things – non-hierarchical, distributed, bottom-up. As a result it couldn't help but appeal to non-military types and, in the last ten years, it has become part of the cultural mainstream.

Thanks to the web (and browsers and multimedia and all the rest of it), the net has experienced phenomenal growth since the mid-nineties and has become the scene of an ongoing battle between big companies keen to control our access to cyberspace (and hence make lots of money). However, things are much more complex than this basic outline suggests. And one of the best places to dig into that complexity is the net itself. Unsurprisingly, there are any number of brilliant resource sites online where you can read about the net's past.

< 413 >

Bruce Sterling's Short History of the Internet –
http://www.forthnet.gr/forthnet/isoc/short.history.of.internet
A sparky account of pre-web times from the garrulous Texan cyberpunk
SF writer.

Hobbes Internet Timeline –
http://www.isoc.org/guest/zakon/Internet/History/HIT.html
Net timelines are popular online. This is one of the best – very comprehensive, with links.

Anthony Anderburg's Net Timeline –
http://www.geocities.com/~anderberg/ant/history
This one is also pretty good.

The Internet Society's Internet Histories –
http://www.isoc.org/internet-history/
Good page of links to accounts written by the main players involved in
developing the net.

Community Memory Discussion List on the History of Cyberspace –
http://memex.org/community-memory.html
The rather overwhelming web site of an excellent mailing list.

Gregory R. Gromov's Roads and Crossroads of Internet History –
http://www.internetvalley.com/intval.html
Yet another history. Worth a look.

< 414 >

A Little History of the World Wide Web –
http://www.w3.org/History.html
The official account of the history of the web, plus lots of links.

Netizens Notebook –
http://www.columbia.edu/~hauben/netbook
Web presence of Michael Hauben and Rhonda Hauben's Netizens – a
bottom-up account of the history of the net and Usenet.

Electronic Frontier Foundation –
http://www.eff.org
Homepages of the digerati pressure group. It's worth investigating the
archives here, especially if you want to look into some of the recent battles
over online privacy and censorship.

If all this isn't enough, search on Yahoo for more Internet history sites.
And go to the Further Reading section, because there are lots of good
books on the subject too. ▲

●●

Do It Yourself

Once you've spent a while sampling the delights of the online world, you
may get the itch to have a go yourself. Looking at some web pages, it's
hard not to come away with the idea that you could do something better.

< 415 >

You probably could. But can you keep it up every week, week in, week out? Are you willing to spend the time learning how to add all the new multimedia features your web page is supposed to have to compete with everyone else's? Are you ready to spend money on web-publishing software? If you really are a Power User, you're probably already desperate to get out and spend some more money on another high-tech toy. However, non-Power Users shouldn't think that taking a more active role online is best left to those who want to spend every waking hour in front of their computer screens. Web gurus say that you need to update your homepage constantly to keep it fresh. But if all you want to do is have a bit of fun putting up something your friends can check out, you can safely ignore them. And the beauty of the web is that, if you're prepared to forgo the high-tech tricknology, it's pretty easy to put up a simple page and then forget about it. It's also relatively easy to set up mailing lists and create alt newsgroups. However, remember that turning these into thriving enterprises will take a lot of effort. ▲

Starting your own mailing list

If you're a frustrated writer, zine publisher or small businessman, a one-way mailing list is a good alternative to the web for getting your thoughts (or product information) out to the rest of the world. The idea is to get a

< 416 >

list of (willing) subscribers and send regular updates to their mailboxes; sending your email newsletter to people you merely *think* might be interested shifts you into the territory of the spammer. You'll need software to automate subscriptions and the like. Getting that to work is relatively easy. The hard thing is publicising your list so that people know it exists and want to subscribe, then keeping up the flow of regular bulletins. A one-way mailing list as part of a general web page can be a great way for businesses to build customer interest and loyalty – as long as it steers clear of spam. Two-way mailing lists (in which subscribers can contribute) are a bit more complicated. You don't just need to know how to work a mailing list program; you need people skills. You need to manage disputes, steer discussions without appearing to censor and generally keep things on track. If your list becomes popular, you'll need to provide digests for people who don't want the full thing. It can take up a lot of time.

If you do want to start a mailing list, first figure out what sort you want to do. Check with your ISP to see if they can host it for you. Then you'll need some software. Listserv is available at **http://www.lsoft.com**; there's an excellent manual here which, aside from technical details, gives you a good idea of the problems you might encounter running a mailing list. The other big mailing list program, Majordomo, is available from **http://www.greatcircle.com/majordomo/**. Check out the Majordomo FAQ for technical help. ▲

< 417 >

Starting a usenet newsgroup

If you really do want to start a newsgroup, there's an easy and a hard way to do it. You can start an alt group. That's the easy way. Alternatively, you can start an official Usenet group, with one of the officially sanctioned hierarchies (**soc**, **rec** and the like). That's the hard way. Trawling through the newsgroups trying to make some sense of it all may be hard work but it's nothing compared to the hassle involved in setting up a 'proper' newsgroup. At least, that's what some people say. Usenet may seem like lawless chaos, but it actually has very rigid rules and people who (perhaps because they can't find much to read in the newsgroups) spend all their time arguing over how to interpret them. Perhaps that's a bit unfair, but it is a lengthy process. You will need to get together enough would-be subscribers to prove that there is interest in your group. You'll need to get the name right and put it in the right hierarchy. Then it has to be approved, announced and voted on. For more on how to do it, go to the UK Usenet homepage at **http://www.usenet.org.uk**. As previously noted the alt hierarchy was set up in protest at attempts by the Usenet powers-that-be to block newsgroups devoted to sex and drugs. As a result, creating an alt group is pretty easy. To find out how to do it, try So You Want to Create an Alt Newsgroup at **http://www.cis.ohio-state.edu/~barr/alt-creation-guide.html**. ▲

< 418 >

Creating your own web page

It's a safe bet that most people who get on the net won't try their hand at starting their own mailing list or newsgroup. That isn't the case with web sites. More and more net users are taking the time to set up their own homepages. It's becoming a pretty easy thing to do. HTML – the language used to format web pages – isn't that hard to learn, but now there are plenty of web publishing software packages which make the whole process as easy as creating word-processor documents. It's easy to get free space for your page – either on your ISP's site or on one of the web communities like Geocities, which will also give you plenty of help with page design and supply templates and the like. If you want to put lots of pictures up, you will need a scanner of some sort. And if you want to do some sort of cutting-edge multimedia extravaganza, you will have to learn some more complex programming (or buy some fairly expensive software). But if you just want to share your thoughts on *The X Files* with the world, you probably have the software you need already and won't need to do that much swotting. Most of the information you need is online. Rather than get into detailed description and advice, the next few sections aim to point you to the information you need.

HTML Basics

As mentioned above, HTML is the language used to create web pages. Basically, it's a set of text commands – known as tags – which determine the

< 419 >

way a document is laid out, the line spacing, placement of images, links to other documents and much else. When a document written in HTML is viewed by a browser, you just see the content the way the designer intended. If you were to open the same document in a text editor, you would see all the tags around the basic content. Actually, you can view the HTML code for any web page you're browsing. In Internet Explorer, select the **View** menu, then **Source**. In Navigator, select the **View** menu then **Page Source**. As you'll see, tags are enclosed by < and >. You may also notice that they generally come in pairs – an opening and closing tag. The closing tag usually features a forward slash, as in </BOLD>. Looking at the source code of web pages can give you a few clues about how to use HTML. However, there are several useful interactive tutorials online which let you mess around with tags and see what they do. For example, try HTML?, a good but basic introduction at **http://www.publib.nf.ca/CAP/west/ CornerBrook/tutorial/index.html** or HTML for the Rest of Us at **http://www. geocities.com/SiliconValley/Lakes/3933/frame.htm**. HotWired does a good introductory tutorial on its web developer site WebMonkey – go to **http:// www.hotwired.com/webmonkey/teachingtool/**. Once you feel like you're getting the basics, go to the NCSA's Beginner's Guide to HTML for some more in depth information – **http://www.ncsa.uiuc.edu/General/Internet/WWW/ HTMLPrimerP1.html**. For a good general introduction to web page design, try Jonny's HTML Headquarters at **http://webhelp.org**.

HTML Editors

Some would argue that beginners don't need to bother with learning HTML at all. There are plenty of WYSIWYG programs (as in 'what you

< 420 >

see is what you get') which will let you design web pages without ever having to expose yourself to any kind of techno gobbledegook. Professional designers argue that you shouldn't rely on these editors because they don't create 'clean' HTML and you will in the end have to go in and sort out the mistakes they introduce. However, this isn't really going to be an issue for ordinary users: they could get by with the latest version of Word, Microsoft's word processing package, which features web page templates you can adapt to your own purposes. It will also let you create documents the way you would normally, then save them as HTML. If you don't have a new version of Word, you should have received something you can use when you downloaded your browser. Internet Explorer comes with Front Page Express. Netscape's Communicator suite features a program called Composer. Both are fine if you're just starting out. There are plenty of other HTML editors/web publishing packages you could try out – Hot Dog Pro **http://www.sausage.com**; Hot Metal Pro **http://www.soft quad.co.uk**; Page Mill **http://www.adobe.com**. Mac users could try BBEdit

Read about it online – Web Design

There are plenty of sites that specialise in advice for professional web designers. Even if you aren't that serious, they can be good places to go to find out what's new and pick up tips. Try HotWired's WebMonkey **http://www.hotwired.com/webmonkey/**, CNet's Builder.com **http://www.builder.com** or Website Garage **http://www.websitegarage.com**. ▲

< 421 >

http://www.barebones.com. When it comes to creating and formatting the visual content of your page (the graphics should be saved as gifs and any photos as jpegs), you could do a lot worse than Paint Shop Pro **http://www. jasc.com**. If you want to see what the professionals use for their flashy sites, go to **http://www.macromedia.com** and look for the links to their web creation package, Dreamweaver.

Some General Advice

Mastering the technology isn't the only problem you'll face when creating your own page. Even if you're just doing something for fun, you do need to think about design. After all, you want people to enjoy your page. And good web design isn't just about aesthetics. You also need to think about how people are going to be viewing your page. That big graphic file may look like the perfect way to open your site, but if it takes several minutes to download no one's going to hang around to see the rest of your site. So think about design, who your page is for and how they'll be accessing it. You can get some advice on web style at **http://www.higfive.com**. Alternatively, just look at the source of pages you particularly like. Some people suggest you help yourself to HTML that you particularly like the look of. In theory, this isn't that big a deal for amateurs. However, there have been cases recently in which professional designers plundered huge chunks of code from others without crediting them. Even if you aren't in it for the money, there is something a bit cheesy about just helping yourself to someone else's hard work. Look and learn by all means. But try to adapt what you find. Some people even suggest that a good way to learn about web design is to look at bad web pages, although what constitutes

< 422 >

a badly designed web page is still open to argument. Decide for yourself and try a site like Web Pages That Suck at **http://www.webpages thatsuck.com**. If you're doing your page as part of a business, you need to devote some serious thought to the project. You can't just put up a page and expect it to start boosting your profits. You need to figure what you want a site to do: is it going to be marketing/PR-based or a transactional site where you'll actually sell things. You'll need to make sure it's integrated with the rest of your business literature/communications. You'll need to keep it well maintained and updated. You'll need to publicise it. In the end, you may decide that you need to get a professional in to do it for you. However, it's always worth learning a bit about HTML and design: at least you'll have a bit more of an idea about what you're paying for.

Publishing and Publicising Your Page

Once you've laid out your masterwork, you need to upload it to your ISP's server or to the site that will be hosting your page. Get in touch with your ISP to find out exactly how to do this. In fact, it's worth talking to them about your page in general. Though all the ISPs now offer free space for web pages, they have lots of little rules that may come into effect if, for example, your page turns out to be either controversial or incredibly popular. Once your page is up, you'll need to make sure the world knows about it. You can visit the sites of the major search engines and submit the details of your page. This can be time-consuming. There are sites which will let you submit the details to all the engines at once – try Submit It **http://www.submit-it.com**. You can also send details to newsgroups or

< 423 >

mailing lists if the site is particularly relevant. But be wary of sending anything that resembles spam. You don't want your site to be taken down by anti-spam activists in its first week. If your site is about a popular topic, you could try joining the web ring devoted to that subject – for more on web rings, go back to the section on search engines on page 144. If you create links on your page to your favourite sites, you can always get in touch with them and see if they'll put in a link to your page. If they do, it might drive a bit of traffic your way. You can also add design touches to your page so that it can be easily identified by search engines – the meta tags discussed in the section on search engines. Remember that abusing meta tags for a few extra visits is bad netiquette. People are unlikely to enjoy your page if they're conned into visiting it. Of course, the easiest way to get traffic is to do something controversial then alert the newspapers so they can run one of their Internuts stories, but if you don't agree that all publicity is good publicity, you might prefer to rely on gradually building word of mouth.

< 424 >

Next Step

You should now know how the net works. It's up to you what you do with it. Have fun. Here's one last tip to be going on with. There's a lot of rubbish talked about net addiction, but there's so much information online, it's easy to get into a 'wood for the trees' situation, visit loads of web sites without actually paying any real attention to any of them, do a vast amount of research and never get round to your actual project, and confuse a vast amount of apparently relevant information with knowledge and wisdom. So take it easy: more information isn't always better. And remember – there is a real world out there. Sometimes the best thing you can do with the net is log off. ▲

< 425 >

FURTHER READING

● ●

The thing about the net is that there's always something new to get your head round. So all books about the net look slightly out of date a few months after they're published. However, if you want to find out what's new online, you could do a lot worse than read the *Guardian*'s Online supplement (it comes out on Thursdays). You can access it on the web via the main *Guardian* site at **http://www.guardianunlimited.co.uk**. The *Daily Telegraph* also does a good computer supplement – called Connected – also out on Thursdays. Again, you can also read it online at the *Telegraph* web site at **http://www.telegraph.co.uk**. It's also worth reading John Naughton's Internet column in the *Observer*'s Review section. The *Independent*'s Network section on Mondays is usually worth a look. Find it on the web at **http://www.independent.co.uk**. Marek Kohn's Technofile column in the *Independent on Sunday*'s Review supplement is always worthwhile – a version is available online at **http://www. poptel.org.uk/technofile**. The *Sunday Times*' Innovation section is also worth reading – it's usually in the Business supplement – again, you can look for it online at **http://www.sundaytimes. co.uk**. Both Future Publishing's *.net* magazine **http://www.netmag. co.uk** and

< 427 >

Emap's *Internet* magazine **http://www.internet-magazine.com** are good places for features on new developments online. As mentioned before, they're also a good source of software via their cover discs.

Of course, if you really want to stay up to speed with changes online, the best place to go is the net itself. Try Cnet **http://www.news.com**, Wired News **http://www.wired.com** and the 21st section at Salon **http://www. salon magazine.com**. Also worth a look is Feed magazine, which specialises in more reflective pieces about general net trends **http://www.feedmag. com**. If you want more technical information, try the weekly geek newsletter Need to Know **http://www.ntk.net** or Slashdot **http://www.slashdot.org**.

OK, so a few books about the net are often out of date by the time they reach the bookshops. But there are lots of titles which will help you explore further some of the issues raised in this book. In particular, there are now some good books around about the history of the net and computer culture in general. It can also be interesting to look back at some of the more hype-addicted net books from a few years ago. Here's a list of a few you might find useful.

Barbarians led by Bill Gates, Jennifer Edstrom and Martin Eller
(Henry Holt)
An account of the way Microsoft works, up to its recent efforts in the browser wars, written by an ex-Microserf and the daughter of a Microsoft employee. Interesting and occasionally funny, if a little rushed.

< 428 >

Being Digital, Nicholas Negroponte (Hodder & Stoughton)
The ur-text of net hype. Interesting reflections on the digitisation of everything, worked into a rather airy grand statement shot through with slightly bizarre fantasies about info-butlers and the like.

Bots, Andrew Leonard (Hardwired Books)
An excellent look at the growing use of automated software programs – aka bots – to perform various functions online. Works as a fragmentary history of recent events on the net too

Burn Rate, Michael Wolff (Weidenfeld & Nicolson)
A rip-roaringly partial account of the mid-nineties web biz. Wolff thought the net was going to make him rich, started various businesses then crashed and burned when the bubble burst. This pokes fun at everyone involved (though Wolff lets himself off rather lightly).

Close to the Machine, Ellen Ullman (City Lights Books)
Not strictly about the net but too good to leave out. Ullman is a programmer who thinks a lot about what she and people like her are doing to the world. Brilliant insights on programming life and the fascinations of computer systems, along with some caustic reflections on the net and browsers.

< 429 >

Cyberville, Stacey Horn (Warner Books)
Horn runs the New York-based virtual community Echo and this is an account of how she has managed to build it up into a thriving digital meeting place for upscale New Yorkers. Great stories – something of an antidote to the Howard Rheingold title below.

Data Smog, David Schenk (Abacus)
There are loads of neo-Luddite rants about the awfulness of the net. This isn't one of them, just a well-argued, critical look at information overload, complete with a few strategies for keeping it in check.

Deeper, John Seabrook (Faber & Faber)
Seabrook received a lot of flak online (often, it seems, for being the *New Yorker*'s man on the net). But this story of his infatuation with the net and search to find a home there – a vaguely melancholy pioneer's tale – is well written and thoughtful.

Escape Velocity, Mark Dery (Hodder & Stoughton)
Excellent acerbic look at the nineties cyberculture – the hype surrounding *Wired* magazine, virtual reality, the net and 'post-humanism' – from a wonderfully wordy American critic.

Hackers, Steven Levy (Penguin)
A look at the early history and culture of hacking – not a book which deals in silly scare stories.

< 430 >

Hard, Soft and Wet, Melanie McGrath (HarperCollins)
One British woman's journey into the net and the American idea of the future. Clever and insightful, this is ostensibly about children and technology but really documents McGrath's gradual disillusion with the net.

Interface Culture, Steven Johnson (HarperEdge)
Johnson is the editor of Feed, one of the better web zines. These are his thoughts on the role of computer interfaces in modern life – everything from the desktop metaphor to the web browser – tied to a suggestion that we need an 'interface underground' to produce something more experimental (and perhaps ultimately better) than the standard desktop windows.

Islands in the Net, Bruce Sterling (Ace Books)
Along with William Gibson, Bruce Sterling did the most to establish the gritty, street-smart strain of SF known as cyberpunk. This 1988 novel is a still interesting attempt to imagine what a globally networked future of info-trading might be like.

Life on the Screen, Sherry Turkle (Weidenfeld & Nicolson)
An extended look at the identity games people play on line – in chat rooms, MUDs and elsewhere – seen from an psychoanalytical/sociological perspective.

< 431 >

The Media Lab, Stewart Brand (Penguin)
One of the starting points for net hype. A journalistic trip round the MIT Media Lab in the mid to late eighties, rounded off with more general thoughts on the coming global networks – interesting as a historical artefact

My Tiny Life, Julian Dibbell (Fourth Estate)
Interesting account of life in LambdaMOO, one of the most famous MUDs currently up and running. Dibbell wrote the famous journalistic account of a 'rape' that took place in LambdaMOO and its effects on the community. Here, that becomes the starting point for a thoughtful meditation on the consequences of creating alternative identities on the net

net.wars, Wendy Grossman (New York University Press)
Excellent history of some of the recent conflicts over the net – everything from the hassles over spam to the online war between Scientology and its critics.

Netizens, Michael Hauben and Rhonda Hauben
(IEEE Computer Society Press)
Bottom-up history of Usenet and the net (along with a few speculations on the future), which began life online and is now in book form.

Neuromancer, William Gibson (HarperCollins)
Gibson changed SF with this gritty noir-influenced piece of futuristic crime writing, first published in 1984. He also came up with the term 'cyberspace' and his vision of a three-dimensional transnational datascape that exists beyond the computer screen has proved massively influential

< 432 >

with both techno-entrepeneurs (who tend to ignore the irony and critical edge in his books) and ordinary net users.

Out of Control, Kevin Kelly (Fourth Estate)
A look at the way the lines between nature and machines are becoming blurred, with several sections on the 'organic' nature of the net. One of the key texts of mid-nineties net hype.

Protecting Yourself Online, Robert Gelman with Stanton McCandlish (HarperEdge)
A manual produced by the Electronic Frontier Foundation, which pushes its soft libertarian line and is fairly American in focus but still pretty useful. Look for an online edition on the EFF site **http://www.eff.org**.

Release 1.0 , Esther Dyson (Viking)
Being Digital Part 2, sort of, though not as hype-y and optimistic as that might suggest, from sometime *Guardian* columnist Dyson who tends to be described as the Queen of the Digerati (she's one of the few high profile women in that particular boys' club)

Sex, Lies and Cyberspace, Jonathan Wallace and Mark Mangan (Owl Books)
Useful American journalistic history of recent legal disputes concerning the net, which covers the controversy over the Clipper chip – the US Government's attempt to introduce an encryption standard – the Communications Decency Act and much else.

< 433 >

Snow Crash, Neil Stephenson (Penguin)
When it was published in 1992, Stephenson's novel about an information virus replaced Gibson on the desktops of netheads and the tech-biz community, thanks to its vision of the Metaverse/The Street, a kind of 3D space on the net where people interacted via realistic physical representations known as 'avatars'.

Speeding the Net, Joshua Quittner and Michelle Slatalla
(Atlantic Monthly Press)
Another hit-and-run history of the browser wars, this time written from the perspective of Netscape. Nicely written and informative, this still feels a little incomplete – even though it only came out in 1998.

Techgnosis, Erik Davis (Harmony Books)
Davis sets out to look at the various spiritual hopes and fears people have projected onto communications/information technology. The end result is a fascinatingly dense tome which covers everything from early ideas of electricity as diving life force to modern day visions of the net as a global mind.

The Virtual Community, Howard Rheingold (Secker & Warburg)
One of the first books to talk up the community-building potential of the net. Obviously a bit dated now – not least in its optimistic view of technological potential – but still interesting.

< 434 >

Webonomics, Evan Schwartz (Penguin)

There are shelves and shelves of net business titles, all promising to help you and your company make millions online. This is a more sober account of business online and the new economy supposedly taking shape on the net. A bit dated – even though it only came out in 1997 – but still useful.

Where Wizards Stay Up Late, Katie Hafner and Matthew Lyon
(Simon & Schuster)

A good attempt to write a considered history of the early development of the Internet in the sixties and seventies. A little dry, but still valuable. Now we need someone to write a decent history of the development of the web.

Zeroes and Ones, Sadie Plant (Fourth Estate)

Out-there mix of theory and science fiction from Britain's premier techno-theorist which looks at women's involvement in computers over history and argues that they are more suited to the coming networked world than men.

< 435 >

INTERNET SERVICE PROVIDERS AND ONLINE SERVICES

• •

There are now hundreds of internet service providers in the UK alone, but the field is dominated by several big names who are getting better and better and providing a decent service. Here are the contact details of a few of the bigger players. However, remember to give local ISPs a chance. They may do a better job of supplying your area than the bigger companies. For a complete rundown of UK ISPs, try the specialist monthly magazines on the net – *Internet* magazine is particularly good here, though *.net* is also worth a look. ▲

• •

Online Services

AOL 0800 279 1234 – **http://www.uk.aol.co.uk**
Compuserve 0990 000200 – **http://www.compuserve.com**
LineOne 0345 777464 – **http://www.lineone.net**
MSN 0345 002000 – **http://www.msn.co.uk**
Which Online 0645 830240 – **http://www.which.net**

< 437 >

Internet Service Providers

BT Internet 0800 800001 – **http://www.btinternet.com**
Cable and Wireless Internet 0500 200980 – **http://www.cwcom.co.uk**
CIX 0181 255 5111 – **http://www.cix.co.uk**
ClaraNET 0171 903 3000 – **http://www.clara.net**
Demon Internet 0181 371 1234 – **http://www.demon.net**
Direct Connection 0800 072 0000 – **http://www.dircon.net**
EasyNet 0541 594321 – **http://www.easynet.net**
Global Internet 0870 909 8041 – **http://www.global.net.uk**
Netcom 0800 980 9107 – **http://www.netcom.net.uk**
NetDirect Internet 0800 731 3311 – **http://www.netdirect.net.uk**
Onyx 0345 715715 – **http://www.onyxnet.co.uk**
Poptel 0171 923 9465 – **http://www.poptel.org.uk**
Prestel Online 0990 223300 – **http://www.prestel.co.uk**
Sonnet Internet 0171 891 2000 – **http://www.sonnet.co.uk**
UUNET Pipex Dial 0500 567000 – **http://www.uk.uu.net**
Virgin Net 0500 558800 – **http://www.virgin.net**

< 438 >

GLOSSARY

● ●

What follows is a round-up of all the jargon definitions that appear in the main part of the book, along with a few bits of net slang thrown in for amusement. It certainly doesn't amount to a comprehensive glossary.

For that, as you might expect, the best place to go is online. Here are a few web dictionaries worth consulting if you find yourself baffled by net terminology.

PC Webopaedia – **http://www.pcwebopaedia.com**
The Jargon File – **http://www.jargon.org**
What Is – **http://www.whatis.com**
NetLingo – **http://www.netlingo.com**

There are also some good print dictionaries around. *Wired Style* (edited by Constance Hale and published by HardWired Books) is aimed at people working in the media but is an excellent introduction to techno-speak. Alternatively, the print version of jargon.org, *The New Hacker's Dictionary* (compiled by Eric Raymond and published by MIT Press) is

< 439 >

worth hunting down. *Wired* Magazine takes a perverse pleasure in generating and logging new sorts of techno jargon. It's a great place for people who take an active pleasure in net slang – the magazine refers to them as 'jargonauts'. Look for their 'Jargon Watch' – a self-styled 'pocket dictionary for the jitterati' (i.e. a collection of computer industry slang) compiled by Gareth Branwyn. (Some the more amusing terms in the following glossary were found there). Wired Magazine also recently put together an 'Encyclopaedia of the New Economy', a useful collection of terms gaining currency in the net biz. It should still be on the magazine's web site – look for a link on **http://www.wired.com/wired/current/html**.

Those seriously interested in geek speak might also want to look at The Microsoft Lexicon **http://cinepad.com/mslex.htm** – a collection of slang generated at the Seattle software company, aka Microspeak. Some of this is familiar stuff – e.g. a Code Warrior is someone who writes code – though a few entries are interesting – at Microsoft, 'dog food' is apparently software that is not fit for the public but OK for internal use.

< 440 >

A ●

Accelerators Add-on programs which aim to speed up your web browsing by retrieving all the links on a page before you actually get round to clicking one. Consequently, when you do click, the page has already been downloaded

ActiveX Control ActiveX is a programming language used to deliver multimedia via the web. A control is Microsoft's version of the plug-in, something you add to your browser so that it can handle a particular type of web multimedia. Programmers apparently refer to it as 'Captive X'

Agents The dutiful servants of the digital age. An automated, autonomous program which aims to perform various online tasks (retrieve web pages, reserve flight tickets, manage your social life for you) while you watch TV

Alpha Geek West Coast slang for the guy/girl in the office that knows the most about (and can do the most with) the computers/network

alt Usenet hierarchy used to signal groups devoted to alternative material. This has now crossed over into mainstream culture as an all-purpose label for alternative – as in alt.culture

Animated GIF Low-tech web animation technique in which several graphic images (i.e. GIFs) are loaded one after the other to create a kind of flip-book effect

< 441 >

Anonymous FTP The procedure which lets you access FTP sites and download files without having to give your real name/address

Anonymous Remailer A server/program set-up to allow anonymous email and one of the more controversial pieces of net technology. Send a message via a remailer and it will take out identifying details before sending it on to the correct address.

Applet A small program written in Java which can be placed on a web page

Archie One of the search tools of yesteryear. Used for finding files on FTP sites

ARPANET – ARPA stands for Advanced Research Projects Agency: essentially the Pentagon's R&D department during the cold war. So, as you might expect, the ARPANET was the network it set up to test out new computer communications technology.

ASCII As in American Standard Code for Information Exchange. Basically, the set of standard unformatted characters and numbers – plain text, in other words – that all computers can understand

Attachments Files, graphics, pictures, sounds, even programs that are attached to email messages and sent across the net

< 442 >

B •

Bandwidth – Network capacity: the amount of data that can be sent over a net connection. The scarce resource of digital age

Betas Test versions of software currently in development and due for eventual commercial release

Binary File A non-text file: everything from sound and images to compressed archives

Bits Used to denote units of data and not to be confused with bytes. One byte consists of eight bits (each either a 1 or a 0). Bits are the measurement used when talking about data transmission speeds – as in 56 kilobit modems. Bytes are used when talking about memory and disk space – as in a 4 gigabyte hard disk

Bot A software robot – i.e. an automated, autonomous program which performs a particular task online (from searching and logging web sites to cancelling spam on Usenet).

Bookmarks A list of the addresses of your favourite web sites set up to allow you to access them a little bit quicker. The term comes from Netscape. Microsoft calls these Favourites. Bookmark is the one that has entered the language. It's also a verb, as in 'please bookmark this site'.

< 443 >

Bounced Mail Email that doesn't reach its destination for whatever reason and is returned to the sender with an error message

Bozo Filter Typically a function on mail programs and newsreaders which lets the user block posts/mail from irritating people – also known as a kill file

Bps Bits per second

Browser The software program you use to move around the web and download and view pages

Buddy Lists Another name for the 'online pagers' (like ICQ) which keep a record of your friends, alert you when they come on to the net and let you send them an instant message

Bulletin Board Service aka **BBS** The precursors to the online services and virtual communities today. A BBS is a computer hooked up to a telephone. You dial it up directly and can upload and download files and post messages for others to read, amongst other things

< 444 >

C ●●●●●●●●●●●●●●●●●●●●●●●●●●●●●●●●●●●●●●

Cache The place where your browser stores all the files (pages and pictures) it downloads from the web. Typically Microsoft has a different word for this, but everyone calls it the cache anyway

Chat Online conversations in which participants exchange text in real time

Chatiquette An informal code of conduct for online chat, i.e. rules about what you should and shouldn't do when in a chat room

Chat Room An online space where you can chat (i.e. exchange text messages in real time) with a group of users

Client/Server Two bits of technical jargon for the price of one. Servers are central computers on which data is stored. Clients are the software programs that access data stored on a server. In a more general sense, client often means any bit of software which accesses information via a network

Clickstream The trail you leave as you move around the web. A word much used by web business types and online ad men, who place great store in analysing user clickstreams

Cobweb An old, outdated web site

< 445 >

Collaborative Filtering Search tools which work by pooling and cross-referencing recommendations from individual users. If one user likes movies X and Y and you like movie X too, the filter may suggest that you might also like movie Y

Compressed Archive One file which contains several other files which have been compressed to make them smaller and hence quicker to send around the net

Content The stuff on the web site that you actually read, look at or play

Cookie Little identifying text files which some sites place on your computer when you visit them. When you go back to a particular site, it will be able to read the cookie to tell what you did there before. It will also be able to add more information

Crossposting The practice of sending articles or posts to several Usenet newsgroups at once. If you're in the middle of a discussion and it strikes you that your contribution might be of interest to another group, you can crosspost it there. Use with discretion

Cybercafé A café complete with a few terminals where you can buy coffee and access the net for a hour or so. Very popular a few years ago, cyber-cafés will need to develop and offer something more than net access if they're to survive over the next ten years

< 446 >

Cyberspace A term first coined by SF writer William Gibson for the consensual hallucination people encountered when they logged on to computer networks. Now taken to mean the place you're in when you're on the net

Cypherpunks Skilled programmers with a libertarian bent who believe in free speech (and the free market, usually) and defend the right of individuals to use encryption technology to protect their privacy online. When they're not writing/distributing encryption programs, they compose rants about the evils of big government, its future collapse and the coming of crypto-anarchy.

D ●

Data Mining The practice of analysing huge databases of information (i.e. records of what people buy at supermarkets) to extract something useful

Dead Tree Edition Snide geek slang referring to information printed out on paper

Digerati, aka the self-styled cyber-élite. A group of software programmers, business people, theorists, gurus, old hippies, rich people and self-publicists who are bravely helping us all out by living the future now – on expenses, naturally.

< 447 >

Digital Signature A way of signing a letter – using encryption technology – which guarantees the identity of the person sending a particular electronic communication

Domain Name System Also referred to as the DNS. The net's system of addresses in which each computer on the net has a unique IP number and domain name

Domain squatting The practice of buying the rights to the online version of famous names/brands in the hope of making some money selling them back to the real-world owners

Download As with a lot of online terms, both verb and noun. If you transfer a file from a computer on the net on to your PC, you're downloading it. If it takes a long time, you can moan about the lengthy download

E ●

E-Cash Electronic Cash. A digital form of currency which will, so gurus say, revolutionize online commerce – once it works

Email Electronic Mail. Messages sent via the net

Emoticons Also known as smileys. Little faces made up of text which are intended to add emotion/tone to online communications and hence reduce the potential for misunderstanding

< 448 >

Encryption A way of encoding online communications and hence keeping them private. This can also be used to sign net messages and so guarantee the identity of the sender

Extension – as in File Extension. A group of letters, which come after the file name and identify what type of file it is

F •

FAQ Frequent Asked Questions. A file of standard queries put together by a Usenet newsgroup. New users are expected to read the FAQ before becoming involved in the group so that they don't bore the assembled sages with enquiries they've heard before

F2F Face to Face. Online slang for meetings that actually take place in the real world

Filterware A software package designed to block access to certain sites – either those that the maker of the program deems unacceptable or sites specified by the user

Flame An abusive/insulting online message often fired off in anger at some mistake or perceived slight. People often get hold of the wrong end of the stick online, get angry and send a response without engaging their brains. Which leads to flame wars – raging arguments, which can disrupt newsgroups and mailing lists

< 449 >

Frames According to some, the invention of Satan. A method of splitting web pages up into separate windows

Freeware If you believe the purists, this isn't really software you don't have to pay for. It's software that is open, software where the source code is freely available, software you can modify

FTP File Transfer Protocol, which allows you to upload or download files to and from the net

Future proofing If you want to buy a computer that isn't (supposedly) out of date next year, you need to future-proof it – i.e. buy a more expensive PC than you might normally, one with the very latest technology (most of which you won't use)

G •

GIF Graphic Interchange Format. One of the most popular formats for putting images on the web, this is typically used for graphics. Photographs are put online as JPEGs

GUI Graphical User Interface. Developed in the seventies at the Xerox PARC research lab, brought to ordinary punters in the eighties by Apple, the GUI made computers user-friendly by replacing text commands with a visual interface made up of icons, windows and the whole desktop metaphor. If you want to look like you know what you're talking about, pronounce it 'Gooey'

< 450 >

Gopher A precursor to the web – a way of storing and finding text documents on the net. Not used much these days outside the academic world

H •

Hackers In the press this has come to mean computer criminals, something which hugely upsets old-school hackers. Originally, hacker meant someone who loved programming and messing around with computers, someone able to make the old machines do all sorts of thing that weren't in the manual. People who identify with this like to dismiss younger hackers who get into headline-grabbing mischief as 'crackers'

Header The basic details about the message – what it's about, who sent it and when. They are not the message itself. You'll need to go back online for that

Helper Apps Helper Applications. Programs which can handle some of the multimedia content you find on the web. Unlike plug-ins, these remain separate from your browser

Hierarchies The thematic categories used to distinguish different Usenet newsgroups – i.e. the little suffixes that appear at the start of the group name – as in rec.football or alt.flame

Hits A crude method of measuring web traffic but a crucial tool for early web hypesters. In the early days of the web, site owners would talk about

< 451 >

the sites generating hundreds of thousands of hits, implying that that figure represented hundreds of thousands of users. It didn't. A hit is generated when a file is downloaded from a page. One page can contain lots of files. So one user viewing a couple of pages on a site could generate hundreds of hits

Homepage A homepage can be (a) the first page your browser shows when it starts; or (b) the first page of a web site. But most non-geeky types now think of a homepage as a personal web site put up by an ordinary net user to reflect their interests and obsessions

Host Another word for a computer connected to the Internet

HTML HyperText Markup Language, the computer code used to create web pages

HTML Mail Email that doesn't come in the form of plain text but is formatted using HTML

HTTP HyperText Transfer Protocol. The protocol which enables communications on the web

Hypertext A method of formatting computer text so that documents are linked to each other

< 452 >

■ ●

Identity Hacking Taking advantage of the relative anonymity of the net to pretend to be someone else

Identity Theft Stealing someone's online identity – i.e. their login names, email address and passwords

Image map Another element of web design that is often misused. A large graphic which contains links to other pages

Instant Messages see Buddy Lists, above. Short messages sent to friends who are on the net, usually with a view to setting up a real-time chat.

Interactive TV Much hyped in the early nineties before the net came along. This was supposed to be a TV set you could use to order pizza and videos and generally control when you saw certain TV shows. Some people think interactive TV was killed off by the net, but it remains the holy grail for certain big tech companies

Interface The thing that comes between you and all the zeroes and ones sitting on your computer (i.e. all those icons, folders and trash cans on the monitor) and helps you actually make use of your machine

Internet Service Provider A company that is attempting to make money by providing people with access to the net

< 453 >

Intranet A private corporate or institutional network which uses the technology and protocols of the Internet

IP (as in Internet Protocol) **address** This is a collection of four numbers, separated by full stops/periods (e.g. 123.4.56.891)

IRC Internet Relay Chat. A method for chatting in real time on the net

ISDN Stands for Integrated Services Digital Network. ISDN lines offer very fast connections to the net and can carry voice calls at the same time

J •

Java/Javascript Programming languages which, among other things, can be used to create interactive multimedia effects on the web

JPEG The letters stand for Joint Photographic Experts Group (honestly). A way of compressing and formatting photographs so that they can be displayed on the web

K •

Kill File see Bozo Filter, above

Killer App 'Killer Application' – the piece of software that works well enough to convince people that they need to spend lots of money on the

< 454 >

hardware required to run it. According to some accounts, the spreadsheet was the killer app which sold the business world on computers

Knowledge Management The term currently favoured by search engine companies trying to sell themselves as something more

L •

Link A connection between one web document and another. Click on it and you move to the linked page

Lurkers Net slang for those who hang around in newsgroups (and chat rooms), read what other people have to say but don't actually post anything themselves

M •

Mailbomb An attempt to crash a particular system by sending it a huge amount of email. Anti-spam activists often try to mailbomb known spammers

Many-to-many network One way of describing the net, which lets lots of people receive and transmit messages – unlike the TV network which is one-to-many

< 455 >

Meta Tags A way of marking a particular web page, so that search engines can more easily identify and log its content. Much misused, especially by people running porn web sites

Micropayments A form of e-cash (see above), much hyped but now seemingly unlikely to take off, the idea being that in the future people might be willing to pay a couple of pence to see a particular cartoon/ column and that struggling hacks might make a lot of money as all those nickels and dimes added up

MIME Multipurpose Internet Mail Extensions. The standard used to handle attachments to electronic messages

Mirror Site A copy of a web site that is situated on another computer in another location. Mirror sites are a way for busy sites to cope with traffic. Many big sites have mirrors in different countries. Sites that are banned are often mirrored in protest by anti-censorship activists

Modem A modem converts the digital information your computer works with into audio signals that can then be sent down a standard telephone line. Apparently the name is a compression of the technical term, Modulater Demodulater

Mouse Potato Computer culture's equivalent of the couch potato – someone who spends all night mesmerised in front of their computer screen

< 456 >

MPEG The letters stand for Moving Picture Expert Group: the standard for compressing audio and video so that they can be sent more easily across the net

MUD Multiple User Dungeons (or Dimensions or Dialogues) are chat spaces in which users have collectively talked up a whole world, with its own rules and customs. Relying simply on text, users create an alternative geography (and alternative identities) where they can play out ideas, theories and fantasies

Multimedia Basically a combination of different media forms (i.e. text, sound, video) in one integrated, interactive whole

N •

Nethead Slangy term for someone who uses the net a lot – rather out of favour now

Netiquette The net's code of conduct

Netizen An active member of the Internet community – a term much promoted by *Wired* magazine

Net Telephony Using the Internet to make cheap long-distance international telephone calls

< 457 >

Newbie Slang term for someone new to the net

Newsgroups Online forums where people discuss a variety of subjects

NNTP Network News Transfer Protocol: the protocol used to handle messages to and from newsgroups

Node Yet another term for a computer connected to a network – though strictly speaking, it can refer to any kind of device that is so hooked up

O •

Offline Browsing A way of downloading web pages so you can read them whilst offline and thus save money

Online Service An organisation which, along with supplying its customers with access to the net, also provides special content, chat rooms, conferences and many other services

Operating System The basic software running on your computer – the program that lets you use all the other programs (or applications). Most computers run Windows 95/98. Other operating systems include Unix, DOS and Linux

< 458 >

P •

Packet Switching When messages are sent via a network, they are broken up into individual packets of bits which are then sent separately. Packets contain details of the place they came from amd the address they're going to, amongst other things

Patch A small chunk of code designed to fix a bug in a larger program

PGP Pretty Good Privacy – a strong encryption program released for free online in 1991 in protest at government attempts to prohibit ordinary users' access to encryption technologies

Plug Ins Programs that you add to a browser, so that it can handle different sorts of files, specifically multimedia files, sound, video and animation

Point of Presence The place, or rather telephone number, you dial to connect to your ISP

POP3 As in POP3 mail. The letters and number stand for Post Office Protocol, version 3. This is the protocol that is used when it comes to receiving email.

Portal The big web biz buzz of the moment. Portal sites are web sites which contain all the services people are most likely to use online – free

< 459 >

email, chat rooms, conferences, homepage facilities, online shopping, search engines, directories and much else. These aren't so much gateways as destinations in themselves and as such seem counter to the free-ranging spirit of the early web

Post A message sent to a Usenet newsgroup – sometimes referred to as an article

PPP Point to Point Protocol: the protocol used to hook computers up to the net

Protocol A shared language used by computers so that they can communicate with other computers

Proxy Servers Local servers which keep copies of the most popular sites. You can set your browser to get these copies rather than going out on to the net proper.

Push A method of sending information to users via the net at regular intervals. Rather than pull down the content you want, it is pushed at you. Much hyped a couple of years ago but now considered to be something of a dud

< 460 >

Q •

QuickTime Apple's way of formatting video for viewing on computer or via the net

R •

RAM Random Access Memory. Best thought of, according to some, as your computer's short-term memory. You always need more of this stuff

RL As in Real Life: the stuff that happens away from the net

ROT13 Simple form of encryption which replaces each letter with the one thirteen steps ahead of it in the alphabet

S •

Screenager Slang term for the kind of high-tech teens who grow up surrounded by TV screens and computer monitors

Scripting Language A set of programming shortcuts which make it a little easier for programmers to create interactive routines

Search Engine Programs which let net users search for pages containing particular words

< 461 >

Shareware Software which you can test out a bit before actually buying it. Typically, evaluation copies of shareware programs are made available for free, but lack certain features or will 'time out' after a month

Sig File As in 'signature file'. A combination of name, address, contact details, amusing quotations and even ASCII art which is attached to email as a way of personalizing it

SLIP As in Serial Line Internet Protocol. The protocol which allows access to the net via a telephone line and a modem. Outdated now and replaced by PPP

Smiley see Emoticons, above

SMTP Simple Mail Transfer Protocol. The protocol used to send email

Snail Mail Snide net slang for old-fashioned mail that comes in envelopes, is delivered by the post office and takes a lot longer than email to arrive. Actually, in the past, some well-known UK ISPs have had problems with mail at particularly busy times of the year and some unlucky users found themselves waiting two weeks and longer for their email

Source The underlying version of a particular web document, a version which contains all the HTML tags which make the page look the way it does

< 462 >

Spam Net slang for unsolicited email sent in bulk to thousands of users at once, i.e. electronic junk email. It's also a verb: you can spam someone as well as get spam. The name comes from the *Monty Python* sketch and is supposed to refer to the way it keeps on coming, or something. Apparently Hormel, maker of real-world Spam, has considered taking action to prevent its product being associated with such a heinous practice

Spamdexing Misusing meta tags on a web page so that it is more likely to be rated higher by a search engine

Spoofing Creating email messages which are altered so that they look as if they were sent by someone else. Though a popular online prank (e.g. sending friends mail from **tonyb@newlabour.org**), this is also used for more malicious cons – i.e. attempts to extract passwords and the like

Spyware Software used by companies to log exactly what their employees do on the net

Standard A format approved and accepted by the computer industry as a whole. Standards serve ordinary users because they mean that products – hardware and software – produced by different companies will work with each other. Ordinary users in the past have suffered because of competing standards (cf. Apple Macs vs. Windows). It was hoped that the web would offer a bright, new, universally compatible future. We'll see

< 463 >

Streaming As in 'streaming video'. Video or audio files which you can play as you download them from the web. You don't have to wait to get the whole file before you can play it

Surfing All-purpose term used to make the business of accessing the net seem more exciting than it usually is. That's if it comes from the thing people do on boards in the sea. There is an argument that it derives from 'channel surfing' – the habit of randomly flipping through TV channels looking for something worth watching – and that as such, it isn't an accurate way to describe the activity of accessing the web

Sysop/Op/Sysadmin A System Operator is usually the person in charge of a BBS. An Op runs a channel on the IRC network. A System Administrator runs a network

T ●

TCP/IP TCP stands for Transmission Control Protocol. IP stands for Internet Protocol. Both 'protocols' (think of them as networking languages) allow your computer to communicate with the Internet

TCP/IP Stack A TCP/IP stack is several bits of software in one – TCP/IP software, packet driver software and sockets software – each of which is needed in order to send and receive data across the net

< 464 >

Telnet. A software program which lets you connect to a remote computer via the net and then use the programs on that computer

Thread The online term for an ongoing conversation taking place in a newsgroup, mailing list or conference

TLA Three-Letter Acronyms: conversational shorthand (BTW equals 'by the way') used to compress electronic messages

Top Down, Bottom Up Two related terms you hear a lot online. The former refers to authoritarian/hierarchical structures in which order (and other things) are imposed by the people at the top. The latter refers to more open grass-roots structures in which order (and other things) emerge from the actions of ordinary users and trickle up

Troll A post to a newsgroup or mailing list that is deliberately designed to wind people up and hence start a flame war

U ●

Unix The computer operating system of choice for hackers and geeks, who spend hours tinkering with its various versions

Upload The opposite of download – i.e. transferring a file from your computer to another computer in a different location

< 465 >

URL Uniform Resource Locator: the address given to computers/files on the web

Usenet The name for the network of newsgroups

Uuencode A way of encoding binary files (e.g. images) so that they can be attached to email and sent across the net. This is gradually being replaced by MIME

V •

Vaporware Slang term for sofware (or any piece of technology) that gets talked about a lot but never actually made

Virtual Community Posh name for a BBS/mailing list/newsgroup which draws a regular set of users who begin to feel part of a group

Virtual Reality A sort of three-dimensional, computer-generated world users were able to enter and interact with, courtesy of goggles and gloves, which was the big techno-buzz before the net took over

Virus A malicious program, usually hidden inside another program. When you run the main program, the virus is activated too and can damage your computer

< 466 >

VRML The letters stand for Virtual Reality Modelling Language – a text-based programming language created in 1994 that is used to create online 3D worlds

W •

World Wide Web The graphical multimedia portion of the Internet

Webmaster The person who runs a particular web site (i.e. keeps it working and updated). The webmaster can be the designer of the page, but not necessarily

Web Pages A document, usually formatted in HTML, which might contain text, images, animations, sound and even video

Web Ring Loose collectives of sites (often personal homepages put up by fans) all devoted to the same basic subject

Websites A collection of pages put up by an individual, institution or business

< 467 >